D0723140

SYSTEMS
OF
MODERN
PSYCHOLOGY

SYSTEMS OF MODERN PSYCHOLOGY

A CRITICAL SKETCH

DANIEL N. ROBINSON

COLUMBIA UNIVERSITY PRESS/NEW YORK/1979

Library of Congress Cataloging in Publication Data

Robinson, Daniel N   1937–
  Systems of modern psychology.

  Bibliography: p.
  Includes index.
  1. Psychology—Philosophy. I. Title. [DNLM:
BF38.R6   150'.19   79-15778
ISBN 0-231-04308-2
ISBN 0-231-04309-0 pbk.

Columbia University Press
New York   Guildford, Surrey

CONTENTS

PREFACE

When I was invited to write this volume for Columbia University Press, I had just completed the last of the twenty-eight Prefaces to the volumes of *Significant Contributions to the History of Psychology* and was, as a result, caught in the grip of remembrances of things past. Having examined thousands of pages from the psychologies of the eighteenth and nineteenth centuries, and having been reminded of the fatal flaws in those great, overarching "systems," I was persuaded not only that contemporary psychology was destitute of *systems* but that, on the whole, maybe this was all for the best. In any case, something seemed odd about accepting an invitation to write on *systems of psychology*, given that I knew of none authored after 1920. An additional source of reluctance was the awareness that much of what I might write had already appeared, here and there, in other books and articles of mine and that, in repeating myself, I would become something of a spokesman for my own "school."

That the present volume is now in print is evidence enough that I was able to overcome my misgivings. But to do so, it was necessary to decline to write a *text* on *Systems of Psychology*. Since the title of this work may, therefore, be misleading, this is the proper place to set forth the appropriate caveats.

The present work is not intended as a textbook, but as a supplementary collection of essays designed to acquaint readers of standard texts with the assumptions—largely metaphysical—on which all contemporary "systems" of psychology rest. The method by which this acquaintance is brought about is that of *criticism* rather than *survey*. It was more than modesty that urged me to include the word "sketch" in the subtitle, for what is offered is, in fact, a critical *sketch*, not a searching and detailed analysis. This may give certain passages a "hit and run" flavor unless the reader is aware of the author's aims. By providing an outline of the essential *terms* of criticism, I attempt to lay foundations for more thoroughgoing analyses.

The first chapter is devoted to the concept of "system." My purpose here is to offer a rather formal sense of the term—to overdraw it, as it were—so that contemporary formulations can be placed against something standing in vivid contrast. In previous centuries, writers were not content that they had produced "systems" of psychology until they had taken into account everything from the formation of a single idea to the determinants of social morality. These were truly grand undertakings, and when they failed, they failed gloriously. The models for such ventures were Copernicus, Galileo, and Newton, whose achievements seemed to have reduced the universe itself to order and predictability. It was Descartes's dream that the biological sciences, too, could be Copernicanized—a dream often revived, and even in periods of rampant anti-Cartesianism.

Contemporary psychology, true to the age in which it finds itself, has substituted realistic technical objectives for the Herculean conceptual ones of the preceding three centuries. Freud, in this connection, is somewhat exceptional, but even the Freudian "system" is modest when compared with those set forth by the *philosophes* of the Enlightenment and, in the nineteenth century, by Spencer, Bain, Fichte, Hegel, and others. The price paid for this substitution has, all too often, been a trivializing of the subject. In its darkest moments, contemporary psychology trades perspective for technique and applies the latter with such mechanical devotion as to exclude itself from the balance of the history of ideas—including the history of scientific thought. In some respects, these moments are occurring with increasing frequency. There is a tendency away from the judgment that a *system* of psychology is an ambitious undertaking and toward the radically different notion that it is merely chimerical. I believe this is a notion to be resisted, but not by deluding ourselves into thinking that current efforts somehow constitute a valid system of psychology.

The closest we have come to a systematic psychology is in the refinement and articulation of global perspectives. In the present volume, these are identified as *physicalistic, behavioristic, cognitive, psychoanalytic, phenomenological,* and *humanistic.* Each of these perspectives contains within it the seeds of a system, but none of them can now claim proprietorship of one. In sketching out the critical boundaries within which systematic efforts may proceed, I have attempted to provide modest direction and to give fair warnings.

There is an additional aim embodied in this small book, but one that may fall beyond the perimeter of the interests of most readers. One of the complaints—and happily I say one of the few complaints—voiced generally by those who have commented on my *An Intellectual History of Psychology* is that twentieth century achievements were not given enough space and attention. To those who were careful and kind enough to submit this appraisal, I offer the present volume as, in part, a postscript to the other one.

As a final word, I should speak directly to those whose

words and works are discussed herein, and qualify the criticism brought to bear on them. I have not included in the present analysis anything I have judged to be of ephemeral consequence; anything lacking in substance, in possibilities, in implications. What I have selected for critical scrutiny is that which merits the attention of all interested in psychology. For any criticism of mine that is based on misunderstanding or misconstrual, I apologize. The book, itself, is something of an invitation to a dialogue. If it excites no rebuttal, it will have failed in one of its central objectives.

Daniel N. Robinson

Georgetown
March 1979

SYSTEMS
OF
MODERN
PSYCHOLOGY

CHAPTER ONE

THE
NATURE
OF
SYSTEMS

The Elements of Systems:

The expression "systems of psychology," is so common in texts and scholarly articles as to suggest general agreement on just what a *system* is. It has become something of a protected term, sanctioned far more by the frequency with which it is used than by the information it conveys. Predictably, public discourse provides no assistance. What, after all, is the common conceptual thread running through "systems of government," "transportation systems," and "the Bell Telephone System"? When we consult the man in the street—that stage-prop in every metaphysical argument—he is confident that he knows what "system" means, but he just can't find words to express his knowledge. Rather, he offers examples: his digestive system, a system for gambling, the solar system, the Columbia Broadcasting System. Any term called upon to do this much work in both the public and the scientific realms is not likely to surrender to the forces of clarity and precision. Certainly the present volume cannot expect to have legislative power. However, since every subsequent chapter will be addressed to "systems" of psychology, it will be useful to set aside some space for an analysis

1

of the concept of "system" as it will be used throughout this work.

Psychology as a discipline is cut from the larger fabric of intellectual history. Accordingly, any "system" it might host will be a *system of thought*. More specifically, it will be colored as a scientific system of thought since the discipline has been patterned after the physical and biological sciences. The earliest record of a scientific system is found among the pre-Socratic philosophies, and presents itself in the form of cosmology. The ancient Greek cosmologies are not only the oldest examples of scientific systems, but are also prototypic of the formal structure of most subsequent speculation in the developed sciences. The point here is not that the cosmologists all said the same sorts of things, for they did not. Empedocles was persuaded that the universe was composed of four primary elements—earth, air, fire, and water— and that the contents of the universe could be explained in terms of combinations of these tetrads. Earlier, Parmenides had proposed a fundamental, unitary "Being" as the monadic foundation of the universe. For some cosmologists, the permanence of the elements indicated that *sensed* change must be illusory; for others (for example Heracleitus), there was only change, and nothing was permanent. But in all ancient cosmological systems there are three essential ingredients: first, a set of universal propositions from which can be deduced all the events occurring in that part of the universe to which the system is applicable; second, a delineation of what counts as an event; third, the stipulation of which portion of the universe is to be embraced by the system.

Each of these features is, of course, steeped in difficulties. From the little that survives of pre-Socratic thought, it would seem that the pre-Socratics were not fully cognizant of the problem of knowledge itself, and were more or less content to let conventional language and ordinary perception operate without serious challenge. There is, then, a fourth ingredient—one not sufficiently respected by the pre-Socratics, and one too often neglected in every epoch of intellectual history including our own. This is the ingredient of *epistemology* which takes the very process and act of knowing as the subject of study. Socrates and his school were more dutiful than all their predecessors in examining epistemological issues. In their recognition that every instance of claimed knowledge involves an interaction between a knowing subject and a thing known, they invented psychology. Epistemology entails psychology.

At first blush, it may seem contradictory to speak of realms of reality while acknowledging that these realms cannot be known. But there are many things we know *about* which we do not know directly; hence, Russell's useful distinction between knowledge by *acquaintance* and knowledge by *description*.[1] One knows his hunger by (direct) acquaintance, but that of another only (indirectly) by description. To say, "I know you are hungry" is not the same as saying, "I know your hunger." Thus, we are not to expect perfect symmetry between the epistemological and the ontological features of a system. There will always be conditions under which we acknowledge the existence of things or events which we cannot know directly, but which can be plausibly inferred from what is known.

The term "discipline" has already been used several times. Note that a discipline cannot come into being until a stand is taken on questions of ontology. There must be general agreement on what is to count as an event, on what is to be taken as having real existence. The first stage in the development of any discipline involves ontological legislation or by-laws. Only *these* and not *those* items, events, entities, and processes are to be included in our discipline. Yet, this is only the first step, for one can settle all the ontological questions and still have nary a system. Astronomers were plotting the transit of stars centuries before there was a Ptolemaic *system* of astronomy. It is in this respect that the very notion of a system implies an organizing and codifying perspective which, in the history of science, is manifested in those universal propositions called the *laws of science*. Each such law begs rather than settles questions of ontology and epistemology. The law becomes possible only when answers to such metaphysical questions are, as it were, taken for granted. This fact is respected by the Duhem-Quine thesis[2] but it is not a sanction for theoretical anarchy. Neither the Duhem-Quine thesis nor Einstein's monumental achievement confers a carte blanche on speculation. To contend, for example, that the descriptions we offer of the universe depend upon where we are within it and our velocity at the time the descriptions are given is not to establish that the universe, itself, varies according to such factors. This is a common mistake among those converted to relativistic epistemology; those who fail to distinguish between epistemological and ontological claims. And it is a tendency which has had especially untoward effects in psychology. It is now more common than ever for psychologists to take a stand on *what there is* in the psychological realm purely on the basis of what the methods of psychology are able to unearth. The extreme expression of this tendency is found in those varieties of behaviorism which deny existence to any state or event falling beyond the shadow of behaviorism's methods. This will be discussed at length in a later chapter. At this point it is enough to recognize that a system is virtually defined by its solution to ontological and epistemological problems; and to recognize further that these solutions are not themselves scientific (nor can they be) but *metaphysical.* New disciplines appear, and established ones evolve primarily as a result of challenges to the latent metaphysical foundations supporting the status quo. Careful observation, often aided by advances in technology, produces a new event; one not contained in the "received" ontological catalogue; for example, the discovery of synapses, the detection of a previously unknown planet, the presence of reflexes in decapitated animals. The older system—which had legislated against all events except those in class X—must contend with an unanticipated phenomenon which now requires an expansion of the ontological range of the system. Then, too, new disciplines come into being and established ones are transformed by methodological advances which alter or challenge the received position on epistemological matters. The committed rationalist who would proclaim on purely deductive grounds that only seven planets are possible—and who then lives long enough to witness the discovery of Ceres with the aid of an improved telescope—might be forced to conclude that in such areas pure deduction is not the method of choice![3]

Except in the outer reaches of theoretical physics, ontological and epistemological issues form the unconscious life of the sciences. As physics presses on toward the boundaries of the microscopic and macroscopic realms, it comes face to face with those ancient questions regarding the relationship between the knower and the known, the knower and the knowable, observations and observables. Physics, that is, becomes metaphysics, and thus closes the circle. Ironically, those newer sciences that are so eager to mimic the methods of physics seem equally eager to divorce themselves from anything bearing the slightest resemblance to metaphysics. Psychologists seem to work with uncommon energy to avoid such issues, although William James knew that they could not be avoided or evaded. Having accepted psychology as a natural science, he noted that this did not guarantee an easy future:

It means just the reverse; it means a psychology particularly frag-ile, and into which the waters of metaphysical criticism leak at every joint. . . . The Galileo and the Lavoisier of psychology will be famous men indeed when they come, as come they some day surely will. . . . When they do come, however, the necessities of the case will make them "metaphysical."[4]

It would be far too congratulatory for any psychologist to suggest that, since James wrote these lines, psychology had hosted a Galileo or a Lavoisier. Yet, there have been impor-tant developments and significant advances in the factual, conceptual, and methodological divisions of the discipline. All of the major proposals—all of the epistemological and ontological biases—articulated in the eighteenth and nine-teenth centuries have now had at least a century to run their course. They have benefited from loyal and industrious fol-lowers in our own century. Thus, the hour is not too early to reexamine the latent metaphysical foundations of contempo-rary systems and to file a progress report with the ghost of James. The report itself will be somewhat thin, for only a small fraction of psychology's now immense handbook even loosely qualifies as a *system*. And this book is concerned only with systems of psychology. To qualify for inclusion, the psy-chological works must possess (a) a discernible *metaphysical* component which establishes the ontological content of the school or theory and the epistemological rules by which method, theory, and evidence are integrated; and (b) a suf-ficiently *propositional* character for the critic to ascertain the claims of the school or theory and the criteria—both eviden-tiary and logical—which the school or theory attempts to satisfy.

Explanation

The function of systems is threefold. A system is designed to organize phenomena, to explain their occurrence, and to establish standards of description which permit unambiguous assessments of the adopted organization and explanation. The organizational function is generally expressed in the form of a classification or taxonomy of phenomena. The explanatory function, at least in scientific systems, is served by theories. The standards of description are embodied in what the system takes as its so-called *methodology*. Any serious critique of a scientific system will include an analysis of all these functions as they are performed by the system under examination. One of the guiding principles of science, at least since the seventeenth century, is that nature is not only orderly but parsimonious. Accordingly, it has been the traditional expectation of scientists that the sobering diversity of natural phenomena ultimately will be embraced by a small set of laws. By this standard, a crude but instructive measure of the success of a scientific discipline is the range of phenomena it is able to cover with a modest and diminishing collection of laws.

The notion of classifying disciplines in terms of the formal character of the explanations they provide is an old one, dating back to Aristotle's famous theory of the "four causes." It is sometimes averred that the modern age of science began with a rejection of the Aristotelian "final causes," and with the stubborn commitment to confine scientific explanations to the language of efficient causes. But Aristotle said as much in his very formulation of the principles of explanation. It was he who noted that we do not expect the same precision of a carpenter that we demand of a geometer,[5] and it was also he who grounded the very distinction between physics and metaphysics in the concept of "final causes."[6]

Aristotle's claim was that a *complete* explanation must include a knowledge of all four causal principles. The claim is tantamount to declaring that no science, no matter how developed, can in and of itself provide a complete explanation of anything. What it can and must provide is a *scientific* explanation. Aristotle distinguished between knowing *that* and knowing *why*, a distinction very much alive in contemporary philosophies of science. To some extent, we are correct in dating the appearance of modern science with the growing doubt that we ever know *why* such and such is the case, and with the growing conviction that universal laws based upon *efficient* causation are the most that can ever be known. But this is not really a rejection of Aristotelianism. Rather, it is a rejection of metaphysics as something with which science must concern itself. Thus, the modern scientist is satisfied when he has provided a purely (efficient) causal account of phenomena.

This, however, is just the place at which a scientific psychology faces its sternest challenge. The challenge is both historical and conceptual, and has taken on a variety of forms throughout intellectual history. In its most philosophical manifestations, it appears as the tension between *rational* and *causal* explanations. The issue of reductionism figures in this tension but is not at the heart of it. What is at the heart of it is nothing less than Aristotle's arguments for teleology, but now in modern dress. The rationalist's position—stated here with a brevity that borders on caricature—takes the following general form:

1. Human actions, in contradistinction to mere reflexes, are directed toward some object which is their goal.
2. Such actions are explained meaningfully only in terms of the actor's *reasons* which are, by their very nature, *psychological*.
3. A causal account of such actions will either be veiled

rational explanation (that is, it will include the actor's reasons in the causal sequence) or it will be a materialistic explanation such as is found in the physical sciences.
4. No explanation based exclusively upon material interactions can preserve, address, or embrace the purely rational. Thus, no such explanation can, in fact, *explain* significant human actions.

The issue of reductionism enters into this dispute principally at (4). Opponents of the rationalistic school traditionally have based defenses of causal explanation in psychology on the claim that reasons themselves are reducible to a causal nexus within which only material entities operate. Thus, to say that Smith has a "reason" is to say only that Smith has a "need" which itself is completely explicable in biological terms. To know the needs at a basic biological level is to be able to predict Smith's behavior without ever taking recourse to Smith's putative "reasons."

Those who subscribe to the rationalistic perspective will reject this rebuttal on several grounds. First, they will insist that such a biological account is, in the vast majority of instances, unintelligible to the actor himself. Smith understands his actions in terms of his *reasons,* and he senses no relationship whatever between these reasons and something taking place in the cells of his body. Thus, even if he accepts the causal (material) account of *what* is going on in his body, he will not accept it as identical to the reason *why* he is acting. Second, the successful material reduction does not explain, but eliminates the very rational antecedent of action which the explanation is to explain. There is simply nothing that matter in motion shares with thoughts and reasons. Even if we grant in principle that, for every reason Smith has there is a perfectly correlated biological event, we are not required to accept that the latter *is* the reason or even that it is the cause of the reason. Third, and related to this point, causes and reasons have different histories: given a cause, the effect follows necessarily, whereas given a reason, the action may not follow. In deploying the adverb "necessarily," the disputant need not subscribe to the formal necessitarian theory of causation. He need not, that is, have to defend the claim that effects follow causes by *physical* necessity.[7] Rather, he may simply note that the very concept of "cause" implies an effect in the way that the concept of a reason does not. Indeed, following Hume, he may treat the notion of causation as the sort of idea we form when our experiences show us that *A* and *B* are constantly conjoined and that *B* always follows when *A* is present. Again, this is not what experience shows in the relationship between reasons and actions.

How one elects to relax this tension determines the system of psychology one will seek or accept. If it is to be a *scientific* system, the pressures are great to evolve causal explanations of the sort encountered in the established sciences. The aim becomes one of articulating universal or "covering" laws from which the data of the science can be deduced. This is the program skillfully defended by Carl Hempel[8] and one which, if only intuitively, the founders and leaders of modern science generally have followed. The resulting *Hempelian* explanations may, of course, possess covering laws written in the language of *reasons*, but the laws must be true, must actually cover the events they are purported to cover, and must in all relevant respects behave the way physical causes do in the established sciences. During the formative periods of a given science, covering laws may be absent and only reliable empirical generalizations may be available. In such periods, the developing science will not be in a position to provide bona fide scientific explanations, but will be able to offer "explanation sketches";[9] that is, incomplete explanations having the form but not the predictive power of scientific explanations. Illustrative of such sketches is the "law of supply and demand," according to which the exchange-value of any commodity is determined by two variables: its relative scarcity and its relative desirability. Somewhat less predictive power is contained in a "law" of the form: "national resources are allocated to military functions in proportion to the perceived military strength of neighboring nations." The role of such propositions is a provisional one. The objective is to incorporate them into more general propositions which ultimately become the covering laws of the discipline. The point here is that in principle rational explanations can form the basis of Hempelian explanation. Yet, few would support the claim that such explanations ever will be sufficiently confirmed *in practice* to have the status of scientific explanations. They seem destined to remain "sketches" in search of a law; to remain, that is, the explanatory devices of disciplines whose relation to science is one of perpetual aspiration.

Several ways around this dilemma can be found in modern systems of psychology. One involves the bold initiative of attempting to convert all the issues of psychology to a purely material-causal form. The second involves the abandoning of the hypothetico-deductive model entirely, and the adoption of a purely descriptive approach to the subject. The third is characterized by the suspension of both rationalistic and physicalistic terms and concepts, and the substitution of ontologically neutral elements. A few introductory remarks are in order on each of these approaches.

The two schools of modern psychology that most consistently reflect reductivism are physiological psychology and behaviorism. In important respects, however, the term "school" is inappropriate. There is, after all, no coherent theory of physiological psychology, nor is there a physiological theory of general psychology. Behaviorism, on the other hand, has found theoretical expression but, with the exception of Guthrie's version,[10] none of the extant theories is significantly reductive. As I shall note in subsequent chapters, current and traditional behavioristic arguments are not theories at all, but are, rather, loose federations of fact, opinion, polemic, and habit. At present, then, neither the physiological nor the behavioral reductivist "school" is sufficiently articulate to allow for critical appraisals. Both derive inspiration from the idea of "the unity of the sciences," and from the successes enjoyed by chemistry and physics. The problem, however, is that the phenomena of *mind* have always stood as the challenges to "the unity of sciences." Thus, to defend reductivism by asserting the truth of the very proposition under examination is to do no more than beg the question.

Matters are strained further by the tendency, more recent than traditional, of defenders of material reductionism to legislate bona fide psychological events off the list of scientific problems, and to proceed to reductive analyses of far simpler events. This is a tendency, not a conspiracy, but the effect is the same, and is brought into being by a not-so-subtle corruption of logic. One begins reasonably enough by acknowledging the difficulty (or present impossibility) of reducing complex psychological processes to physiological or behavioral principles. One then proceeds to make significant strides in reducing simpler and only quasi-psychological processes to their neural or "operant" substrates. But *then,* on the strength of this successful reduction, one insists either (a) that the complex processes are but ensembles of these simpler ones or (b) that the so-called complex processes are will-o'-the-wisp, an unnecessary legacy of the ages of spiritism and "mentalism." Such arguments are convincing until we recognize that they are neither logically nor empirically supported by the facts unearthed in the reductive analysis of simple processes.

The strategy involving the abandonment of the hypothet-ico-deductive model is perilous for an aspiring science, for it disconnects it from the balance of scientific reasoning and scientific achievement. Subjects such as comparative anat-omy and taxonomy derive their scientific standing from the relationship they bear to a larger, hypothetico-deductive science. Evolutionary biology, for example, constitutes the implicit foundation of modern comparative anatomy. Were there not an overarching set of covering laws—a larger theo-retical context—the purely descriptive activities of anato-mists would amount to no more than exercises in naming. The point here is not that psychology *cannot* elect to forego hypothesis and theory, but that if it does it will, ipso facto, remove itself from those endeavors, both historic and cur-rent, that comprise science itself.

It is also worth noting that the apparently antiseptic term "purely descriptive" is something of an oxymoron. The very act of describing involves any number of steps and decisions which, properly understood, are metaphysical, epis-temological, and theoretical. One does not describe *every-thing*, but only certain things; and one does not offer just any sort of description, but descriptions of a specified kind; for example, quantitative, qualitative, statistical. When *behav-ior* is the subject of descriptions, a decision has been made as to which genre of behavior counts, and this decision comes at the end of many others: the species, age and gender of the organism; the particular task required of the orga-nism; the means of counting, measuring, or otherwise re-cording the behavior under investigation. Each of these deci-sions is based upon considerations of an essentially theoretical nature such that the ultimate descriptions are anything but "pure."

The election of neutral theoretical terms and concepts has much to recommend it, not the least of which is an escape from the problems associated with reductionism and "pure" descriptivism. But as this strategy avoids the pitfalls present in the other strategies, it also denies itself their assets. Illustrative of what might best be called neutralism is the psychophysical function. The observer is exposed to a series of physically graded stimuli and is instructed to report when a stimulus is "seen." A function results that describes the growth of perceptibility coincident with, for example, the physical intensity of the stimuli. In the end, the investigator is able to offer a general, mathematical statement; for example

$$D = f(I)$$

where D represents detectability (percent "seen"), I represents the intensity of the stimuli, and f stands for the mathematical function by which the equality is established. For example, f may stand for $\log_{10}$.

In this example, the expression $D = f(I)$ is a *transfer function* by which the perceptual outcomes and the stimulus values can be interchanged. Note that the expression is neutral in regard to neurophysiological mechanisms, theories of perception, the ontological status of flashes of light, the reducibility of psychological processes. Indeed, the D in the expression may just as well refer to a photocell, the retinal receptors of the frog, or the performance of a traffic-control officer at a busy airport. The expression, moreover, is not a "description," but a relationship. It is precisely because it is neutral with respect to the source of D and the mechanism by which D and I come to be related that, in fact, it does not describe anything. Rather than a description, it is an assertion.

Let us expand the experiment to include flashes of light that vary in wavelength. It is now found that D is also a function of this variable, so that a more complete expression takes the form:

$$D = f(I; L)$$

where L is the wavelength of light given in millimicrons. To be more accurate, two expressions are required since the functional relationship between D and I is different from the functional relationship between D and L. Thus:

$$D = f_1(I)$$
$$D = f_2(L)$$

The ability of any sensing device to detect radiation is a function of many variables, and this is as true of the human eye as it is of radars, sonars, photocells, and thermometers. Yet, the basic approach to understanding the system in question is indifferent to the material composition or the behavioral nuances of the system in question. The "radar equation," for example, is a mathematical statement of the functional relationship among such variables as (a) the cross section of targets, (b) the power of the transmitted radar signal, (c) the distance between the receiver and the target, (d) the area of the antenna. From the *systems analysis* perspective, a radar installation has been "explained" when the radar equation has been given. That is, the explanation is no more than those transfer functions which establish equivalence between the response of the system and the physical features of the external world. Note, then, that the forthcoming "explanations" will be the same for radars of different sizes, ages, locations, uses, shapes, and configurations. Just as the Pythagorean theorem is true of all right-angle triangles, the radar equation is true of all radars.

The chief difficulty of this neutral, systems-analytic approach, is that it does not yield the sorts of explanations ordinarily required by those who wish to know *how* and *why* things are the way they are. When we discover, for example, that the relationship between detection and intensity is given by a logarithmic function, we tend to consider the fact as something less than an explanation. To learn further that optic nerve discharges also increase logarithmically with increases in the intensity of stimulation is to learn more about *how D* and *I* come to be logarthmically related. For most contemporary psychologists, therefore, the neutralistic position is a preliminary one; one worth adopting on strategic and experimental grounds, but one whose final justification awaits successful redescriptions in behavioral or physiological terms. Most, that is, would subscribe to W. V. O. Quine's claim that "to be is to be the function of some variable"[11] but would ask of psychology more than such ontological purity.

Issues, Fashions, and History

In succeeding chapters, the principles set forth above will be brought to bear upon specific areas of contemporary psychology. Clearly, a book of modest size cannot be expected to have something to say about all areas of psychology, or even about most of them. Psychology has not developed to the point where fads and fashions are immediately distinguishable from bona fide issues. Perhaps the surest guide as to where such distinctions must be attempted is history. Once we move beyond the established sciences, the most dependable sign that a set of questions and perspectives constitutes an issue worth addressing is that both questions and the perspectives were present in every period of intellectual vitality.

Some might argue that the historical test is not applicable in the present circumstance because psychology is so "young." The position one takes on the age of psychology is determined by one's position on the formal character and the proper subject matter of the discipline. It is true, for example, that the experimental analysis of animal behavior is less than a century old. Yet it is not true that the perspective on which this analysis is based is only a century old. And, since the perspective itself has not changed significantly as a result of sixty years of data gathering, there would seem to be no reason to defer a critique of the perspective until additional data have been accumulated. Whether one is addressing behaviorism, or psychoanalytic theories, or theories of cognitive function, or theories of social interaction, the "data" are only marginally relevant since, were there not abundant facts standing in support of the theory, criticism would amount to mere dismissal. The part to be taken by the critic, therefore, is one involving an analysis of the assumptions upon which the fact-gathering itself is based; the implications drawn by the fact-gatherer from the data into a larger and more speculative realm; the logic of inference and explanation reflected by this or that system of psychology. Useful criticism is not exhaustive but suggestive. To establish that a given system is fundamentally flawed in its methods or its explanations is enough to suggest that all systems based upon it will also be flawed in these respects. Thus, the following chapters are based upon the most significant perspectives in modern psychology. They do not attempt to provide a handbook of contemporary interests.

Another feature of modern psychology—as distinct from the established sciences—is that its various schools, systems, and orientations exist largely as independent principalities, nearly completely separated from one another conceptually and semantically. This makes it difficult to choose a defensible progression of topics. Of the several plausible formats, the molecular-to-molar seems best suited to the purposes of this text. The choice, however, is not a veiled endorsement of reductionism—as the chapters themselves will make clear—but an attempt to prepare the reader for discussions of complex phenomena by introducing various analytical methods within the context of simpler ones.

CHAPTER TWO

THE PHYSICALISTIC POINT OF VIEW

Historical Background

Physiological psychology is the oldest of experimental psychology's special branches and continues to be the most interdisciplinary. There are the usual and the many ancient "fathers" of the subject, but its modern history is generally dated with Descartes' *Meditations* and his *Passions of the Mind.*[1] Descartes (1596–1650) sought to found the biological sciences on the same hypothetico-deductive base that Galileo and Kepler had established for physics. To achieve this, and to confer on natural philosophy the rigor and realism of both mathematics and science, he was persuaded that all earlier authorities must be rejected. While pledging himself to the laws of his country and the truths of his religion, he invoked the *method of doubt* as a means of acquiring self-knowledge. This is all spelled out in his *Discourse on Method*[2] where Descartes promises to accept as true only that which cannot plausibly be denied or denied without self-contradiction. It is in the same *Discourse* that the commitment is made to reduce all concepts to their elemental constituents, and to build up elementary propositions until they take the form of exceptionless laws.

The official skepticism adopted in the *Discourse* led Descartes to doubt even his own existence; to conjure, for argument's sake, an evil spirit conspiring to delude him. Alas, even to be deceived is to *be*. Accordingly, Descartes was able to accept his own existential status on the grounds that he could doubt it. *Cogito ergo sum*.

Now equipped with existence, Descartes was able to proceed in his investigations of "self," and to raise the question, How does the mind come to be the way it is and come to know what it purports to know? His answer to this question was very much in the tradition of that medieval Aristotelianism which he had set out to avoid and oppose. He assumed (with Aristotle) that the contents of perception permitted the inference that there were external causes. Yet, we do not directly experience what is "out there," but only what is in our minds. Moreover, there is no conceivable way of determining how good a "copy" of reality is made by the mind. In any case, the ancient metaphor of the "wax impression" seemed serviceable. According to this account, objects are impressed upon the sensory organs which transmit the impressions to the brain via the nerves.

It is worth pausing here to examine a difficulty recognized by Descartes and elevated to the level of a metaphysics by George Berkeley (1685–1783). If we grant that we only have *direct* knowledge of our own thoughts (sensations, feelings, ideas)—that is, that we know immediately and without the need for inference of any kind only that which is in our minds—a question arises as to how we ever come by the notion of *matter* in the first place. Note that it won't do to claim that we *inferred* matter from the very fact of experience, for this requires us to have the concept of *causation* independently of experience. We do not "see" causes. Descartes could discover only one way to solve this dilemma, and that was by positing an innate disposition, grounded in our very nature. Over the centuries—and in far too many contemporary texts—Descartes is accused of having a theory of *innate ideas*, a theory which he explicitly rejected.[3] He did not propose in any of his essays that infants enter the world in possession of factual knowledge or of deductive proofs. Rather, he noted a number of truths of which every mature and reasonable person is aware although such truths could not possibly be *given* in experience. *Matter* is but one of these. Our immediate experience consists only of what is in our minds, thoughts, and percepts. From such experience, the inductive leap to an assumed *material* world is possible only if we grant the idea of *matter* a priori. The concept of matter, then, is *logically* prior to our experience of it.

For Descartes, the idea of *God* was of the same sort. No single experience and no combination of experiences will conduce to such an idea, yet it is an idea shared by men and women throughout the world and over the ages of recorded history. Since experience cannot grant such an idea, and since it is (nearly) universally held, it must be innate. But again, the term "innate" was not intended by Descartes to suggest neonatal wisdom. Rather, it refers to a feature of our very nature; something inextricably tied to the mind of a rational being.

These comments provide a sample of Descartes' *rationalistic* psychology, and are offered to offset the frequent claim that, underneath it all, Descartes was a mere (and radical) materialist. However, when we move from the realm of metaphysical and theological truths to that of factual knowledge, Descartes's epistemology becomes increasingly materialistic, sensationistic, and reductionistic. In his posthumously published *Treatise on Man and the Formation of the Fetus* (1664) the materialistic side of his psychology is the dominant one, whereas in *The Passions of the Mind* biological explanations are reserved primarily for the routine sensations and motions of men and animals. The latter work presents one of the earliest reflex theories of sensory-motor integration. It is essentially a theory of automatons, stretched to cover the behavior of animals and nearly cover the behavior of persons. Human beings are exempted on the grounds that no robot would attain to the idea of God, or engage creatively in speech, or possess a comprehension of higher moral and mathematical principles. But aside from these complex ideas, the psychology of man and that of beast are explicable in terms of similar processes and laws.

It was in the Second and the Sixth of the *Meditations* that Descartes advanced his solution to the Mind/Body problem most explicitly, and in Articles 35 and 39 of *The Passions of the Mind* that he offered his psychobiological theory of sensation and action. In regard to the latter, it is only necessary to recall that, to Descartes, the pineal gland served as the structure by which the soul regulated the affairs of the body, not as the *place* where the soul resided. The Cartesian soul is immaterial and, therefore, unextended. Clearly, it cannot be a *place*. And, since it is not a place, it cannot be affected by any *extended* thing; that is, by matter. It makes no more sense to say, for example, that an idea is "here" than it does to say that an idea is heavy, blue, tall, or soft. It does, however, make sense to say that, if Smith has the idea that he is late, then Smith makes his feet move more quickly. It was this sort of reasoning that led Descartes to conclude that the relationship between mind and body was one of *one-way interaction*. The mind (soul)—by bringing its influence or power to bear upon the brain (specifically, upon the pineal gland)—is able to control the actions of the body. But the body can have no influence on the mind (soul).

Opposition to Descartes's theory was immediate and formidable. Pierre Gassendi (1592–1655), one of the most influential philosophers of the seventeenth century—and an ordained priest—judged the *Meditations* to be unintelligible. It made no sense to argue that a material body cannot affect an immaterial soul while insisting that the latter can control the former. Gassendi was alert to the fact that Descartes had relegated causal authority to the body when it came to *all* the actions of animals and most of the actions of human beings. Thus the burden of proof now rested with Descartes to show why *any* process, mental or otherwise, could not be accounted for in these same physiological terms.[4]

The success of the Gassendist position throughout the eighteenth century was confined largely to France and to that celebrated circle of Enlightenment men and women known as the *philosophes*. The sense-based psychologies of Francis Bacon and John Locke were in complete accord with the larger social and political aims of the French libertarians. Locke's *Essay Concerning Human Understanding* was translated by Condillac (1715–1780) whose own *Essay on the Origin of Human Knowledge* remains one of the most cogent defenses and one of the clearest expositions of empiricistic philosophy. Condillac's metaphor of the "sentient statue"— an entity that gains psychological characteristics through the incessant barrages of a stimulating environment— became one of the idols of the *philosophes*.

In the nation of its birth, empiricism was not rigidly tied to materialism. Neither Locke nor Hume was much given to speculation on the possible physiological foundations of mental life, and Berkeley—a radical empiricist—went so far as to withhold existential status from matter entirely. Among the British philosophers of the eighteenth century, only David Hartley (1705–1757) offered a systematic materialistic psychology.* His *Observations on Man* (1749) combined Hume's associationistic principles, Descartes' primi-

---

* Joseph Priestly's efforts in this connection were less psychological than cosmic. His *Disquisitions Relating to Matter and Spirit* (1777) remains a cogent polemic against dualism.

tive reflex psychology, and Newton's gravitational laws into what was nearly a modern psychobiological theory of man. But in this Hartley was departing from the philosophical traditions of Britain, and I say this even with Hobbes's *Leviathan* (1651) in mind. Hobbes put forth a mechanistic theory of society which proposed to account for social organization in terms of the instinct to survive. His epistemological orientation was actually more in the rationalist than in the empiricist tradition and his "biopsychology," such as it was, is more backward- than forward-looking. There is no denying Hobbes's influence on subsequent materialistic theories, but *Leviathan* cannot be said to have the same status as *Observations on Man* among those texts upon which physiological psychology ultimately came to depend, as we shall see later in this chapter.

It is not easy to explain briefly how materialism and empiricism became so firmly welded in eighteenth century France. An important factor was the general opposition to Cartesianism in all its forms. Thus, Locke's empiricism was chosen over Descartes' rationalism; Newton's physics over the Cartesian *vortices;* finally, Gassendi's biological theory of mind over Descartes's dualism. Less easy to establish is the mixed part played by England's Royal Society which, since its founding in 1662, vigorously resisted the temptation to "philosophize." Locke and Hartley were elected as Fellows of the Royal Society, but this was exceptional—and remains so. Neither Berkeley nor Hume nor John Stuart Mill was elected. Indeed, no one after Locke was ever elected for purely philosophical contributions to the world's fund of knowledge. Isaac Newton's maxim "I frame no hypotheses" aptly summarizes the historical position taken by the Royal Society on just what counts as science. The results of this have been mixed in the sense that philosophy, over the centuries, was at best a sideline in the British scientist's endeavors. Often the most scientifically astute worker refused on principle to "frame hypotheses," or simply ignored the use to which scientific findings were being put by the philosophers. In France, on the other hand, there was much more traffic between the arenas of science and philosophy and, as a result, French science in the eighteenth and early nineteenth centuries was far more philosophical—again, with mixed results. In this connection, it is worth recalling that the *philosophes* who were most directly influenced by and in command of Locke's writings—and here I refer to Condillac and Helvetius—were least given to physiological theories of psychology, although even Helvetius seems to have taken such theories for granted. The rest, however—Diderot, Holbach, Voltaire, Condorcet, La Mettrie—subscribed in various degrees to the physiological point of view.[5]

Coextensive with these philosophical developments were the strides taken in the study of anatomy and physiology. The seventeenth century was very much a century of optics and hosted the founders of microscopy: Leeuwenhoeck (1632–1723), Malpighi (1628–1694), Hooke (1635–1703). The gross descriptive anatomy of the nervous system that had been bequeathed by Vesalius was now surrendering to the more refined surgical methods of men such as Thomas Willis (1621–1675), whose remarks concerning the dependence of mental functions on pathways and structures within the brain were sufficiently specific to serve as a primitive physiological psychology. But if neuroanatomy entered its modern phase in the seventeenth century, neurophysiology waited for the eighteenth. It is true that the Royal Society had been treated in the seventeenth century to a demonstration by Robert Boyle of the survival of reflex motions in the decapitated frog, but the earliest systematic efforts along these lines must be credited to Robert Whytt (1714–1766), physician to the King of Scotland. It was Whytt's research that established the relationship between the intensity of stimulation and the vigor of reflex movements; the role of the spinal "marrow" and spinal nerves in the initiation of involuntary movement of the skeletal muscles; the power of reflex mechanisms to overcome ". . . any effort of the will."[6] Later in the same century Galvani all but proved that the mechanism of the reflex was electrical, thereby replacing concepts such as the *vis nervosa*, the "vital principle," and the *spiritus animus* with one drawn from the purely physical world. Galvani's notions were resisted for a while even by the scientific community, in large part because of the absence of a coherent theory of electricity. But this was all remedied in the first decades of the nineteenth century through the efforts of George Ohm (1787–1854) and Sir Humphry Davy (1778–1829).[7] It remained for Carlo Matteucci and Emil Du Bois-Reymond to assemble the rudiments of a polarization theory of bio-electric phenomena; rudiments which, as the nineteenth century ended, were combined into a theory of neural conduction not unlike the modern theory.[8] Together, the anatomists and the physiologists, by 1800, had "fleshed out" Descartes's automaton and had contributed a degree of credibility to mechanistic philosophies of mind.

What seemed credible to some in the eighteenth century gradually seemed obvious to many in the nineteenth. It was in the nineteenth century—the century that invented physiological psychology as we now know it—that data from the clinic, from the laboratory, and from the dissecting table converged. The ill-fated *phrenology* launched by Francis Joseph Gall (1758–1828) and refined by John Caspar Spurzheim (1776–1832) was significant. Gall was not the first to propose a strict *localization of function* hypothesis to account for psychological, moral, and intellectual faculties, but he was the first leading and recognized scientist to advance such a hypothesis against a background of relevant clinical and experimental findings. Willis' earlier efforts were modest and halting by comparison.

Phrenology attracted the devotion of many laymen and, early on, a fair number of capable scientists. Gall's major works appeared between 1810 and 1825. By 1830, there were over a dozen journals devoted to phrenological "science," and a small army even prepared to revamp institutions along phrenological grounds. The bare bones of the theory can be set forth in a fashion capable of inducing laughter, but a tolerant reading of Gall's and Spurzheim's texts is enough to engender respect. The "bumpology" portion of phrenology is, of course, ridiculous, but setting it aside we discover the three claims upon which phrenology rested its case: (1) that for every discernible psychological trait, faculty, or capacity, there is a definable region of cerebral cortex uniquely involved; (2) that, *within* a given brain, the relative contribution of mass to a given faculty, the relative preponderance of that faculty; (3) that the intellectual, moral, and broadly psychological characteristics of man are innate.

There were many telling criticisms advanced against phrenology soon after the publication of Gall's earliest statements of the case. *Phrenology Examined* (English translation 1846) by Pierre Flourens is illustrative of the best rebuttals, but even Flourens based much of his criticism upon a defense of free will and on the insistence that "self" is an undivided substance; defenses of a metaphysical and not scientific nature.[9] Nonetheless, owing to the controversy between Gall and his detractors, significant research was undertaken in an attempt to test the hypothesis of functional localization of psychological processes. Such research also had predated the controversy, and certainly not every nineteenth century investigator justified his efforts in terms of a pro- or antiphrenology perspective. Rather, phrenology brought to a head a materialistic orientation that had been swelling for decades. More than any other influence, phrenology made the Mind/Body problem a *scientific* one—or so it seemed.

Accompanied by less fanfare than phrenology, discoveries in the neural sciences in the nineteenth century helped to fashion the essential features of modern physiological psychology. Sir Charles Bell in 1811 and, independently, Francois Magendie in 1822 demonstrated the anatomical separation of sensory and motor functions in the spinal cord; that is, the Bell-Magendie Law. By the 1830s, Marshall Hall in England and George Prochaska in Prussia had integrated this law into studies of reflex organization and were, as a result, laying the foundations for Pavlov's psychological "reflexology." In the 1850s, Helmholtz provided measures of the velocity of nervous conduction—such conduction previously thought to be nearly instantaneous. Pierre Broca introduced his famous "speech center" in 1860, and ten years later Fritsch and Hitzig demonstrated that movement could be induced in a dog by electrically stimulating the exposed cortex on the contralateral side. Their demonstration also included the fact that the dog's body was *topographically* mapped on the "motor" cortex. Thus, in 1876, David Ferrier's *Functions of the Brain* was able to present findings in the neural sciences generated by a wide variety of methods: surgical destruction, clinical examination, electrical stimulation. A little more than a century earlier, La Mettrie had declared in his *L'Homme machine* (1748) that the soul was but "an enlightened machine," a declaration that forced the author to find refuge in Prussia. In 1876, Ferrier could calmly observe, "That the brain is the organ of the mind is a universally accepted axiom."[10] It is clear, then, that physiological psychology existed at least as early as 1876, even if Wundt had yet to give it a name.

Contemporary Formulations

Although physiological psychology has perhaps the broadest factual base of all the branches of psychology, it is surprisingly lacking in theoretical integrations. There is, to be sure, that overarching perspective according to which all psychological phenomena are but expressions of neural processes, but this is hardly a theory. In terms of the criteria of a system set forth in the first chapter, there have been only three systematic physiological psychologies advanced in the twentieth century: Pavlov's and Hebb's connectionistic theories, and the recent "holographic" theory proposed by Pribram. Before examining these, it will be profitable to review the facts that any developed system of physiological psychology must be able to embrace.

Perception: Experimental studies of human perception are the oldest in the history of psychology and continue to provide the most reliable findings. The basic functional relationships between, on the one hand, signal detection and discrimination and, on the other, such independent variables as the physical features of stimuli, and the age, species, and level of adaptation of the subject (observer), are the most precise and numerous in all of experimental psychology. In addition to such traditional topics as color vision, pitch perception, tactile sensitivity, and others, the experimental analysis of perception includes complex perceptual processes: pattern perception, "constancy" phenomena, a wide variety of illusions, perceptual consequences of alterations in motivation, attitude, set, and past experiences. Although a physiological theory of perception is not required to account for all of the items cited, it must not stand in conflict with the facts as gathered psychophysically. For example, a physiological theory of perception that accounted for the discriminations made at the long-wavelength end of the spectrum, but did so in terms that made short-wavelength discriminations impossible, would not be acceptable.

Behavior: Nothing more than neurobiology is needed to account for the contraction of skeletal muscle, for the initiation of reflexes, and for the response of sensory organs and systems to stimulation. A theory of physiological *psychology* must account for *learned* behavior, including those lengthy chains of behavior involved in adaptation to complex and changing environments. To the extent that such behavior is shown to be dependent upon motivational variables, or affected by arousal, attention, curiosity, and the like, the physiological theory must address these factors. The theorist may—by invoking a version of the First and Fifth Amendments—choose to confine "behavior" to a small and otherwise unrepresentative pool of the organism's overall behavioral reservoir, but he does so at the risk of rendering his theory trivial.

Cognition and Language: Although it is generally granted that an understanding of lower organisms is of value in its own right, there is also a general expectation that theories based upon studies of lower organisms are intended to be of some value in our attempts to understand human psychology. This is not to say that every theory must explicitly address complex human characteristics. However, if the theory proposes that the more complex characteristics are to be understood in terms of interactions among those simpler processes and mechanisms contained in the theory, then there must be some argument or evidence by which the claimed generality can be defended. Thus, a physiological theory of, for example, maze learning—which purports to be a simplified model or reduced theory of cognition—sustains the burden of demonstrating the equivalence of maze learning and cognition. Similarly, the theory that accounts for vocalization can only be viewed as a primitive theory of language to the extent that language is shown to be but a developed form of vocalization.

Emotion: Physiological theories of emotion are obliged to disclose the quality and range of emotion embraced by them. Demonstrating, for example, that certain species engage in copulatory behavior following stimulation of a region of the brain does not ipso facto shed light on the possible neural mechanisms of "love."

This list is offered to illustrate the grounds for critical appraisal and not as a complete enumeration of the states and characteristics to be embraced by a physiological theory of psychology.

Methods

As in all experimental sciences, physiological psychology relies upon correlational data and upon statistical estimations of the dependencies displayed among variables. Causal inferences drawn from these findings are on the same epistemological footings as those found in the physical sciences.

In clinical research, diagnostic tools are employed to determine the nature and the location of insults to the nervous system, and these insults are ordinarily interpreted as causal factors in relation to observed psychological deficits. The diagnostic tools are numerous and are often used in combination. They include instruments able to disclose anatomical irregularities in the brain as well as devices for recording the intrinsic activity and elicited responses of the brain. The *cerebral angiograph*, for example, is a visualization of the major blood vessels serving the cerebral circulation. Displacement of any of these vessels is a reliable sign of a space-occupying lesion; for example, a tumor. The record is obtained by injecting a substance into the cerebral blood supply. The substance chosen is one that renders the blood relatively opaque to the passage of radiation, such that the cerebral circulatory system appears with the same vividness as does the skeletal system on an ordinary x-ray.

A more direct method for detecting tumors is the *brain-scan*. The basic principle is that rapidly growing tissue (such as a tumor) has a higher metabolic rate than normal tissue and will, therefore, "take up" more of a radioactive substance. After such a substance is injected, the cranial surface is scanned by a modified Geiger counter, and regions of high uptake are sketched by a printer.

The intrinsic activity of the brain is recorded by the *electroencephalogram*. In the normal states of wakefulness, arousal, and sleep, the electroencephalographic record displays characteristic frequencies and amplitudes. These features are also known to follow a particular developmental course and to be sensitive to such factors as fatigue, stress, drug toxicity, and certain diseases of the central nervous system. There is no neurological disorder which is definitively diagnosed by the EEG, but, together with other diagnostic procedures, the EEG often yields evidence that is important and not provided by any other means.

As the EEG is a record of the intrinsic, self-generated electrical activity of the brain, the *evoked response* (ER) is the electrical correlate of the brain's transient adjustments to an arriving stimulus. The normal EEG recorded from a relaxed, adult human being is dominated by the *alpha* rhythm: an oscillating wave of activity whose frequency falls between 8 and 13 oscillations per second and whose amplitude, at the surface of the scalp, is approximately 50 to 100 microvolts. The evoked response, however, provides a far weaker signal—often less than 5 microvolts—and is otherwise masked by the ongoing EEG activity. With computers it has become possible to obtain running averages of the ER such that the background EEG is effectively canceled. To date, the averaged ER has been used imaginatively in basic research, but only rarely (though productively) in clinical neurology.

The most venerable of the clinical methods is, of course, the so-called "clinical examination" which permits the experienced diagnostician to trace out the anatomical integrity and functional status of the principal sensory and motor pathways. Going even beyond evaluating the relatively uncomplicated sensory and motor mechanisms, expert clinical examinations can unearth the neurological foundations of disturbances to learning, memory, problem solving, and related higher functions.

The court of last resort in experimental-clinical neurology is the pathologist's microscope. Post mortem examination of the brain provides direct evidence of the degree and nature of destruction sustained by neural tissue, as well as remarkably precise estimates of the age of the destructive process. The value of this information in terms of physiological theories of psychology cannot exceed the accuracy and the completeness of information describing the psychological correlates of neuropathology. It is not enough to know what has happened to neural tissue; it is also necessary to know what the consequences were to the psychological makeup of the patient.

Put briefly, the status of clinical investigation in the neural sciences is that of a guide, not a founder. For centuries, clinical data have been accumulating and we are now in possession of a large number of reliable correlations. Nonetheless, nature—as the expression goes—is a clumsy surgeon and a disorganized researcher. No two lesions are identical in location or extent or duration. No two patients are identical in their preclinical experiences or postclinical deficits. And there is never enough known about the patients to permit more than a good guess as to the extent of the changes presumed to have been caused by disease. These limitations can only be overcome in the laboratory.

Methods of research in physiological psychology have increased in number and in precision throughout the twentieth century, although most of them were at least anticipated in earlier periods. And, despite the great variety of specific techniques, the entire arsenal of methods can be reduced conceptually to one: some disruptive event is produced within the nervous system, and some measure of the consequences is taken. The disruptive event may be as innocuous as the application of a stimulus (for example, a flash of light) or as extreme as the surgical removal of the entire cerebral mantle. The measure of the effects may be as removed from the nervous system as a verbal report (for example, "I see the flash") or may be taken directly from the tissue of the brain, spinal cord, or nerves.

Each of the modern methods enjoys assets and suffers liabilities. The method of surgical destruction or removal (*ablation*) of regions of the brain is designed to alert the investigator to the functions served by that region before surgery. To some extent, however, the brain functions as a whole—or at least in large ensembles of "subsystems"—such that it is always hazardous to base claims regarding function on the consequences of ablations. Microscopic surgery offsets a number of the problems associated with the destruction of large masses of brain, but in the process faces the problem of sampling. That is, once the investigator confines his studies to the behavior of just a few neural units, it is unlikely that the functions of the brain *as a system* will be unearthed.*

It is now common to record the electrical activity of brain cells or entire subsystems of the brain, and to do so in a manner that is only marginally destructive. This technique has produced a number of reliable findings, particularly those which describe the "coding" of sensory information. In addition to recording the activity of various nervous structures, physiological psychologists also initiate activity through the use of stimulating electrodes. A thick handbook of findings already exists as a result of this research. Regions of the brain have been identified that appear to be causally involved in complex perceptions, memory, emotional responses, eating, drinking, copulation, and such basic regulative functions as the maintainance of body heat, blood pressure, sleep, and arousal. The literature here is a vast one, defying even a summary. Nevertheless, it has yet to be integrated into a general theory of psychobiology.

Available methods are precise, but they are not free of difficulty. The major current problems of interpretation are due in part to the following factors:

1. Only rarely are the same procedures—both physiological and psychological—brought to bear upon more than a single species by the same investigator. Accordingly, even at a purely descriptive level, *comparative physiological psychology* is relatively undeveloped. Rats, cats, and several varieties of monkey dominate the experimental populations. However, even where findings from several species have been obtained under (loosely) comparable conditions, there is no *theory* of comparative psychology by which meaningful interspecies comparisons can be made.

---

* One tends to think of single-unit recordings as nondisruptive. They are, of course, only moderately disruptive, but some destruction of cells is unavoidable.

2. Gross, functional neurophysiology has not advanced to the point at which instructive comparisons can be made of the psychological effects produced by different methods. It is well known, for example, that highly similar effects can be produced either by stimulating a region of the brain or by removing the same region. In the absence of a theory of brain function, such findings are merely paradoxical. Worse than this is the fact that, in the absence of such a theory, there is very little guidance in the matter of choosing an experimental method. Whether the researcher employs surgery, stimulation, electrical recordings, or pharmacological agents seems to be more a matter of individual taste than scientific injunction.

3. Until quite recently, the science of genetics has been nearly unheard of in physiological psychology. There is, of course, overwhelming evidence showing the dependence of any number of psychological processes upon the genetic composition of the organism.[11] Yet, few studies in physiological psychology directly compare groups of genotypically varied organisms. What is needed, of course, are estimates of the *heritability* of effects produced by specific ablations, stimulations, drugs, etc. As of now, however, the literature is exhausted by studies which (a) "control" genotype by studying only the highly inbred strains of a given species or (b) ignore genotype entirely. Thus, as there is no comparative physiological psychology, there is also no genetic physiological psychology. Because of this, the specialty remains strikingly divorced from two of its most natural partners in the biological sciences.

4. Far more care is devoted to the selection and implementation of the physiological procedures than to the choice of psychological (dependent) variables. The maze, the "Skinner box," and the delayed-response apparatus continue to dominate the physiological psychology laboratory. Only rarely are experimental subjects placed in natural settings— ethologically significant settings—and even here the behavior studied is generally confined to mating, feeding, and

nest-building. In those instances involving more complex processes (for example the effects of lesions upon social hierarchies among primates) the full range of the organism's abilities are ignored as the investigator records the one effect he set out to study.

Each of these shortcomings applies to the systematic attempts to be discussed below. Indeed, because of these experimental deficiencies, theorists have been called upon to do the impossible: to provide a general theory of processes and phenomena only incompletely known even at the descriptive level.

Theories of Perception
Physicalistic theories of perception* may be divided into two broad classes: *sensationistic* and *constructive*. The term "sensationistic" is used here to refer to those attempts to account for the facts of perception in terms of the known electrophysiology and biochemistry of sensory systems. The term "constructive" refers to those theories which go beyond the known properties of sensory physiology and seek to establish models of neural function by which an equivalence of neural and perceptual processes is implied. The two approaches are conceptually different but are not necessarily in conflict. What divides them is often little more than a question of emphasis. The emphasis, however, generally betokens a deeper metaphysical rift which will be explored below, after representatives of the two approaches have been discussed.

The psychology of perception is intimately tied to the *problem of knowledge* as such. This, of course, is the most

---

* Physicalistic here is used as that which is opposed to phenomenological. A physicalistic theory need not be *physiological*. Thus, for example, Gibson's theory is discussed under this heading.

vexed issue in the history of philosophy, and we are not to expect it to be settled by the experimental psychologist. Nor would it be possible to discuss the issue at any appropriate length here. Yet, the ultimate significance of experimental work in perception will be judged in terms of its contribution to a clarification of this issue and, for this reason, a few comments on the philosophical side of the matter are in order.

How much trust are we entitled to have in our perceptions? This ageless question is ignored by everyone in the day-to-day affairs of life, but it stands at the very center of metaphysics and epistemology. Before we can take a position on what there is in the universe we must settle the question of what we are able to know in principle. Historically the welter of answers to this most basic question can be reduced to a few isms. The one that appeals to the ordinary citizen—and even to philosophers in their nonprofessional hours—is what has been called *common-sense realism*. What there is in the world is just what we see (hear, taste, touch, or smell). The "thing" before me, which is called a typewriter, is 18 inches wide, 1 foot deep, has black keys and a little ball on which are embossed the letters of the alphabet. The answer to the question, *What is it really like?* is: "It is 18 inches wide, 1 foot deep . . ." etc.

Realism of this sort has much to recommend it, not the least of which is the nearly unanimous adherence of active parties in the nonspeculative arenas of life. But a moment's reflection admits a legion of troubles. First, everything I report regarding the characteristics of the typewriter is based upon the evidence provided by my eyes, fingers, and ears. In every perception there is at least one third term in addition to "thing" and "knowledge of the thing." The third term, whether acknowledged or not, is *sensation*. It is the central tenet of the philosophical school known as *phenomenalism* that all we can ever know *directly* are our own sensations (and the ideas fashioned out of these sensations) and that, accordingly, we can never know the external world directly and *in itself*. This is at the heart of Kant's famous distinction between the "noumenal" and the "phenomenal" worlds, the former referring to "things in themselves" and the latter to our perceptions of them. It is also the cornerstone of the *phenomenalism* defended by Hume and by Mill, and the *immaterialism* advanced by Berkeley. The roots of phenomenalism are deep enough to reach the pre-Socratics. In the hands of Socrates, the essential truth of the phenomenalistic position was enough to lead to a rejection of purely perceptual knowledge and the commitment to turn philosophy into a search for those "True Forms" ever beyond the range of the (mere) vulnerable senses.

Realism has not always quailed in the face of phenomenalism. The realist's reply to the claim that the senses are often deceived or that some perceptions are illusory is that the very concepts of deception and illusion entail valid perceptions. In this dispute, realists have often obtained support from the naturalistic perspective. Setting human perception aside, the realist points to the balance of the animal kingdom in which survival depends upon adapting behavior to the perceived realities of the world. Were there no correspondence between the world as it is and the world as the animal senses it to be, the animal's life would be over before it began. On the realist's account, the senses are reporting *something* and the report must faithfully reflect the physical features of that which initiates the sensory response.

One of the most compelling defenses of realism was provided by Thomas Reid in his *An Inquiry into the Human Mind*, the essay designed to overturn Hume's skeptical philosophy.[12] Reid judged Hume's radical empiricism to be based upon two major metaphysical premises: that all we can know are our own ideas, and that these are but "copies" of our sensations. Reid's rebuttal takes as an illustration the drawing of, for example, a right-angle triangle on a sheet of paper. What "sensation" results when we examine this drawing? Given the facts of physiological optics—including the shape of the cornea and the retina—the peripheral "sensation" is one involving a spherical triangle; one whose sides are curved and whose angles sum to more than 180 degrees. But what is *seen* when we examine the figure? The answer, of course, is a right-angle triangle. On Reid's theory of perceptual realism, the mind is so constituted that it constructs the real object *given* the transformed information delivered by the senses. In Reid's terminology, the sensory reports serve as "natural signs" of the actual object and the mind is able to pass from the "natural sign" to the thing signified. In this we have an illustration of *constructive realism* advanced against Hume's *sensationism.*

In contemporary psychology, the principle sensationistic theory is that developed by J. J. Gibson.[13] The argument in defense of the theory and the data on which it is based would require many pages to present, but the theory itself can be summarized in a short sentence: *Perception is a function of the stimulus.* Gibson's point is that we need not invent "mental" operations to account even for the facts of complex perceptions. The perceptual outcome is *determined* by the physical properties of impinging stimuli, and the task of psychology is to identify the specific feature or features of stimuli by which the percept is thus determined. Gibson's formulation of the hypothesis is as follows:

(F)or every aspect or property of the phenomenal world of an individual in contact with his environment, however subtle, there is a variable of the energy flux at his receptors, however complex, with which the phenomenal property would correspond if a psychophysical experiment could be performed.[14]

Interestingly, Gibson's sensationistic theory shares many elements found in Reid's constructive realism. Gibson does not attempt to account for every illusion, hallucination, or daydream, nor does he attempt to specify the neurophysiological operations at the root of perception. Nevertheless, his theory is explicitly physicalistic and implicitly physiological in that physiological variables are taken as the ultimate causal agents in the chain leading to *every* perception. His theory, then, is sensationistic, realistic, and physiological. It requires the investigator who would challenge it to produce reliable perceptual data which cannot be correlated with known variables of "the energy flux."

Although sensationistic, Gibson's theory is not *elementaristic* in that it specifically legislates against attempts to understand the perceptual enviroment in terms of particles of stimulation. For Gibson, the physical stimulus is the *totality* of environmental impingements, and the perceptual response is the response of the relevant sensory *systems*. The point here is not that the whole is greater than the sum of its parts, but that the whole cannot be explained by reference to any single or small fraction of the elements of the system. There is nothing mysterious or "transcendent" about a radio. Yet, were we to leaf through pages of descriptions of each component of a radio—descriptions of the pressed cardboard serving as the speaker, the diodes providing amplification, the crystals which function as transducers—we would have no understanding of the *radio* as such.

A fuller understanding of Gibson's theory can be obtained through an illustration; that of "prismatic adaptation" as studied by Ivo Köhler.[15] Subjects required to wear distorting lenses for prolonged periods (weeks or even months) soon adapt to the optically transformed world, and begin to see it normally. Once the prisms are removed, there is a lingering displacement of the real world. That is, a period of readaptation is now necessary, and may last for weeks. When the prisms are removed, however, the curvature perceived in straight objects is actually greater when the eyes are turned to the right than when they are turned to the left—an effect which is reverse of the actual curvatures induced by the prisms during the period of initial adaptation. Findings of this sort have generally been offered in support of perceptual theories opposed to sensationism. The data clearly illustrate that adaptation and readaptation cannot be based upon elementary receptor processes or on the fixed anatomical projections of the visual system. They have been interpreted, instead, as evidence for a kind of spontaneous reorganization of the field, where field refers either to a field of brain activity or to some more "cognitive" space in which perceptions are organized. Gibson, however, judges these same data to be in conformity with his central thesis:

Note what the formula implies: that a psychophysical correspondence between *values* of stimulation and *qualities* or *intensities* of experience is not permanent. There are no fixed pairs of connections between them; the connections are altered by a few minutes' exposure to special stimulation.[16]

Gibson's theory, then, is not a rigid stimulus-response theory or a connectionistic one. It is, to use a much misused word, *dynamic* in its description of the adaptive responses of perceptual processes to altered environments.

The strengths of Gibson's theory are precisely the sources of its weaknesses. It begins with the somewhat startling claim that every perception is explicable in terms of the energy flux contained in impinging stimulation. This is the usual (traditional) opening round in which the sensationist lays the groundwork for a rigorously reductionistic psychology. Yet, Gibson does not propose to reduce perception to physics, for he promptly installs such variables as the "totality" of environmental stimulation, and such Delphic variables as "what happens in the cortex."[17] Gibson also acknowledges the part played by attention and "set," and appreciates the role of imagination, learning, heredity, motivation, and emotion. This is all to the good, but it somehow dilutes the very provocative initial hypothesis with a rather prosaic collection of qualifying clauses. If, for example, there is a way to hold constant such variables, states, and processes as motivation, emotion, attitude, expectancy, imagination, prior learning, heredity, level of adaptation, and memory, then indeed we have every reason to expect that identical energy fluxes will yield identical perceptions; that changes in the energy flux will produce equivalent alterations in perception. In fact, the past century of psychophysical research has made it abundantly clear that the well-conducted study of sensory thresholds will yield precise, reliable, and informative data which can be safely generalized not only across subjects but even across species. However, to obtain such data it has been necessary to reduce the stimulating environment to its barest elements, and to confine evidence of "perception" largely to reports of a "yes–no" nature.

Gibson's theory and his own exceptional studies have called attention to a number of stimulus variables too often neglected in research on perception. As a result of these contributions, researchers must now recognize such factors as texture gradients, eye and body motion, and optical "slant" in the determination of perception. Gibson has also added to healthy doubts about treating sensory processes as the means by which we make "copies" of the external world. Those influenced by Gibson are now persuaded that the mission of physiological psychology in relation to perception is one of discovering the functional relationships between environmental impingements and perceptual outcomes. This, of course, was Fechner's dream and has been an abiding feature of the history of sensory research, but Gibson has added an articulate defense of the need to specify the adequate environmental stimuli.

As a physiological theory of perception, Gibson's fails, but for reasons Gibson would surely accept. In none of his many articles or several books has he attempted to specify with any exactness ". . . what happens in the cortex." He takes for granted that the sensory nervous system, from periphery to brain, is the efficient causal link in every perceptual outcome. This, however, is no more than subscribing to psychological materialism and is, therefore, merely a metaphysical bias, not a theoretical term. Moreover, in none of the statements of his perceptual theory has Gibson incorporated the principal facts and hypotheses emerging from the neural sciences. Neurophysiology is rather taken for granted on the assumption, it would seem, that any fact produced by it will conform to the Gibsonian theory. This assumption is warranted in a telling way, for as the theory has been presented it is confirmed by *any* neural response reliably tied to *any* change in the "energy flux." The theory, to put the criticism briefly, offers no direction to sister disciplines. It acknowledges the part taken by learning and motivation in perception, but does not specify the relationship between these processes and perception itself. It confers causal status on the nervous system, but does not propose questions or methods by which the neural foundations of Gibson's version of perception might be established. It is worth repeating that Gibson has not attempted to provide a developed theory of the *physiology* of perception. His thoughts are included here because they *do* take the physiology for granted: without the neural equipment, contact with the environment is impossible. This is Gibson's claim, and it is this claim that makes his theory relevant and of interest to, and finally assimilable by, the neural sciences. Note, also, that it matters very little that Gibson speaks of neural "correlates" or perceptual-neural covariances, rather than of the neural *causes* of perception. He has taken the position that every perceptual event occurs at the end of a chain of events all of whose links except the first are biological. Again, this is not a theory but a vote for the prevailing scientism. It does not address the Mind/Body question, but begs it. Similarly, in the matter of epistemology, it is not enough to note that perception is not a copy of the real world, but only a function of it. To claim that X is not a copy of Y requires minimally that both X and Y are known. For Gibson to claim, then, that our perceptions do not give us faithful reproductions of "things in themselves"—Kant's *noumena*—is implicitly to claim some knowledge of these. To claim further that two persons should not be expected to have the same perception even under conditions in which the "energy flux" is the same requires some specification of what the differences are likely to be, and some specification of what would have to be done for the differences to be eliminated. Otherwise, what is the significance of the "law" according to which which all perception is a function of stimulation?

Gibson has defined his theory as a psychophysical theory of perception and a biophysical theory of stimulation.[18] It is in his approach to the specification of relevant features of the environment that the originality of the theory becomes most evident. It is in just this respect that the term "sensationistic" is to be applied with caution and qualification. Gibson himself would probably reject the adjective, and argue that his major proposition is that perception cannot be understood as the outcome of cell-by-cell discharges. But it is important to recognize that sensationism and elementarism are different perspectives on perception. Their connection is historical, not logical or scientific. It is something of a comment on the march of ideas in this area that, in 1978—a century after Wundt planned the Leipzig laboratory—psychology still finds itself quibbling over the distinction between sensation and perception. The usual differentiation is based upon the putatively greater complexity of the latter; the relative dependence of the latter on "organismic" rather than stimulus variables; the relative durability of the latter in the face of fluctuations in the stimulus; for example, "size constancy." Philosophers have added to the confusion by admitting such terms as "sensa" into discourse concerning the nature of experience. Here the "sensa" refer to such raw and neutral experiences as patches of light, pressures on the surface of the skin, fields of homogeneous illumination. The sensa, then, are to be contrasted with *percepts* of the actual material things which are the objects of perception—chairs, apples, textbooks. Perhaps Gibson's most salutary contribution has been the argument favoring a realistic approach to the selection of stimulus variables, and the related arguments against assessing stimuli from the receptor's point of view! Yet, with this ecological orientation, the theory has become even less biological, largely because the neural sciences themselves have not been able to embrace those transactions between the unconstrained organism and its natural environment. But an ecological orientation is not opposed to sensationism necessarily, and Gibson's form of perceptual ecology is actually quite at home with sensationism. The phenomena to be addressed by Gibson's theory are all those involving *contact* between the organism and the environment. The theory seeks to explain adjustments to the environment in terms of the sensory processing of impinging stimuli. This is the sensationistic side of the theory, and it survives no matter what position is taken on the question of the reducibility of sensory responses to a more elementary (receptor) level of processing.

It is precisely because Gibson opposes elementaristic reductions while defending an essentially sensationistic approach that the theory has failed to direct physiological psychologists. First, even the experimeter who studies the individual receptor is not committed to the view that perceptual outcomes can be found in the responses of single units. To this extent, Gibson's criticism is a useful reminder to those who, in a moment of weakness, might be misguided by the physiology of receptors, but it is not enough to offer mere reminders. What a physiological theory of perception must provide—if one of its central tenets is opposed to elementarism—is the sort of evidence which is fundamentally unexplainable in elemental terms. However, much of the evidence adduced by "Gibsonians" in support of *holism* * can be explained by theories based upon the pooling of receptor responses; a pooling that involves both inhibitory and excitatory mutual influences exerted by units on their neighbors. It is one thing to proclaim that "Stimulation for the *animal* is not the same as stimulation for a *cell*" [19] but quite another to establish precisely the difference between an animal engaged in perception and the sensory-neural apparatus of that animal as it is engaged in perception. The latter certainly involves more than "a cell," but does it involve more than the cells of the relevant sensory system? If so, what more? Indeed, is there any operational means by which to distinguish between (a) a large pool of mutually interacting receptor units and transmission units and (b) a field of perceptual activity whose total response cannot be matched by a complete description of the unit-activity occurring within the pool?

---

* Here the term *holism* is meant to serve as the antonym of *elementarism*. The requirement that stimuli be specified according to the entire perceptible array of arriving energy—and further specified according to the level of adaptation of the awaiting sensory system—is *holistic*.

This question is not merely rhetorical. Over the past twenty years a number of models have been put forth to account for complex perceptions by assembling the known characteristics of receptors and neurons. The most direct impetus has come from the seminal research of H. K. Hartline and his collaborators working on the peripheral physiology of invertebrate vision, and the highly suggestive research of David Hubel and Thorsten Wiesel on the electrophysiology of central mechanisms of vision.[20] Of Hartline's many fundamental discoveries, the one most relevant to perception is that which accounts for enhancement effects—a kind of image-intensification—produced by inhibitory processes in regions surrounding the locus of stimulation. In the arthropod, these mechanisms operate in the periphery, although there is some evidence to suggest that even in human vision both inhibitory and disinhibitory mechanisms also exist in the retina.[21] Hubel and Wiesel have demonstrated the presence of specific, geometric arrangements of cells in the visual cortex; arrangements that are uniquely responsive to visual stimuli varying in angular orientation, in shape, and in rates of movement. Such findings have made it more plausible to discuss complex perceptual processes within the context of pooled unit-activity, and to propose models of "feature analysis"* that are able to confront perceptual data reductionistically and without embarrassment.[22] What such models have trouble with are phenomena

SIHT SA HCUS

where, for example, the "programming" of a given columnar organization of cortical cells should be of no use—but where perceptual adjustments to the reversal occur in a matter of seconds.

* But consult the important criticisms of William Uttal in *The Psychobiology of Mind* (1978), pp. 498–505.

The properties of the illustration given above which do not change when such a reversal occurs are those associated with the *spatial frequency* of the stimulus. The words SUCH AS THIS can be seen against the white background of the page as a result of contrast. One way of quantifying this is by measuring the number of light/dark transitions occurring per unit-distance. This measure is the spatial frequency of the stimulus and it can, of course, vary in magnitude as well; that is, the changes may be both frequent and of high or low contrast. Note that in the transitions from SUCH AS THIS to snɔH ʌs ⊥HIS or to Hɔns sʌ sIH⊥ neither the spatial frequency nor the contrast intensity changes, whereas a slightly different spatial frequency results from SUCH AS THAT. It has been proposed that neural pools, differentially sensitive to various spatial frequencies—that is, "tuned" to given ranges of spatial frequency—may be responsible for the facility with which subtle alterations in otherwise complex stimuli are discriminated.[23] It is well established that the human visual system is optimally suited to respond to temporal and spatial periodicities when the stimuli involved are limited to large, unstructured fields.[24] These same characteristics, these "resonance" features of the visual system, certainly are operative when complex and structured fields are perceived.[25]

As important as these findings are, they have yet to be incorporated into a general theory of perception. Hartline's studies, masterful in design and rigor, are concerned with neuroelectric mechanisms engaged by contrast at borders. Rudimentary aspects of form perception and brightness discrimination can be addressed by the model developed by Hartline and Ratliff, but these investigators have not suggested that the model is directly applicable to the most complex perceptual processes. D. Hubel and T. Wiesel, who have created a generation of "Gestalt physiologists," can be credited with identifying cortical correlates of such perceptions as slant, motion, and depth, but none of this work has led to a bona fide *theory* of perception. It is no disservice to their exemplary research to note that the correlates obtained experimentally might just as well have been hypothesized for the purpose of theory construction. In other words, *since* we perceive changes in the angular orientation of stimuli, we certainly must have *some* equipment in the visual cortex able to register these changes. It is of undoubted value to know something about this equipment, but this can be no more than a footnote to any general theory of the physiology of perception.

This criticism turns out to be more to the point than those ordinarily directed against sensationistic and reductionistic approaches to perception. As I have noted already, there is no a priori justification for rejecting a physiological theory of perception merely because it rests on the analysis of neural or receptor units. Historically and currently, the problem has been a rather different one: those engaged in analyses of this sort have simply failed to provide general theories of perception. Typically, a physiological measurement has been made; for example, the velocity of propagation of the neural impulse; the rate of impulse-initiation as a function of the intensity of stimulation; alterations of background (EEG) activity in the nervous system following the application of various stimuli; destruction of sensory "centers" and correlated deficits in perception. And just as typically, the account ends once the fact has been announced. But, again, all such findings can be *stipulated* for the purpose of developing a general theory. The point here is that the physiological details are of less significance than is ordinarily appreciated. The phenomena to be explained are *perceptual,* and are easily and reliably demonstrated. They do not derive their validity from the discovery of physiological correlates. *They would retain all their validity were there no nervous system at all!* But the strong tendency in physiological psychology—to the extent that there is any tendency to theorize at all—is to attempt to construct hypotheses regarding brain function from the facts of perception; not to develop theories of perception in light of the facts of brain function. Such efforts have not met with much success, in part because a given perceptual outcome can (in principle) be achieved in a nearly infinite number of ways, whereas the brain functions the way brains function. I should clarify this with an example. To attempt to discern how a given perceptual effect is achieved is akin to determining how a given game of chess was won. This requires a knowledge of the laws of chess which, here, we may call the "theory" of chess. Nothing is gained by a knowledge of the composition, style, color, or size of the actual chess pieces. In fact, the entire game could have been played out verbally, with no actual pieces. Now, by the same token, to determine how a given set of chess pieces were moved, we need not ever consider the "theory" of chess. A complete causal account can be achieved with no more than the laws of mechanics. But let us take the case a step further. In one column, we record the move-by-move locations of every piece on the chess board. In a second column, we record the verbalized "moves" announced by Smith and Jones. Comparing the entries, we discover that there is a perfect correlation between the positions of the pieces and the record of the verbalizations. In such a case, we properly conclude that *this* particular game of chess was the one played by Smith and Jones. Now let us return to the matter of physiological correlates of perception.

The neural elements of the sensory systems are seldom quiet. They vary in their patterns of discharge, in the D.C. potentials found at synaptic junctions, in their metabolic activity. When stimuli are applied, large numbers of these elements undergo changes in activity. For any given feature of Smith's perception, there will be many neural, chemical, and (even) structural correlates. Discovering such correlates is not enough, except where the most rudimentary perceptions are involved; for example, that of an increase in the intensity of a disc of light. But where the percept includes something like a house or strawberry shortcake or a bird in flight, we need more than neural correlates. We need the same two columns that were required when we set out to determine if, in fact, the movement of the chess pieces constituted the *game* that was *played* by Smith and Jones. That is, beyond neural correlates, we must have a description of the *logic* of the neural sequences to determine if this logic can be mapped on to the logic of perception. The word "logic" here is used to convey rule-governed structures or symbols or codes. Theories attempting this sort of mapping are *constructive* in the sense that they seek to build within the nervous system those rule-governed structures, symbols, or codes which match the logic of perception.

The grandfather of all modern constructive theories of perception is, of course, Gestalt psychology which, from its inception, has been distinctively physiological. During the past half-century of its evolution, Gestalt theory has been both a reaction to behavioristic and sensationistic alternatives and an active force in shaping psychology's methods and perspectives. Epistemologically, it is a theory in the tradition of common-sense realism,[26] and although it is physicalistic, it is not rigidly mechanistic. The "field theory" of physics has been most relied upon by Gestalt theorists. Accordingly, their interest in the central nervous system has been confined principally to those neuroelectric "field" effects manifested in such phenomena as gross alterations in the D.C. potential of the brain as a whole, or of large cortical regions of the brain.[27]

The word "Gestalt" lends itself to a variety of interpretations, most of them not compatible with Gestalt psychology as developed by Köhler, Wertheimer, and Koffka. The theory does not assert—as is often claimed—that "the whole is greater than the sum of its parts," but that perceptual "wholes" are *different* from elementary sensations.[28] Thus, Gestalt theory is not tied to the eccentric notion that, in the act of perception, the percipient somehow mars or distorts reality by staining it with his own idiosyncrasies. Gestalt psychology is, as I have said, in the realist tradition of epistemology. The perceptions with which it is concerned are perceptions of real things in the real world. To this extent, there is close correspondence between Gibsonian and Gestalt theories. Both are comfortable with the general law according to which perception is a function of stimulation, provided that stimulation is defined (a) according to the overall environmental context within which perception occurs and (b) according to the known organismic variables by which any perception becomes possible in the first place.

Unlike the Gibsonian theory, however, Gestalt theory is explicitly physiological, such that the physiological aspects of the theory are at least in principle testable. The central physiological concept of the theory is that of *isomorphism*. As the term suggests, the proposition is that, in any perception, the fundamental form or structure of the percept is matched by underlying neural processes possessing the same form or structure. Note, however, that isomorphism is not a "copy" theory. The rules of chess are *isomorphic* with every legitimate move made in a game of chess, but the rules as such do not "look like" chess pieces. Similarly, the sentences:

"It is red."
"Es ist rot."
"C'est rouge."
"Id est rubrus."

are isomorphic grammatically, as well as identical semantically, even though all the predicate adjectives are literally different; even though no sentence is a literal "copy" of any other.

The neuro-perceptual isomorphism advocated by Gestalt theory is illustrated by the figure given below, a standard "reversible" figure. If one observes figure 1 for 20 or 30 seconds, the larger sectors will replace the smaller ones in the apparent foreground. Under continuous observation, the sec-

tors occupying the apparent foreground will undergo periodic reversals. What occurs at the phenomenal level is the self-obstruction of a figure during prolonged inspection; a sort of fatigue-process that renders a given portion of perceived space less able to excite or sustain perception. According to the principle of isomorphism, the cortical correlate of this effect is one that

raises a local obstruction to its own continuation, and so weakens itself until, as a consequence, this process suddenly moves from its original location into the other possible area, and so forth.[29]

The "local obstruction" in this case refers to certain cortical "currents" assumed to be established by stimulation. To the extent that the perceptual effect is one of self-obstruction, the (isomorphic) effect in the brain must also be one of self-obstruction. Tests of the *mechanism* proposed by Köhler have not confirmed the theory. Electrical fields in the brains of experimental animals have been disturbed through the use of implanted metallic foil,[30] by the application of aluminum hydroxide,[31] and by the surgical scoring of the cortical surface.[32] Despite measurable alterations of the EEG and the overall D.C. level of the field under investigation, animals so treated have failed to display the predicted disruptions of their perceptual capacities. Such studies tell equally, of course, against sensationistic and elementaristic hypotheses by demonstrating the survival of perception under conditions in which the cellular configurations of sensory systems are completely disrupted.

The fact that the mechanism of isomorphism has not proved to be the one proposed by Gestalt theories has not led to the abandonment of the concept of isomorphism itself. Recently, Karl Pribram has combined this durable notion with the theory of *holography* and has set forth a constructive theory of perception which he calls the holographic theory.[33] The inspiration here comes from the pioneering efforts of Dennis Gabor in applied optics. Gabor's aim had been to improve the detail of photographs obtained from electron-microscopic studies of cells. In order to enhance detail, it was necessary not only to preserve the patterns of light and darkness, but also to retain the *phase* information contained in the light refracted by thin slices of tissue. What Gabor proposed in 1941—based upon a mathematical model—was to be realized some 25 years later with the development of the laser. The Gabor principle may be simply (if perhaps simplistically) described as the reconstruction of object-images by the coherent illumination of their interference patterns. If the wavefront produced by refracted light passing through thin tissue slices is photographed directly, only a blur results. However, the same wavefront illuminated by coherent light* forms, through the interaction, an interference pattern in which both the phase and the amplitude information of the wavefront are contained. Subsequent illumination of a transparency of this pattern—provided that the illumination again is with coherent light—produces the *hologram* which contains the *whole* of the original scene. A striking feature of holograms is that any "piece" of one contains nearly all the information one can extract from any other "piece" or from the entire record. The physics and mathematics involved in all this is very complex, but a homely analogy may be helpful. Suppose there were a device which, when a blend of several colors of paint was poured into it, separated each of the constituent colors from the rest such that, at the output end, only pure colors emerged, each in a separate channel. Optical systems, including the human eye, form clear images of distant objects by preserving not only the wavelength and amplitude information (color and brightness), and not only the spatial information (such that the top of the arrow remains at the top, and the bottom, at the bottom) but also the *phase* information that expresses the time of arrival of various waves at the same or neighboring location. However, a photograph cannot preserve such information since, from the film's perspective, all waves arrive at the same time. The film then, referring to the analogy, "sees" only the outputs of the channels containing pure colors. If one of the channels is clogged, there will be no evidence that that color had been part of the blend. In other words, no single piece of the output will contain information regarding any other piece. But suppose we enter the system

---

* Coherent light here refers to light of a single wavelength (i.e., monochromatic light) all of whose rays are parallel to each other.

before the final processing has been done; that is, at the stage at which the blended colors are all homogeneously mixed together. At this stage, any sample of the mixture, when properly analyzed, will contain all the information present in the entire mixture. With holograms, there is an optical equivalent of entering the system prior to the final "processing." The objective entity, for example, an apple, reflects light from every vanishingly small portion of its surface. The image of the apple on our retina is a *processed* image in that the radiation has been passed through cornea, lens, and the fluids of the eye. The photographic image is also processed, but with all of the temporal (phase) interactions converted into variations in brightness. Thus, the apple's depth and texture are greatly reduced. But if before the apple has been focused by a lens—that is, when everything is "blended"—we approach its wavefront and illuminate it with coherent light, an array of interference effects will emerge such that amplitude and phase will be spread throughout the illuminated scene. Thus, any sample will for all practical purposes be the entire sample.

Holograms are not limited to optical information and, at the present time, many of the original constraints (e.g., laser illumination) have been removed by advances in technology. These matters, though interesting in their own right, are not relevant here where we are concerned with physiological theories of perception. What is important, however, are those features of holography which permit a plausible theory of perception grounded in physical processes. And in this connection, the most important features are (a) the hologram's ability to store nearly all information contained in the object everywhere within the hologram and (b) the hologram's record of spatial, temporal, and magnitude information. The importance of these features is rooted in two of the most consistent facts regarding the physiology of perception:

first, that extensive destruction of the sensory portions of the central nervous system may have only marginal effects on perception [34] and, second, that the pulse coding provided by neurons has never been able to mimic the richness, the variety, and the "realism" of perception. What holography has shown, however, is that immense quantities of information can be optically stored in very little space; that a given object can be holographically stored *throughout* the hologram; that the extraordinary detail generally missing from photographic records can be retained by a holographic photograph.

Perhaps it was Karl Lashley who first anticipated the sort of theory that holography has made possible [35] but Pribram should be credited with developing the concept and with combining the actual theory of holography with the physiological and experiential aspects of perception. The great difficulty, of course, is in determining where and how in the physiology of sensory systems something like a holographic construction might take place. Pribram has proposed that the junctional potentials—the electrical events at the neural synapse—may serve as the equivalent of wavefronts, and that neural inhibitory mechanisms may provide the necessary *interference* effects. Note that Pribram does not suggest that holograms of the optical sort are constructed "in the head," or even that a point-for-point relationship exists between holograms and neural processes. Indeed, where Köhler was specific in his statement of the electrophysiology but evasive on the question of theory, Pribram has been generally confident in the holographic theory but properly diffident on the matter of specific physiological mechanisms. The theory is too recent to have received the range and number of experimental tests and challenges needed if we are to gauge its long-term usefulness. Yet, it is the only physiological theory of perception able to embrace without embarrassment the following facts and principles:

1. Perception is largely unaffected by destruction of primary and secondary sensory "centers" in the nervous system.

2. Lesions that do disrupt perception tend to display "field" type effects more complex and "informational" than would be expected were perception only the result of a transmission-line process.

3. Perception often remains constant under conditions in which the physical dimensions of the stimulus undergo radical transformations; for example, in the phenomena of size and distance "constancy."

4. Perception is uniquely *contextual* such that the properties of the entire perceptual *field* are determinative of perceptual outcomes.

5. A fair and meaningful fraction of perceptual principles (depth perception, size and distance constancy, shape discrimination) are operative in neonatal organisms, suggesting that the mechanisms of perceptual organization are not merely innate but functional at the start of life.

6. Despite the known distortions imposed upon the objective world by the peripheral mechanisms of sensation, perceptions display high ecological validity, suggesting that the world which must be dealt with by the organism and the world perceived by the organism are isomorphic—even if not "copies" of one another.

7. Although there is profit in examining psychological functions one at a time, the organism that perceives also learns, recalls, is moved to action, and is given to states of emotionality. Nothing in the holographic theory of perception is inconsistent with these other functions, and certain features of the theory are particularly well suited to such functions as associational learning and memory.

Before concluding this section on physiological theories of perception, a few remarks are in order on the theory of *adaptation level* (AL) initially advanced and frequently discussed by Harry Helson.[36] It is a general theory of psychology, not just a theory of perception. In the broadest terms, it is a theory of adjustment which includes learning, motivation, perception, emotion, and memory among the *means* available to the adjusting organism. The adaptation level, itself, is defined as (in principle) the "weighted log mean of all stimuli affecting the organism."[37] As in Gibson's theory, attention is given to the full ensemble of impinging stimuli and to the condition of the organism at the time such stimuli arrive. Also as in Gibson's theory, AL theory is at base a physiological theory but is not explicit in stipulating specific neurological mechanisms. Rather, the underlying physiology is, as it were, taken for granted. The theory has explanatory merits in dealing with such phenomena as positive and negative aftereffects in the perception of color and shape, but its promise seems to be of a limited sort. AL theory is not to be confused with the old notion of "homeostasis," in that it does not reduce all psychological processes to the organism's need for "equilibrium states." But like homeostatic theories, it is so general in its reach and so lacking in quantitative laws that it is better viewed not as a theory of psychology but as a perspective on behaving organisms.

To summarize:

1. Physicalistic theories of perception are uniformly destitute of bona fide covering laws beyond those which are purely physiological, or which are mere restatements of the traditional psychophysical laws.

2. Except for the holographic theory, attempts to account for perception in physiological terms have been frustrated by the failure to propose biological mechanisms able to match the known complexity, dynamics, and variety of perceptual experience.

3. The holographic theory is less a theory than a model, since the proposed mechanism of neural construction—the "junctional potentials"—has not been shown to operate according to holographic principles in the required sense.

4. Physicalistic theories of perception—if we may so call the works discussed in this section—tend to be confined to a single perceptual system (usually vision) and generally offer no guidance for getting from one system to the others. Gibson's theory and Helson's AL theory are *general*—as is Pribram's—but the empirical foundations are drawn almost entirely from studies of visual perception.

5. By the standards that have become traditional in the developed sciences, there is no physiological theory of perception, although there are many well-confirmed hypotheses of *sensory* coding in all the perceptual systems.

Theories of Learning and Memory

A physiological theory of learning and/or memory must take for granted the perceptual component since, as we have seen, there is no coherent, law-based, and general physiological theory of perception. Before examining specific attempts to provide a physiological theory of learning and memory, it will be useful to enumerate those fundamental facts and issues which any such theory must confront and ultimately explain:

1. All findings support the proposition that the class of adaptive behavior ordinarily described as "learned" is quantitatively dependent upon the species of organisms and their stage of maturation.

2. Operant conditioning has established that the persistence of learned behavior is a function of the schedules of reinforcement employed during initial acquisition of the behavior in question.

3. Among the higher species (and even fish!) practice at the solution of a given problem typically results in greater facility in solving problems of the same genre.

4. Among the higher species, learning is not merely associative, but also *relational*. Thus, the child who is taught to

name the melody "My Country 'Tis of Thee . . ." will recognize the melody played in any key, even though the actual notes change from key to key.

5. To the extent that rewards and punishments are known to have profound effects on performance, a physiological theory advanced to account for the acquisition of such performance must also contain within it (if only implicitly) a theory of *motivation*.

6. Memory, as studied at the level of human beings, involves at least two distinguishable processes; one involved in short-term or "buffer" storing of recently presented material, and one involved in the lifelong retention of information. A physiological theory of memory must make provision for such effects.

7. Memory is affected by previously acquired information in a way that is either detrimental or facilitative, depending upon the nature of the previously acquired information.

There are, to be sure, many other facts and principles established over the past century but the foregoing offer a sufficiently stern test for any theory of learning and memory. Only the theory able to accommodate these need be tested for greater power, and the theory unable to do so need not be tested further.

As with perception, the processes of learning and memory have been dealt with theoretically either in elementaristic or in holistic terms. The first systematic attempt at providing a physiological theory of adaptive behavior was made by David Hartley whose *Observations on Man* (1749) was inspired both by Newtonian physics and Lockean epistemology. Hartley was not the first to rely on the principles of *association* to account for the formation of ideas, nor was he the first to propose that perceptual and cognitive processes could be explained through recourse to the nervous system. But his *Observations on Man* was a lengthy and sustained defense of the psychobiological perspective and was certainly the first treatise of such comprehensiveness arising from this perspective.[38] Associationism is found in Locke's writings—especially his briefer works on education—and figures even more centrally in Hume's. But we owe it more to Hartley that this ism has become a fixture in theories of psychology. Such nineteenth-century psychologists as Alexander Bain,[39] J. F. Herbart,[40] and J. S. Mill were uncompromisingly associationistic though their respective psychologies differed in other important respects. And twentieth-century psychology was virtually baptized by Ivan Pavlov's radical associationism which, revealingly, was at the core of his equally radical materialistic psychology.

It is no discredit to Pavlov to observe that, by the closing years of the nineteenth century, "cerebral" theories of psychology were abundant. Most of the members of the scientific community were now persuaded that any developed science of psychology would be entirely dependent upon neurological findings and principles. Freud was as wed to this view as Pavlov was. Nor do we depreciate Pavlov's accomplishments by noting that associationism was also a commonplace in the nineteenth century. Pavlov's unusual contribution was twofold: first, his experiments on conditioned salivation were original and provocative; second, with the very limited data growing out of these experiments, he assembled a general theory of adaptive (and maladaptive) behavior in which old notions such as "association" were finally reduced to quantitative specification. His writings are punctuated with missionary zeal—just the sort of thing we come to expect of founders of "schools."[41]

I will discuss "associationism" at length in the next chapter. For the present, let us simply take the ism for granted and examine the sort of work Pavlov required of it. He had a reliable experimental finding: the frequent pairing of (un-

conditioned) stimuli known to affect the gastric physiology of dogs (e.g., powdered food placed in the mouth), with (*conditioned*) stimuli not having such effects, soon resulted in the latter coming to have the ability to elicit the responses formerly elicited only by the unconditioned stimuli. To this, Pavlov added another important and reliable finding: once a conditioned response had been established to a specific conditioned stimulus (a tone, for example), the amount of conditioned response was systematically lessened in the presence of stimuli progressively more different from the conditioned stimulus. The fact that stimuli of the same class but different in value could elicit conditioned responses was dubbed *stimulus generalization.*

Pavlov explored the possibility of curtailing such generalized responding. He discovered that, if the unconditioned stimulus (for example, food) was withheld during initial training on all trials when stimuli other than the conditioned stimulus was present, subsequent conditioned responses would not be as readily elicited by stimuli different from the conditioned stimulus. In other words, *generalization* would give way to stimulus *discrimination.*

To explain such effects, Pavlov took recourse to associationistic principles and applied them to the cerebral cortex. On the assumption that a given stimulus excites a specific region of the cortex, and on the additional assumption that such excitation spreads to neighboring regions, Pavlov attempted to explain generalization on the basis of *cortical irradiation.* Briefly, the theory takes the following form: (a) the conditioned stimulus (e.g., a tone of 500 cycles per second) is unfailingly presented one second before powdered food (the unconditioned stimulus) is placed in the dog's mouth; (b) this tone, theoretically, comes to activate a specific region of the cerebral cortex, but the activation spreads with diminishing amplitude to surrounding regions; (c) since surrounding regions are "tuned" to neighboring frequencies of sound, *some* association is forming between the unconditioned stimulus and tones similar to the 500 cps tone; (d) on tests of generalization, the amount of salivation diminishes as a function of the difference between the conditioned stimulus and the test stimuli.

Analogous processes were hypothesized to account for discrimination. Now, however, *inhibition* was proposed as the opponent of excitation. On trials involving the withholding of the unconditioned stimulus, cortical *inhibitory* processes were hypothesized. Illustratively, we might offer 100 trials involving a 500 cps tone accompanied by food interspersed with 100 trials involving a 1,000 cps tone in the absence of food. What the theory calls for is a region of maximum excitation in that portion of the cortex where 500 cps is "represented," and a region of maximum inhibition in the cortical regions associated with 1000 cps. Suppose, now, that tones of 900, 800, 700, and 600 cps are interspersed with the 1000 cps tone—again, with no food presented after any of these. With enough training (conditioning) of this sort, Pavlov was able to condition salivation to a specific tonal frequency and to prevent salivation in the presence of frequencies only slightly different from the conditioned stimulus; that is, he was able to create very sharp *discriminations*. Attempts to establish even finer discriminations—discriminations beyond the dog's capacities—were observed to result in hyperemotional responses; urination, quivering, defecation, irascibility. Pavlov judged this to be evidence of "experimental neurosis," and speculated on the possibility of all mental disorders being the result of analogous histories of conditioning.

More than half a century has elapsed since Pavlov's influential works were first made available to the English-speaking world of science[42] and in that time literally thousands of experiments in classical conditioning have been conducted and published. Most recently, the very trendy field of "biofeedback" has revived some of the older Pavlovian findings, although the new bottles have added much to the price but little to the flavor of the old wine. Our interest here, however, is not in the number of findings generated by the Pavlovian perspective or with the interesting applications of it to medicine or general health. Rather, we must ask whether the premises are sound, whether the theory is coherently related to available facts, and whether the overall approach taken by Pavlovian psychology is likely to be fruitfully brought to bear on the problems of learning and memory. As it happens, the answers to these questions are (a) No, (b) No, and (c) therefore, probably not.

Apart from the problems inextricably tied to the very concept of "association"—problems to be examined in the next chapter—the mechanisms proposed by Pavlov simply do not stand up to the neurophysiological facts. Pavlov's was a *connectionistic* neuropsychology, and it is fair to say that Karl Lashley's entire scientific career made such a neuropsychology untenable.[43] The connections proposed by Pavlov were anatomical ones, a proposition leading to the prediction that extreme alterations of the anatomy of the cortex would have profound effects not only on "connections" already formed but on the capacity of the cortex to form new ones. Moreover, the theory of conditioning advanced by Pavlov required specific sensory elements to make functional contact with specific motor elements, with the cortex serving as the anatomical connecting link. In the case of conditioned salivation, for example, the conditioned stimulus (e.g., the tone) and the conditioned response were to become associated by the process of *stimulus substitution;* that is the tone, presumably, came to be a *substitute* for powdered food.

Again, this substitution, on the Pavlovian account, had to occur anatomically.

Lashley's tests of these propositions were numerous, imaginative and telling. Perhaps the most simple required an animal to learn to choose one of two stimuli while wearing a patch over one eye. Once criterion performance was reached, the patch was removed and placed over the other eye, and the animal was tested to determine transfer effects. Predictably, information acquired by one eye was readily available to the animal when the patch was shifted. The point here was simply to underscore the fact that, whatever sort of connections may be involved in learning, they surely are not connections between *specific* sensory and motor units. More dramatically and convincingly, Lashley undertook an extensive series of *ablation* studies in which primary visual, auditory and tactile "centers" were destroyed. In nearly all cases, such destructive lesions neither (a) prevented animals from acquiring sensory discriminations, nor (b) eliminated such discriminations in organisms that had acquired them preoperatively.

To these physiological inquiries are to be added any number of purely behavioral data emerging from studies of *transposition*. The basic paradigm in such research is as follows:

1. Animals are trained to choose stimulus X over stimulus Y, where X and Y differ by k units of intensity.
2. Stimulus Y is replaced by stimulus Z which is as much greater than X as X was greater than Y.
3. Animals are then tested on their choices, given (2) above.

Time and again, it has been shown that in such situations, animals—pigeons, dogs, monkeys, rats, cats—tend to respond to stimulus *Z*, a stimulus never present during initial learning. That is, they choose stimulus *Z* over the specific stimulus *(X)* that had been reliably associated with reward. The conclusion advanced in the face of such data is that what the animals learned initially was not a particular stimulus, but the *relationship* between stimuli. Thus, the animals learned "brighter than," not "*k* units of intensity." The *irradiation* hypothesis cannot account for such effects, nor can any of the historical connectionistic theories. What is to be said of Pavlov's theory, then—and with proper admiration for his studies and his pioneering methods—is that it is wrong.

The most influential quasi-connectionistic theory proposed after Pavlov's is D. O. Hebb's, which first appeared in relatively developed form in *The Organization of Behavior* (1949). Years later, Hebb would reflect on the state of affairs prevailing in the 1940s: "[C]onnectionism had no defenders, and the psychological world had tacitly conceded the argument that such explanations of behavior were not possible."[44] What Hebb attempted was to preserve the advantages of a Pavlovian type of connectionism without having to adopt those of its limitations already exposed by Lashley and the Gestalt psychologists. In place of the Pavlovian reflexological and radically reductionistic hypotheses, Hebb installed the genuinely psychological variables of attention, "set," perception, cognition, and goal-directed behavior. And in place of the rigidly localized Pavlovian processes, Hebb remained intentionally indefinite on the matter of just *where* in the nervous system the various processes occurred. The reader should note that I could have introduced Hebb's theory in the preceding section addressed to perception, but Hebb himself has acknowledged that his theory is first a theory of *learning*[45] in which perception occupies the first stage.

At the most elemental level of the theory, the mechanism of the *cell assembly* is presented as the functional unit of psychophysiological processes. It corresponds to a given sensory event and constitutes the physiological substrate or representation of an image or an idea.[46] The size and number of cell assemblies are determined by associational operations, the mechanism of which is decreased "synaptic resistance" or, perhaps, decreased synaptic size.[47] The hypothesis is that, under conditions of repeated stimulation, the neurons comprising the active cell assemblies undergo growth at their terminals such that the distances across the activated synapses are diminished. Hebb offers this as but one of a number of possibilities. The coherence and explanatory power of his theory do not depend ultimately on the validity of these hypothesized changes in the anatomy of neurons.

Cell assemblies not only increase in number but, through relevant experience, become integrated with other assemblies. Thus, in time, a large number of assemblies may become engaged and may "discharge" sequentially. Such a series of integrated assemblies is referred to as a *phase sequence* which Hebb has graphically described as "one current in the stream of thought."[48] Conflicting phase sequences, according to Hebb, provide the neural correlate of emotional disturbances, particularly those which take the form of arrested or uncoordinated activity. Given the great number of phase sequences established in the mature organism, the possible combinations are staggeringly large. There is, then, always the possibility of new combinations being elicited—or even being spontaneously emitted—and some of these combinations will turn out to have adaptive value. Hebb judges this to be at the base of so-called "insightful" behavior; that is, originality. Finally, the process of *attention* now can be reduced to the effects of established and on-going phase sequences on subsequent phase-sequence activity. The novel stimulus alters the activity of the central nervous system such that additional cell assemblies are engaged, others are inhibited, still others are added. Hebb has insisted that the concept of the phase sequence, like that of the cell assembly, ". . . is a psychological construct, not a physiological one."[49] The microscopic analysis that would be required to unearth such events is, according to Hebb, both unpractical and impracticable. It would seem that Hebb views such processes as occurring in a whirl and din of activity, while the (complex) organism goes about adjusting its behavior to an environment whose psychological demands are extraordinary and unceasing. According to Hebb, then, the hypothetical physiological mechanisms are to be judged in terms of their ability to be reconciled to the facts of *behavior* as that behavior is emitted by the whole organism.

Because of the foregoing qualifications, the physiological features of Hebb's theory are simply untestable, although certain inferences are possible. For example, Hebb accounts for the persistence of behavior (and the persistence of memory) in terms of *reverberatory circuits* of electrical activity. Studies demonstrating the disruption of learning or memory produced by the introduction of convulsion-producing electrical shocks[50] or by the application of chemicals causing waves of cortical depolarization[51] tend to support the theory. Other research, however, which finds no effects on retention after periods in which all electrical activity has been eliminated (by freezing the animal)[52] serves as a challenge to the theory.

On purely formal grounds—apart from the presence or absence of experimental confirmations—Hebb's work is severely deficient, as Hebb himself has not been reluctant to acknowledge.[53] It is properly viewed as a pretheoretical sketch designed to allow a certain kind of conceptualization; a conceptualization of neurobehavioral correspondences sufficiently broad for the hypothesized neurology to keep pace with the observed behavior. There are no "covering" laws— or laws of any kind—nor are there systematic deductions from higher-order principles or axioms. Even as a theory of operant behavior there is little connection between, on the one hand, the "phase sequences," "reverberatory circuits," and "cell assemblies" and, on the other hand, such established effects as those associated with schedules of reinforcement, delayed reward, and varied magnitudes of reward. In other words, the constructs of Hebb's theory do not make contact in any rigorous way with the more reliable findings emerging from experimental analyses of operant behavior. All we receive from these constructs is a set of *possible* mechanisms which may form the neural substrate of trial-and-error learning and other habits. The difficulties here are not especially endemic to *connectionism*, but are due more to ambiguity and incompleteness.

Gestalt and holographic theories of learning and memory are more properly reserved for the next chapter since, unlike their approach to perception, their contact with neurophysiology is oblique in the areas of learning and memory. They are mentioned here only to note that they do not address the issues of motivation and emotion in relation to memory or learning. Thus, even in the realm of the behavior of organisms, the Gestalt theory remains largely a theory of perception, as Hebb's is primarily a theory of rudimentary problem-solving. But in the thirty years since Hebb's influential text, laboratories have not been inactive. Two major branches of physiological psychology have steadily compiled a large amount of data relevant to the generalities set forth in *The Organization of Behavior*. Thus, while we no longer speak of "reverberatory circuits" and the like except in quasi-historical terms, we do discuss the statistical and temporal patterns of neural discharges recorded from large populations of cells as animals acquire information and store it. We also discuss the role of various chemical "transmitters" in the processes of memory—transmitters whose functions are now thought to be not unlike those required by Hebb's model.

The most refined theory of memory based upon gross electrophysiological recordings is presented in E. R. John's *Mechanisms of Memory* (1967). The data-base upon which the theory rests consists principally of electroencephalographic and evoked-response recordings. The technique, applied in a variety of experiments, is one of correlating these electrical patterns with specific features of stimuli, and with such behavioral measures as correct vs. incorrect choices. John and his associates have shown that such gross electrographic measures are reliably correlated with geometric and informational features of stimuli[54] as well as with the correctness or the failure of the required responses.[55] The theory developed around these facts is of the *constructive* variety. John proposes that large populations of neurons reproduce that electrical pattern or wave shape initially induced by the applied stimulus or configuration of stimuli.[56] Memory, on this account, is akin to a readout which contains—within determinable statistical limits—a duplicate of the electrical codes by which the input was originally represented. John's theory is not connectionistic in that he specifically rejects the claim that memories are stored "here" or "there." His conception of brain function is more allied with Lashley's. The brain tends to operate as a whole, or at least as an ensemble of large and interconnected subsystems which are to be assayed in statistical rather than deterministic fashion. The associations formed between, for example, conditioned and unconditioned stimuli in the Pavlovian experiment are not *structural* associations or, for that matter, associations of any kind. Rather, the unconditioned stimulus produces (throughout vast reaches of the brain) patterns of activity which must be described probabilistically. As the number of pairings of conditioned and unconditioned stimuli increases, the probability rules followed by those neural pools responding to the conditioned stimulus become more like the rules followed by the network responding to the unconditioned stimulus. We can clarify this notion with an illustration. Consider a matrix of bulbs, 10×10, which can be lit in any order and any combination. Let us place two such matrices side by side. Let us also impose "noise" as a variable such that, at any given instant, a few of the bulbs may light up spontaneously or may fail to light when current is delivered. Thus, we can never predict perfectly what a single bulb will do. Let us also run a wire from each bulb in matrix A to the corresponding bulb in matrix B, but with a capacitor in the circuit such that the first discharge by a bulb in matrix A will not succeed in lighting its paired member in matrix B. Only after some number of discharges will the stored volts in an A bulb be released. But, as a further refinement, let us assume that the number of charges stored in matrix A becomes progressively less with each complete discharge. Suppose, that is, that initially there must be 10 pulses delivered to a bulb in matrix A before it discharges its volts to the corresponding bulb in matrix B. However, after this first discharge, only 9 pulses must arrive at the capacitor in order for it to discharge its contents; after this second discharge, only 8 pulses are needed, and so forth. Now let us light up matrix A in such a way as to form the letters "U.S.A." Without laboring over this point, it should be clear that, after a number of such "read-in" steps, matrix B will "read-out" the letters "U.S.A." on every occasion on which matrix A has been thus stimulated. However, on any given trial, a given bulb in matrix B (or A) may be unresponsive or improperly responsive. Thus, a unit-by-unit analysis may tell us very little. However, were we to plot the probabilities of firing for all the bulbs in matrix A and all the bulbs in matrix B, gradually the two probability distributions would become identical, since the noise imposed on each would be the same and could, therefore, be treated as a subtractable constant.

The advantages of John's theory are similar to those enjoyed by the holographic theory of perception. The theory is not vitiated by the retention of learned material following destruction of specific regions of the brain. Yet, the theory is equally compatible with data describing deficits after such destruction. That is, John's theory does not *proscribe* localization of functions, it merely does not require it. Nor does the theory rely upon the known physiology of neural units—a physiology simply incapable of "coding" what we already know about learning and memory. The theory, moreover, is not a "copy" theory; it does not assert that the brain somehow makes an electrical image of the external world, for how could we make an electrical image of an odor? All the theory seeks to establish is a plausible mechanism by which qualitatively and quantitatively distinguishable stimuli can be differentiated within the brain.

The disadvantages of the theory are also significant. First, it is not enough to speak of "transition probabilities." What is required is an unambiguous statement of the relationship between specific features of the input and measured alterations of the electrodynamics of the participating neural pools. It is interesting to discover that objects of different shape produce brain responses that are distinguishable from each other, but this is scarcely a *theory* of perception. It is also suggestive that certain "wave shapes" develop in regions of the brain during conditioning, and that these shapes are strikingly similar to those initially produced by "tracer" stimuli or unconditioned stimuli, but this is scarcely a *theory* of learning. What such correlations lack, in addition to covering laws and relevant deductions, is a specification of *mechanisms*. The theory avails itself of EEG and evoked response data, but we still lack a theoretical account of the EEG itself: its physiological origins, its functional significance, its relationship with other aspects of neurobehavioral and neuroperceptual processes. Then, too, John's theory makes little direct contact with those motivational and affective variables known to have profound effects upon adaptive behavior; less contact with the large and growing literature devoted to human learning and memory; no contact with that admittedly vexed area known as personality. None of this is intended as a criticism of John, for it would have been uselessly speculative had he attempted to extend the available data to cover these other processes. It is intended instead to underscore the underdeveloped state of physicalistic theories of learning and memory.

When we turn to the biochemistry of learning and memory, matters are even more tangled despite the spate of findings and daring guesswork of the past decades. The most secure finding to emerge from twenty years of study is that conditions which preclude the formation of ribonucleic acid (RNA) or certain brain proteins have adverse effects upon the retention of recently acquired responses.[57] Representative studies may be consulted for the details of research of this sort[58] but only a general description of the procedures is required here. Typically, the "learning" selected for study is limited to such unitary and stereotypical responses as escape, body or limb flexion, maintaining balance on a suspended wire, and shock avoidance. An overwhelming percentage of the pertinent literature is confined to studies of rats, or animals even lower on the taxonomic scale. The experimental methods generally boil down to one or another version of measures of performance before and after the administration of an agent known to affect the metabolic physiology of neural tissue. The claims emerging from this research may be summarized thus:

1. Systematic training (conditioning, learning, paced exercise) produces alterations in the chemistry of the brain, and these alterations serve as the "code" for memory of the behavioral patterns in question.
2. Agents that facilitate synaptic transmission or that increase the concentration of specific neurochemical or biochemical substances result in more rapid acquisition of learned responses and more durable retention of these same responses.
3. Agents that prevent the formation of specific biochemicals or that retard synaptic transmission result in defective learning and memory.
4. The effects of training require a period of time for "consolidation" within the brain. The deficits noted in (3) above occur only when the debilitating agents are administered before this consolidation has occurred.
5. Naturally produced codes can be extracted from the brains of trained animals and injected into the brains of naive animals, and the latter will display enhanced performance on measures of learning and memory.

These findings have been recruited in 'support of a biochemical theory of learning and memory which, briefly stated, reduces these processes to an ensemble of neurochemical codes capable of activating specific structures within the brain, thereby producing (reproducing) the original patterns of behavior. Research in this area is still relatively recent, but even at this early date it is clear that the sort of theory likely to be spawned by such studies will be rife with difficulties. Chief among these is the problem of generalizing effects such as those enumerated above to the facts of *human* memory. But apart from this, there are fundamental conceptual problems which have rarely been addressed. First, psychology on the whole has yet to settle on a definition of memory capable of establishing the boundaries within which behavior of a given genre qualifies and beyond which all other behavior does not. Minimally, these boundaries will exclude (a) reflexes, (b) instinctual patterns of behavior, (c) habituation, (d) hypersensitivity, (e) mere exercise or activity. If there is to be a biochemical theory of *learning* and of *memory*, the behaviors involved must offer unequivocal evidence of problem solving. Moreover, the chemical codes must be systematically related to the measures of learning and memory. Thus, if it is proposed that memory is coded by substance X, there must be a functional relationship between the amount or concentration or molecular configuration of X and measures of the accuracy or persistence of memory. Additionally, the role of substance X must be uniquely related to memory. The life of the brain requires oxygen. Accordingly, removal of oxygen will necessarily retard learning and memory—as a trivial corollary of death! Furthermore, proposed substances must naturally occur in brain cells or, if produced outside the brain, must be able to pass through the blood-brain barrier. The chemical "code" or "engram" of *learning* must be a chemical molecule or compound (a) able to assume a variety of configurations, (b) able to sustain new configurations, and (c) sufficiently complex to code the great variety of behaviors coming under the heading, "learning." Similarly, the molecule or compound proposed as a code for memory must be sufficiently *unstable* so that repeated experiences will alter it, and then sufficiently *stable* for the effects of experience to be retained.

These qualifications apply to the chemistry of proposed codes. Let us now turn to qualifications based upon characteristics of the organisms.

There are no more reliable facts in the literature of experimental psychology than those that describe the dependence of learning and memory upon the age, species, early experiences, and genotypic constitution of experimental animals. Any plausible theory of learning and memory based upon neurochemical mechanisms must account for these dependencies. Thus, the theory must be able to explain such phenomena as (a) "critical periods" during which certain behaviors are most easily acquired and most durably retained, (b) strain differences which result in radically different performances by animals of the same species but of known genetic disparity, (c) alterations in learning and memory from infancy to maturity, and from maturity to agedness. To these variables must be added the importance of motivation, emotion, and attention—three states of the organisms which profoundly influence the acquisition and retention of adaptive behavior.

In light of these considerations, the list of findings cited above is of doubtful significance, interesting though the findings are. At a purely *descriptive* level, research on the neurochemistry of learning and memory is commendable. But at a *theoretical* (explanatory) level, it leaves matters pretty much where they stood before the first study was ever conducted. There was never any serious doubt but that the chemistry of the brain is affected by stimulation, behavior, disease, maturation. At least since the nineteenth century, the scientific community has been generally persuaded that all psychological functions are mediated by the anatomical, physiological, and biochemical features of the nervous system. To discover, then, that learning occurs more efficiently when brain stimulants such as Metrazol, picrotoxin, strychnine, or caffeine have been administered is to add detail to a general perspective, not to provide a theory of learning. As with electrophysiological data, the findings from neurochemistry have not been incorporated into a theoretical system which offers a biochemical process for each major behavioral process; that is, a specific code for (a) discrimination learning, (b) extinction, (c) conditioned avoidance, (d) classical conditioning, (e) latent learning, (f) transposition, and so forth. There is, then, no physiological *theory* or *system* of learning and memory, only a substantial and growing collection of findings loosely connected by a generally accepted materialistic metaphysic as pervasive as it is unchallenged.

Theories of Motivation and Emotion

Psychology has had a traditional problem in coming to terms with its terms. *Motivation* and *emotion* are woeful illustrations of this. Everyone—including the layman—has a sense of what these words mean, but no one has advanced precise and universally accepted definitions of them. Motivation is usually treated as a "state" which impels the animal to action and which is tied to a specific goal. But emotions, too, often trigger activity and often are tied to specific objects or circumstances.

No science or systematic body of knowledge can be abandoned until complete semantic purity is attained. Even physics must live with the somewhat unsettling fact that "force," "mass," and related terms resist precise, non-tautologous, and physically grounded definitions. Therefore, it is not an evasion on the part of psychologists to continue to study motivation and emotion even as they acknowledge the ambiguities surrounding the terms and concepts to which the terms refer.

The perspective in physiological psychology is essentially

Darwinian. Accordingly, motivation and emotion are treated as part of the adaptive equipment of the organism. The terms do not refer to "things" or to "parts" of animals. Instead, they are code-words designed to reflect complex interactions between animals and environments. On this account, "motivation" is no more than a word used to refer, in shorthand fashion, to those biological states causally related to changes in the level of activity and in the directional properties of behavior. Lurking behind every specific "motive" is the Darwinian supreme motive: the motive to survive. This is as true of the individual organism as it is of the entire species, although no *conscious* recognition of the fact is implied. The law under which all life must live is one that regulates biological processes in such a way as to increase the chances that given gene-combinations will remain within the gene-pool of the species. Extreme or even subtle novelties introduced into the environment will find certain organisms (genotypes) better adapted, others less adapted, some utterly unadapted. Thus, new species arise out of those that failed, which is to say only that new genetic combinations are now more populously represented in the overall pool of genes comprising the kingdoms of life.

Against this overarching conceptual background, studies of individual organisms are designed to establish specific neurobehavioral correspondences by which the survival of *these* organisms is made more likely. These considerations are behind the stubborn commitment of physiological psychologists to confine studies of motivation and emotion to conditions involving (a) thirst, starvation, and copulation; (b) punishment and tissue damage; (c) maternal behavior; and (d) aggression. For all intents and purposes, the psychophysiology of motivation and emotion is exhausted by the processes of procreation, nutrition, and defense. The relevance of these to the domain of human conduct is defended—when it is defended—on the grounds that even the most complex human motives and feelings are (somehow) fashioned out of these basic, primitive dispositions. The human family, then, comes to be viewed as no more than a kind of "nesting behavior." Society and politics, law and morality, strivings and yearnings, are now the subjects of "sociobiology," and are to be comprehended in Darwinian terms.

At the level of fact, there is a manifest incompatibility between the Darwinian metaphysics and what the laboratory has actually produced. Let us summarize the most reliable findings, again referring the reader to specific publications for the details.[59]

1. The "appetitive" behavior (eating and drinking) of several species (primarily rats, cats, and monkeys) can be altered radically by stimulation of or surgical intrusions upon specific structures within the brain. In this connection, the nuclei of the hypothalamus are especially significant. When these are stimulated or removed, animals nearly cease eating (or drinking) or, on the other hand, eat and drink insatiably until their weights are doubled. However, these effects can be overcome by careful handling and retraining, although the restoration of totally normal appetitive behavior is rare.

2. Those behaviors which, in the natural state, are interpreted as signs of *rage* can be elicited by stimulation of specific structures in the brain. Again, the hypothalamus (the posterior third of it) appears to be particularly implicated, as are nuclei within such structures of the limbic system as the amygdala and the septum. Removal of certain structures of the limbic system generally produces uncharacteristic docility, hypersexuality, and what seem to be visual-interpretive disorders of an agnosic variety. However, these effects are, themselves, dependent in part upon the organism's history of experiences prior to the surgical or stimulative procedure.

3. Animals will work to stimulate specific regions of the

brain, and to terminate stimulation of other regions of the brain. This has suggested to many that the brain itself possesses reward and punishment centers. The reward centers include the septum, dorsal thalamus, medial forebrain bundle (MFB), hypothalamus, and tectum. The punishment centers appear to be part of the overall pain-pathways and associated nuclei (for example, medial lemniscus, posteroventral thalamic nuclei). On those occasions when it has been possible to stimulate these regions in the brains of human patients, the reward centers have elicited statements of well-being; the punishment centers, expressions of apprehension, nausea, or fright.

4. Sexual behavior is the outcome of a causal chain whose principle links are the hypothalamic nuclei, gonadotrophic hormones secreted by the pituitary gland, and gonadal hormones. The effects of surgery or stimulation here depend upon the age, sexual experience, and gender of the organism. But with such factors set aside, copulatory behavior can reliably be elicited by stimulation of hypothalamic nuclei or by chemically induced pituitary secretions.

5. Maternal behavior (nest building, nursing, protection of the litter) can be eliminated by surgical destruction of specific limbic structures.

6. The social organization within a colony of animals can be disrupted by surgical destruction of limbic structures in the brains of animals at various levels of the natural hierarchy.

7. Most of the effects produced by stimulation and surgery can be brought about by the injection of specific and naturally occurring brain chemicals, particulary acetylcholine, norepinephrine, and related transmitters and inhibitors.

Any number of hypotheses have been advanced to account for these general findings. No single theory has been advanced to cover all of them, but conceptual integrations in this area have been attempted. Those which stand in closest agreement with the facts incorporate the following propositions:

1. A given species is equipped genetically in such a manner as to connect specific central nuclei with specific regulatory functions.
2. Each central regulatory structure is paired with or contains within itself an inhibitory partner such that regulation is achieved both by activating and by inhibiting functions.
3. The effective stimuli by which these central mechanisms are engaged are chemical, are delivered through the cerebral circulation, and originate in those peripheral systems associated with digestion, respiration, and copulation.
4. The built-in systems are modifiable by experience as well as by disease, drugs, surgery, and maturation. Thus, even the regulatory activities of the central mechanisms are responsive to "learning"; that is to progressive adaptation as a function of environmental pressures.
5. The organization of central regulatory mechanisms is that of interdependent systems activated by feedback and feedforward loops of both an anatomical and a neurochemical nature. Accordingly, the overall responsiveness of any subsystem depends upon the general level of *arousal* of the organism, a level set chiefly by the ascending reticular arousal system (ARAS). This system, in turn, can be activated by central subsystems associated with hunger, thirst, emotionality, etc.

Within limits, all this is, of course, quite true, but it does not yield a *theory* of motivation and emotion. Instead, it is a description of the observed effects of surgery, stimulation, and alterations of the chemistry of the brain. What frustrates theoretical integrations in this area is the lack of a general physiological theory of perception, learning, and memory. Take, for example, the well-established relationship between hypothalamic activity and appetitive behavior. When the "eating" center is stimulated, the animal does eat available food. But if food is not available—and water is—stimulation of the "eating" center produces *drinking*.[60] Another illustration can be drawn from studies of aggression. Whether or not stimulation of "aggression" centers results in aggressive behavior depends—at least in the case of cats—upon whether one is dealing with tame, laboratory animals or cats dragged in off the streets.[61] Now, without a theory by which to explain the effects of experience on aggression, such findings are simply uninterpretable.

Then there are the conceptual and empirical problems associated with the very idea of a "center." These problems are permanently installed in the annals of neuropsychology under the title "localization of function." More than a century of research has made it clear that the concept of specific centers is not likely to derive support from the facts, once we move beyond basic sensory and motor processes. That is, the more "psychological" the phenomenon of interest, the less specific are the "centers" associated with it. This is just the place at which we might expect help from the Gestalters, but all Gestalt theory offers is a theory of representation or registration. It is not a theory of *action;* it is even less a theory of motivation or emotion. The same can be said of its Hebbian and holographic relatives.

One of the persistent claims made against physiological accounts of motivation is that the effects of direct stimulation of the brain do not mimic rewards and punishments as these are known to operate in the conditioning laboratory. For example, the animal able to stimulate its own brain tends to do so insatiably when the stimuli are delivered to a "reward center." But presentation of external rewards leads to satiation. Similarly, it is difficult to establish low rates of operant responding under conditions of self-stimulation of the brain, whereas the so-called DRL schedule (a schedule of reinforcement that allots reinforcers only for low rates of response) readily controls animals in the usual conditioning setting.

Criticisms or reservations of this sort are not unimportant, but they miss a far more significant point: operant conditioning itself has not succeeded in establishing the range of goal-oriented behaviors witnessed throughout the animal kingdom. Thus, the problem is not simply one of getting brain-stimulation data to mimic data from the Skinner box, for if that problem were solved there would still be the far greater one of getting the data from the Skinner box to mimic the facts of nonlaboratory learning, human learning, insightful leaarning. Indeed, the physiological psychologist studying central mechanisms of reward and punishment, and motivation and emotion, has been far too resistless in the face of behavioristic psychologies. As we shall see in the next chapter, the behavioristic accounts of learning, memory, motivation, emotion, attention, and language are severely limited, and there is no way a physiological psychology wedded to these accounts can escape the same limitations.

Language and Cognition

Since the discovery of "Broca's area" in the nineteenth-century,[62] the possibility of explaining language in terms of physiological processes has impressed many. Although the picture is more complicated than was originally thought, there are reliable relationships between linguistic and general "symbolic" functions on the one hand, the relatively defined regions of pathology in the cerebral cortex on the other. In the matter of complex cognitions, there is the inevitable mingling of learning, memory, attention, motivation, and even emotion—particularly when cognitive functions are examined in patients suffering from one or another neurological impairment. Similarly, *language* is more than the mere articulation of words or proper responses to verbal information. Purely *verbal* language would appear to be but the most developed form of a general capacity to deal with symbolic representations organized according to rules. The rules of grammar are illustrative but not exclusive. Discussing language and cognition together, therefore, is defensible not only on the grounds that many cognitions are verbally mediated, but also because all complex cognitive events involve the manipulation of symbolic elements which, on conceptual grounds, are kindred to linguistic elements.

Although this general view is comprehensible and is shared by many who study language and cognition, the problem of defining precisely both language and cognition is a vexing one. Many interesting studies have been reported in which nonhuman primates are said to have mastered a rudimentary language.[63] In the usual setting, the animal is called upon to select a particular symbol, to string together a number of such symbols, and to interchange the symbolic elements of such chains in order to obtain rewards. To date, none of these performances provides evidence of bona fide *connotations* recognized by the animal. Even the lowly frog will behave in a discriminating way in the presence of light of one color rather than another; that is, the frog somehow is able to perform in a manner that is concordant with what light *A denotes* and what light *B denotes*. But language is more than a collection of denotative symbols; it is also a system of *meanings*, including meanings that have no individual, material referents. Some meanings reside occasionally in the *relationships* among such referents as in the case of *stealing:* One is engaged in *stealing X* when one's *taking X* occurs in the relational context of *X belonging to* someone else who has explicitly or implicitly not surrendered his *ownership* of *X*. Terms such as "belonging to" and "ownership" refer not to entities but to concepts or relationships. This will be discussed further in chapter 4 and is noted here only as an excuse for not including in this section research on the physiology of vocalizations, bird songs, mating calls, and the like. For present purposes, *language* is limited to the unequivocal employment of symbols in *both* denotative and connotative ways—limited, that is, to *human* language.

Cognition is even more difficult to define. Psychologists typically invoke the term when treating of "higher-order" processes, but since there is no universally adopted taxonomy of behavioral—let alone "mental"—processes, it is entirely unclear as to what "higher-order" means. As we shall see in chapter 4, cognitive psychology has absorbed "information processing" into its lexicon but, properly speaking, every transaction between organisms and environments involves "information processing". Again, this is not the place in which to attempt to unravel these issues. Here, we will treat as "cognitive" the sorts of processes judged by physiological psychologists as being "cognitive".

Setting language aside, we learn that the most reliable cognitive deficits obtained by experimental neurosurgery—and observed in the neurological clinic—are those involving (a) the failure to retain recently learned information, that is, deficits in "short-term" memory; (b) the failure to respond to goals recently concealed from view, that is, failure to solve "delay of response" problems; and (c) the failure to employ cues and other signals in a meaningful and successful manner, for example, visual agnosias, or the failure to choose from a collection of alternatives all of which are otherwise correctly perceived.[64] The cortical regions most often identified with these deficits are association cortex, infero-temporal cortex, and frontal cortex.[65]

Explanations of such effects have yet to rise to the level of *theory,* and are usually only restatements of the observed findings. As in so much of physiological psychology, the guiding principle seems to be the one repeated by the eminent biologist, J. Z. Young, in his Hitchcock Lectures:[66] "In the last analysis, the most severe criterion by which we judge our understanding of a system is our ability to take it to pieces and then put it together again, or make one like it." But this is not the criterion that prevails in the developed sciences, and is not a "severe" criterion at all. A youngster destitute of all comprehension of a system—for example, an internal combustion engine—can be taught to take it apart, put it back together, and make another like it, without his ever entering on the path of understanding. As I said in the first chapter, we judge our *scientific* understanding of a system by our ability to subsume its activities under general laws. This is the sense in which we understand celestial mechanics, even though we are unable to take the sky apart and put it back together, or make another like it.

The psychophysiology of language has also been denied theoretical integrations. Attempts, notably by E. Lenneberg, have been made to connect the rhythmic components of speech to underlying electrical rhythmicities, and to connect the principles of grammatical organization to some underlying neural logic.[67] Such efforts have not so much failed as been ignored, and the field remains one cluttered with correlations. The cortical areas associated with expressive and receptive *aphasias* are better delineated than they were in Broca's time. This is attributable not to theoretical advances but to larger samples and more refined techniques in histology and radiography.

Perhaps the most celebrated addition to the psychophysiology of language is that made possible by studies of patients who have undergone therapeutic transection of the *corpus callosum.* The hemispheres of the brain are connected by bands of fibers running densely at five levels of the brain.* It is through these *commissures* that signals from one half of the brain find their way to the other half, although there are alternative means of transmission as well. The corpus callosum is at the highest level, and connects the left cerebral cortex with the right.

Pioneering research by Sperry[68] established that complete commissurotomies resulted in two *functionally* distinct hemispheres. Animals that had learned a discrimination with one eye covered were unable to perform correctly later when the "educated" eye was covered and the "naive" one uncovered. Thus, the representation of learned material in the educated hemisphere was not transferred to the naive hemisphere. Interestingly, the animals displayed no significant deficit other than these peculiar lacks of interhemispheric transfer.

On the strength of Sperry's findings, surgery has been performed on a number of patients suffering from a form of epilepsy both dangerous and, in these cases, unresponsive to more conservative approaches. The disorder in question is one involving erratic electrical discharges from one region of one cortex. The behavioral and general abnormalities associated with this condition do not appear, however, until the erratic "focus" spreads to the corresponding location in the other hemisphere. Thus, the decision to perform commissurotomies seemed warranted. The aim was to eliminate the fiber paths along which the seizure patterns travel in establishing a "mirror focus" in the opposite hemisphere.

Patients who have undergone this surgery display a variety of interesting characteristics. It is well known that dis-

---

* In addition to the *corpus callosum* the major commissures include the *massa intermedia* (joining the hemispheres at the level of the thalamus), the anterior and the posterior commissures, and the fiber-bundles at the level of the (midbrain) tectum.

turbances of language almost invariably are confined to lesions in the *left* hemisphere—even when the sufferer is left-handed. Ordinary speech, therefore, seems particularly tied to the left hemisphere, even when the left hemisphere is not the "dominant" one, where "dominance" is determined by handedness. Because of the anatomy of the visual system, objects falling on the temporal (ear-side) portion of either retina will be registered in the visual cortex on the same side. Thus, objects falling on the temporal retina of the left eye will be registered in *left* visual cortex. Objects falling on the nasal region of either retina will be registered in the contralateral visual cortex since the fibers originating in this region of the retina cross to the contralateral side in the *optic chiasm.* In the normal case, of course, *both* hemispheres receive information delivered to either eye since we view objects foveally and the fovea projects to both hemispheres, and because left-hemisphere information is transferred to right-hemisphere (and vice versa) through the commissures.

When objects are presented to the commissurotomized patient in such a way as to fall on the nasal half of the right retina, the patient has no difficulty seeing or naming the object. However, when the image of the same object is made to fall on the temporal half of the right retina, the patient claims to "see" the object, can point to it accurately, can recognize it by *feeling* it, but cannot *name* it. What has taken place is this: under the latter arrangement, the object is registered in the "nonverbal" hemisphere and, as a result of the commissurotomy, the registration cannot be transferred to the "verbal" hemisphere. Thus, an object that is recognized palpably cannot be identified verbally.[69]

A fair amount of metaphysical furor has been extracted from these findings. Some have proposed that the "verbal" hemisphere, like Western civilization, is verbal and analytical whereas the other hemisphere is somehow more "Eastern."[70] Others have reasoned that, since the patient does not "know" in his right-brain what he "knows" in his left, there must be two "selves."[71] I have addressed these odd notions elsewhere[72] and would prefer now to limit attention to the facts themselves.

First, at the grossest level of analysis, the effects of commissurotomy confirm (once again!) the long-recognized fact that certain functions are *lateralized* in the brain. This lateralization, by the way, can be shifted. For example, preverbal children who have undergone complete hemispherectomies in which the entire left hemisphere has been removed have subsequently developed normal speech.[73] Nonetheless, it is almost invariably the case that linguistic function is mediated primarily by neural mechanisms operating in the left hemisphere, and this fact was unchallenged before commissurotomies were dreamed of.

Second, to locate a region in which X occurs or upon which X depends is not the same as providing a *theory* of X. It is clear that adults require a left hemisphere if they are to speak coherently. They also require vocal cords, tongues, lungs, and lips—not to mention words. Nothing in the "split-brain" literature goes beyond a physiological theory of articulation unless it includes a theory of language itself. That is, unless this literature is prepared to assign to the left hemisphere (and not merely assign functions but also mechanisms) responsibility for grammatical rules, connotative formulations, and linguistic learning, this literature can only be added to the large and equally interesting literature pertaining to the neuropathology of *speech*. This is *not* to say that no more than articulational deficits are suggested by the "split-brain" findings, but that no more can be made of them in the absence of a theoretical model of language itself.

Summary

The principal generalizations made possible by a century of research in the physicalistic tradition have been examined in this chapter. We have seen that this specialty has yielded a wealth of factual material, much of it highly reliable and suggestive. However, the facts have not been incorporated in such a manner as to produce a theory of perception, learning, memory, motivation, emotion, cognition, or language. Pribram's *holographic* theory and Hebb's *connectionistic* theory may be partly exempted from this criticism, but the former awaits more precise formulation and the latter has never claimed to be more than an imprecise formulation.

The absence of theoretical integrations renders physiological psychology destitute of explanatory power. Existing correlations permit predictions of a gross nature, but even these must be qualified because of an equivalent lack of theory regarding the role of heredity, learning and social interactions.

At more fundamental levels—the levels of ontology and metaphysics—modern physiological psychology leaves the Mind/Body problem undisturbed. Nothing in the thick book of neurophysiological fact requires one to abandon monism, epiphenomenalism, psychophysical parallelism, or (even) an immaterialism of the Berkeleian stripe. More to the point, however, at least from the psychologist's point of view, modern physiological psychology shows distinct tendencies in the direction of eliminating *psychological* issues from its physicalistic pursuits. There is some indication that the future of the specialty may be within the purely biological sciences.

CHAPTER THREE
THE BEHAVIORISTIC POINT OF VIEW

There is no doubt but that the behavioristic perspective has been the dominant one in modern psychology, at least in the English-speaking world, for the past thirty years. Despite the somewhat monolithic expression it has been given by its several influential spokesmen, it is a highly varied and shifting perspective. Behaviorism is not a single ism standing in defense of a short list of propositions. It is more a "culture" within psychology than a "school," more a habit of thought than a system. It is, therefore, with caution that one goes about stating what behaviorism is. In my own cautiousness, I find it useful to start with a discussion of what behaviorism *was*, while recognizing that children do not always take after *either* parent.

Undergraduates are taught that John B. Watson was the "father" of American behaviorism, that Ivan Pavlov was, somehow, another father—perhaps the grandfather—and that E. L. Thorndike's *Animal Intelligence* [1] provided something of a nursery for the quickly developing ism. As with most claims of intellectual priority, these are partly true and partly false, both revealing and misleading. In significant respects, the modern behavioristic perspective under consideration here differs from that adopted by Pavlov and promoted by Watson. And, to the extent that the current perspective can be said to be at all "Pavlovian" or "Watsonian," its roots go back much further than the works of either Pavlov or Watson. What is shared by Pavlovian, Watsonian, and modern behaviorisms is a desire for explanatory parsimony coupled with a not too veiled impatience with *psychological* psychologies. To these characteristics may be added an uncommon interest in practical applications—that is, a decidedly *pragmatic* bent—and a confidence bordering on faith in reductive analyses of human and animal conduct. But it is precisely these features that can be found in every period of speculative discourse on the nature of man and society. Beyond these features, and at a more technical level, twentieth-century behaviorisms are also bound to the past through their explicit or quiet acceptance of one or another form of *associationism* by whose ageless maxims practice makes perfect.

It is not a criticism to observe that a contemporary idea has ancient roots. After all, men and women had witnessed falling bodies for many millenia before Newton arrived with a scientific explanation. Thus, the mere fact that rewards and punishments have been applied throughout history to domesticate children and other small creatures in no way depreciates modern advances in the *technology of training.* Nor should contemporary behaviorism's reliance on the old "pleasure principle" lead inevitably to scorn. Indeed, if this principle does account for conduct within the animal kingdom, it is to the credit of the ancients for having recognized the fact, and not to the discredit of moderns for accepting it.

But these are all generalities. Once we move past them and begin to assess the specific hypotheses and arguments generated by them, matters quickly become tangled. If modern behaviorism stood for no more than the truism that much of what we do is governed by real or imagined or expected rewards and punishments, if it proposed that one—or even the major—source of our knowledge, concepts, ideas and the like was "association," and if on the strength of these propositions it went on to defend a general theory of *performance* in terms of rewarded practice, there would hardly be room for debate. Indeed, were these the only claims set forth by modern behaviorism, there would be no such ism, for all this had been said before, countless times. What makes behaviorism formidable, what establishes it as something to be dealt with, is its adoption of associationistic and hedonistic principles to the exclusion of all others. I must quickly insert the reminder that there are several different behavior*isms* to be addressed in this chapter, including varieties which place less stress on the role of reward and punishment; still others which are less mechanically associationistic. But on the whole, what presents itself as modern behaviorism—the behaviorism of B. F. Skinner and his many followers—is an associationistic and a hedonistic psychology promising to account for the full range of animal and human conduct by taking recourse to no consideration beyond the "reinforcement history" and whatever more or less fixed genetic nuances have to be included to account for exceptions. Before assessing this and several other modern formulations of the behavioristic perspective, it will be helpful to review the concepts of "association," "reinforcement," and "conduct."

Associationism

From Hellenic times to the present, theories of learning have been based upon some form of the principle of *association*. Perhaps the most influential version in modern times comes from Hume, the author of an uncompromisingly *psychological* epistemology. The famous Humean account of the manner in which simple ideas become parlayed into complex ones invokes the principle of *contiguity*. When *A* and *B* are spatially and temporally contiguous, and when their occurrences are sufficiently frequent, the mind is so constituted that, on receiving an impression of either, it will automatically call up the other.

The Humean mind is furnished by *impressions* and *ideas*, and the former of these consist entirely of *sensation* and *reflection*. As Hume put it, ". . . every simple idea has a simple impression which resembles it and every simple impression, a correspondent idea."[2] The fundamental difference between a sensation and an idea, aside from the fact that sensations precede ideas, is that the latter are weaker and less vivid "copies" of the former. However, in the matter of *complex* ideas, there is a compounding; a network of relationships such that little of the originating sensation may be evident in the ideas themselves. As for these relationships, they are no more than those of resemblance, contiguity, and cause and effect.[3] Two ideas become more strongly associated (a) when there is a degree of resemblance between them, that is, when they share certain properties; (b) when they are spatially close to each other; (c) when one invariably precedes the other. The *belief* that attaches to our ideas is grounded in *feeling*, for there is nothing in the pure, physical objects of our perception which can command such belief or, for that matter, serve as the stimulus for belief. We do, then, form opinions about our knowledge, and these opinions are fashioned out of tests of *constancy* and *coherence*. I *believe* that the house in front of me is the same house I looked at yesterday because its essential features have remained constant, and because the relationship between this house and its surroundings reflects the same coherence as was present in the earlier experience.

That this epistemology conduces to skepticism was clear

to Hume and has been clear ever since. On the Humean account, the very idea of *causation* is *only an idea* whose existence can be traced to the experiences of constant conjunction and succession. This theory permits, as Hume acknowledged, *anything* to be the cause of anything else, as long as the two are constantly conjoined, and as long as one always follows and the other always precedes. To say that one billiard ball is the *cause* of the movement of another is only to say that such a relationship has never been violated in past experience, and to *surmise* that it will not be violated in the future. All we *know*, however, is that ball *A* moved, collided with ball *B*, and that ball *B* then moved. Our experience does not also include a "cause." Thus, the concept of causation is merely an inference from the perceived facts, and not itself either factual or demonstrable. A cause cannot be experienced and it cannot be deduced; it can only be inferred.

The heart of Hume's epistemology—and of the phenomenalism of J. S. Mill and others in the patrimony of Hume—is a combination of associationism and impressionism. Both of these elements have suffered under close philosophical analysis, but both have survived, in one or another form, in modern philosophy and in behaviorist psychologies. The impressionistic elements, as I noted in the second chapter, were tellingly challenged by Thomas Reid who argued that our experience of objects is not the experience of the "impressions" such objects make on the sensory organs, but the experience of the objects themselves. Reid also criticized Hume's theory of causation on the grounds that causality is never inferred in some cases involving constant conjunctions and invariable succession, for example, the setting of the sun and the rising of the moon. No one thinks that the setting of the sun has *caused* the moon to rise. Similarly, when it comes to those things that *we* do as causal agents, we do not make inferences about our causal role: we know *absolutely* that we are the causes. Take, for example, our writing of a book. We do not wait for all the pages to come together under one cover before concluding that *we* are causally responsible, nor is our sense of this responsibility merely "probable."

There are other well-known problems with Hume's account of causation but they are beyond the scope of the present chapter. Even his principle of *succession* is problematic—as Kant was wont to show—for it entails the concept of *time* which must be granted if any experience is to be ordered *in time*. Time is not "given" by anything on the billiard table. Rather, it is a property of perception or of the mind itself such that, without this property being granted a priori, there can be no "succession."[4] What is important here is that Hume's theory of causation takes mental associations for granted, and that his theory of mind is based upon his theory of causal relations. We come to have the idea of "cause" through a history of reliable, associated experiences, and we come to have complex ideas through the compoundings of such ideas which, themselves, are held together by causal relations. If, therefore, Hume's theory of causality (or just his theory of reasonings about causality) is flawed, any cognitive pyschology based on it will be infected with the same failings.

This brings us to the matter of association as a psychological principle. Psychological materialists such as Pavlov, Bain, and Hebb have generally assumed that the basis of associations is structural. Repeated experiences somehow alter the structural features of the activated neural elements. But even those who have been less explicit on the question of mechanism have discussed associations in such a way as to suggest some sort of "bonding," "binding," and "building."

Architectural metaphors have been common in this literature.

If we assume that the process of learning—the process of forming ideas—is an associative one, and that the finished product is some sort of ensemble of more elementary "pieces," we quickly find ourselves on the horns of a dilemma. Let us take the example of a concert pianist. We listen to his performance of the last movement of the *Moonlight* Sonata. The time required for a signal originating at the tip of the left index finger to travel to the sensory cortex, and for the motor signal originating in the motor cortex to travel down the spinal cord and out to the next finger to be moved is far longer than Beethoven will allow. Thus, our "machine" (the concert pianist) cannot wait for the sensory consquences of an earlier response to determine the next motor event. His performance, quite simply, is not the outcome of unitary "associations," but of clusters of responses which are somehow "read out" of the system all at once. Then there is the added problem of the pianist's virtuosity. He completes the movement without error. If, however, we return to the architectural metaphor—which would have such a performance composed of separate movements just as a house is composed of separate bricks—we would expect the pianist to repeat all the errors that were committed on the way toward mastering the piece. The difficulty courted by associationistic theories is that they often fail to distinguish between what is involved (or may be involved) in the process of *acquisition* from what is involved in the final *composition* of the idea, performance, or response. It may be that Smith acquired his pianistic skills associatively, but it is scarcely true that in performing the *Moonlight* Sonata, Smith is merely unwinding the entire history of mistakes and nonmistakes acquired along the way.

It is also the case that the term "association" is not as psychologically neutral as it appears on first inspection. To say that a stimulus and a response have become associated is a highly indefinite assertion, for *stimulus* may pertain to any feature of the physical universe to which the organism's senses are responsive, and *response* may pertain to any number of neural and muscular discharges. When, therefore, we say that the dog has learned to "associate" the sound of the bell with the presence of food in the mouth, we are (grudgingly or otherwise) speaking in *psychological* terms, not neutrally physical ones. Sound, as an experience, entails an experient. And what the animal experiences is determined by a variety of considerations not the least of which are attention, motivation, and emotion, that is, other psychological processes.

Contemporary psychology in the associationistic tradition too often takes the stimulus for granted, and fails to recognize that the associationistic theory of learning rests upon a theory of perception which itself may be poorly formulated or fatally flawed. One may speak of "stimuli" in the abstract, but once an organism is placed in front of such physical entities we need a theory of perception or sensation by which to explain what now is to take place. It is clear, for example, from the experiments of Michotte on "launching" and "entraining" that we have direct impressions of causation—that there is a phenomenal causality—even in situations in which the physical facts do not satisfy the Humean conditions of causal inference.[5] And, of course, there is the entire corpus of Gestalt research and theory establishing the interactive determinants of experience. Quite simply, there is enough evidence to raise grave questions about an elementaristic theory of perception. As long is this is the case, associationistic theories of learning and cognition are suspect.

If the *stimulus* receives little attention from associa-

tionists, the *response* does not fare much better. A rat pressing a lever is not engaged in a unitary response, but in a
complicated chain of sensory-neural and neuro-muscular
sequences. Is it the entire chain that becomes associated
with a stimulus? Clearly it is not, for the rat taught to run
through a maze will swim through the same maze even
though entirely new response elements are now required.[6]
Traditionally, the concepts of "stimulus generalization" and
"response generalization" have been invoked to account for
such plasticity of learned behavior, but these notions merely
beg the larger question. The concept of generalization is only
modestly mentalistic when confined to such stimulus dimensions as intensity and wavelength, but most of the generalizations of interest in human psychology are generalizations
of a conceptual nature where no physical continuum is involved at all. A child learns that tabbies, lions, tigers,
pumas, leopards, and jaguars are "cats." What stimulus continua are relevant here? Size? Color? Shape? And in what
sense is a "swimming response" but the "generalization" of
a "running response"? And what "generalization" is involved when a rat—taught to run down a runway and to
make a right turn to the goal box—now runs diagonally
across the top of the cage once freed from the maze?

To all this must be added distinctions that obtain between
the idea of responses and that of *action*, where the latter contains or is animated by the additional notion of *intention*.
The difference between a pot falling from a window and one
being thrown from the window may elude the laws of dynamics. Yet we all know that, though the rate of descent is
the same in each case, and though the damage done is the
same, there is a difference. The difference is that in one case
the outcome was *intended* by an agent-actor and is, therefore, an *action*. In the other case, all we have is an *event*,
though, no doubt, a *caused* event. Now, the committed behav-

iorist may ask whether we have actually added anything to the *observable* situation by taking recourse to the notion of intention. To this we have every right to reply that the issue under investigation is just the issue of whether a plausible system of psychology can be confined to "observables." In invoking the actor's intentions, we have provided an *explanation* not contained in a merely descriptive account of the "observables." We may be wrong in imputing a given motive to the actor, but this does not prove that there were not intentions behind the actions. Indeed, to insist that one may choose the *wrong* motive is to accept that there are correct choices available.

The so-called "volitional theory of action" has been attacked by behavioristic psychologists and philosophers vigorously over the past thirty years. Gilbert Ryle's *The Concept of Mind* (1949) must rank as the most influential and coherent of these attacks, but the central ideas advanced in it have been given both ancient and modern expression by many others (e.g., Zeno, Democritus, Gassendi, La Mettrie, Helvetius). The core of the complaint is that volitional explanations are both spiritistic and prone to infinite regression:

> Volitions have been postulated as special acts, "in the mind," by means of which a mind gets its ideas translated into acts. I think of some state of affairs which I wish to come into existence. . . . So I perform a volition which somehow puts my muscles into action.[7]

Ryle's wariness in the face of volitional explanations is similar to Gassendi's. How can putatively immaterial "desires" move material muscles? And if it is necessary for me to will to do something in order for me to do it, must I also will to will to do it? If the answer to the second question is of the sort, "No, I merely will the event once, and it is my *self* that brings willing about, not some other act of will," then we face the problem of disembodied "selves" able to have effects on arms and legs.

In my judgment, far too much time and effort have been devoted to the problem of infinite regression which, after all, is conceptually specious and factually absent. No one who thinks of himself as intending to do something is perplexed by his failure to discover a prior intention to intend. Each person recognizes himself as an intending agent in the same way as he recognizes that he is hungry. He grants intentions to others on the same grounds as those he uses to grant hunger to them, even though he has no direct knowledge of their intentions or their hungers. The individual is no more doubtful of having aims and goals than he is of having a headache—whether he knows the causes or not.

To have a motive or intention is said to be akin to having awareness, and is said to invite the puzzling query. "Am I aware that I am aware, and aware that I am aware that I am aware?" Aside from the fact that awareness is known directly only by the individual who is aware, and that the individual is simply not plagued by such metaphysical problems, there is the additional fact that no such regression is required by the claim. We sit before a column of numbers and begin to add them. Let us say the column contains 20 entries. After we get to the sixth entry, someone asks, "Are you adding or are you adding your addings?" Most goals or aims require a number of steps each of which may be misperformed. Through a kind of tracking behavior, we find our way to the intended place although, all along the way, new information may call for new steps and new subgoals. To say that I have an intention to go to the concert hall is kindred to saying that I had my first toothache when I was four years old. No one expects me to have a toothache in order to have another one, and no one should expect me to have an intention before I can have another one. There can be a first intention and a first toothache in every life. To "have" an intention is to have knowledge of a goal. To act on that intention is to have a belief that such actions will bring the goal closer, or bring "some state of affairs . . . into existence." There is nothing odd about my volition putting "my muscles into action," any more than my toothache, as it were, putting me into the dentist's chair. I surely do not get to the dentist's chair by virtue of my dental nerves, but by virtue of my hands, feet, Volkswagen, and ignition-key.

Some will protest that the toothache-to-dentist's chair sequence is not analogous to the volition-to-performance sequence, for in the first case all the terms are grounded in neurophysiology whereas volitions are only "in the mind." But of course toothaches, too, are "in the mind"—even if teeth aren't—and it remains a matter of some controversy whether everything "in the mind" is also (or only) "in the brain." One who reports intentions is not obliged to solve metaphysical problems of Mind and Body in order to be believed; less in order to believe himself. It may be that I do not know how my volition "puts my muscles into action." For that matter, I do not know how my motor cortex puts my muscles into action; I know, however, that it *does*. Some have proposed, following William James, an *ideo-motor* theory of volition whereby the willing of action X is the appearance of a mental image of action X and its desired consequences. On this account, the volition is something of an image of the willed response in action.[8] An interesting feature of theories of this sort is that it becomes impossible to will actions without histories. Thus, to will that I fight bravely is to have an image of those responses which experience teaches to be brave actions. But to will that God be different from what God is is impossible, since nothing in experience teaches what God is. Yet we often *wish* that a novel had a different ending, even if we are not prepared to suggest one and even if we cannot conceive of a preferred alternative. Wishing, then, becomes willing *with the image of response removed*. If this is so, however, then it is possible to have desires of a specific, cognitive nature without having corresponding and relevant images of responses that might satisfy such desires. That is, one can desire *in vain* and knowingly. It would appear, then, that although images of responses *may* often be associated with volitions, they need not be. Otherwise, it would be impossible to desire that which has no precedent.

The past fifty years of behaviorism has produced a tangle of dependent and independent variables. Associationism has been employed simultaneously in the service of theories of knowledge and theories of conduct, seldom making clear the connecting links between what an animal *has learned* and what the animal *does*. As noted, this has yielded propositions regarding *performance* which confuse the process of acquisition with the actual nature of what now is known or can be done by the animal. And by stripping such accounts of a volitional component, these same propositions have no conceptual bridge uniting animal·learning with human conduct. Skinner, as we shall see, has built many bridges, but these have been polemical, not conceptual. Let me now turn to specific behavioristic systems. Following custom, I will discuss these under the headings of *Contiguity* models and *Reinforcement* models, and will follow these with *Relational* models.

Contiguity

The essential feature of all contiguity models of learning is associationism. Stimuli come to have their evocative powers by association with responses and by association with each

other. What distinguishes such models from so-called reinforcement theory is that the latter incorporates the operations of reward and punishment as a means of accounting
for the formation of associations, whereas the contiguity
model contains no such requirement. Theories of behavior
based upon the concept of reinforcement are generally contiguity theories also, but are not *merely* contiguity theories.
The most influential of the contiguity theories is that advanced by E. R. Guthrie. Guthrie has expressed his "primary
law of association" thus:

> A combination of stimuli which has accompanied a movement will on
> its recurrence tend to be followed by that movement. Note that noth-
> ing here is said about . . . reinforcement or pleasant effects.[9]

Guthrie goes on to say that this formulation is not intended
as an explanation of any single instance of learning, but only
as a general law serving as a guide when we seek to unravel
the determinants of goal-directed behavior.[10] Another interesting aspect of Guthrie's theory is that it rejects the concept
of learning as something gradually acquired and replaces it
with the concept of *one-trial learning:*

> a stimulus pattern gains its full associative strength on the occasion of
> its first pairing with a response.[11]

Accordingly, learning is not the *continuous* accretion of partial associative bonds, or the gradual strengthening of associational "connections," but the establishment of a functional tie between a "stimulus pattern"* and a given
response on the first occasion of their concurrence.
    The empirical challenges facing such a theory seem, on

---

* Guthrie recognized the impossibility of specifying accurately and exhaus-
tively every unitary stimulus in the relevant environment of the organism.
Because of this, he adopted the term "stimulus pattern" as a short-hand
way of conveying the environmental complexities and subleties with which
behavior becomes associated.

first inspection, to be formidable. Traditional learning curves, as well as the accumulated experience of the human race, make the strongest case for *gradual* learning, and the weakest case for *one-trial* learning. Guthrie's theory seeks to answer these seeming counterinstances with the hypotheses of *negative associations* and *associative inhibition:*

Every instance of learning involves both positive and negative association. For every response attached to a cue, some former response has been detached.[12]

Associative inhibition is produced when a different response (call it R_2) becomes associated with the cue (call it C_1) to which another response (R_1) had been associated. No longer does C_1 elicit R_1, for the latter has now been replaced by R_2. Measures of learning suggest gradual acquisition because, in the course of actual learning, the desired responses must vie with competing ones. Associative inhibition represents a kind of confusion-matrix within which the "correct" Cs and Rs must somehow find each other. This same associative inhibition is at the root of *forgetting* as well. Mere "empty" time causes no one to forget anything. The cause of forgetting is *interference* produced by new associations and brought to bear on older ones.[13]

There is very little biological speculation in Guthrie's theory. The usual concepts of drive, motivation, and reward are reduced to purely associational principles. Stimuli result in behavior, a fact with which Guthrie's theory begins, and one which the theory does not seek to explain except in loosely Darwinian fashion. Each response occurring at the time of some stimulus-event becomes associated with that event. Some of these associations—for example, eating food—*solve the problem.* That is, the stimuli which happen to be correlated with food deprivation disappear once the deprivation no longer exists. Eating, which was the response associated with those (visceral) cues we call hunger, stops when the cues are no longer present. Guthrie can find no more in the "law of effect" or the principles of "reinforcement" than just these associations: ". . . the law of effect is reducible to and conforms with the principle of association by contiguity." [14]

In such a complete reduction of learning to associative processes, a notion such as *intention* is not likely to retain much of its historical and philosophical vitality. In one of his earliest publications (*General Psychology*, 1921),* Guthrie attempted to provide an "objective" theory of intentionality. The thesis may be summarized as follows: (1) a given stimulus pattern persists, and the responses which once removed it are somehow blocked; (2) prior associational bonds commit the organism to action, even though the particular response is now obstructed; (3) prior associations constitute a condition of "readiness" such that the organism is prepared for the consequences of the alternative actions about to be emitted. Note that this is something of an ideomotor theory of intention as a result of (3). What is supposed to make this an "objective" theory is that all references to intention are *behavioral* since even the state of preparedness is defined in behavioral terms.

The experimental support for Guthrie's theory is broad if not deep. Studies of human memory, for example, have demonstrated time and again that the mere passage of time has little effect upon paired-associates retention, but that the acquisition of new paired-associates has great interference effects.[15] Research addressed to the "reinforcing" effects of such nutritionally barren substances as saccharine has been interpreted as evidence against the theoretically essential role of drive-reduction in learning and, therefore, as evi-

* Written with Stevenson Smith.

dence favoring Guthrie's contiguity theory.[16] Guthrie's own studies of cats in boxes indicate that the animals will learn to escape from the box in a single trial if, in fact, on that single trial the emitted response is successful.[17] In the more traditional Skinnerian setting, H. S. Terrace has shown that errorless learning can be achieved by pigeons when the training begins with very easy discriminations and proceeds gradually with the introduction of more difficult discriminations.[18] W. K. Estes has also shown that paired-associates learning conforms to the contiguity model and not the reinforcement model and has insisted, in Guthrian fashion, that ". . . repeated reinforcements simply (give) repeated opportunities for the formation of an association between a stimulus pattern and the reinforced response."[19]

A contiguity theory having both historical and conceptual ties to Guthrie's has been proposed by W. K. Estes, and named by him the *stimulus sampling theory*.[20] It will be useful to summarize it here before turning to an analysis of contiguity theories in general, even though there are differences between Guthrie's and Estes' formulations.

Estes' theory, like Guthrie's, takes into account the practical and theoretical problem of itemizing relevant and unitary stimuli. Where Guthrie speaks of the "stimulus pattern," Estes speaks of S-*variables* and defines them as typically subtle environmental events of which only a small number are effective at any given time. The effective stimulating condition, then, is but a *sample* of the overall environment in which the organism is located. On the behavioral side, Estes makes the useful distinction between what he calls an R-*class* and an R-*occurrence*.[21] This distinction honors the fact that unitary responses are (probably) never identical and that, in any case, we would not be able to ascertain such identities were they to occur. Instead, the psychologist must confine his analysis to the *R*-class—the ensemble of behaviors that produces measurable and repeatable effects on the environment. Estes' theory, therefore, pertains to correlations between *stimulus-samples* and R-*classes*. The principle of contiguity, as employed in his theory, dictates that learning is but a systematic change in the probability of a given R-class as a result of its contiguous association with a stimulus-sample. The dependent variable is *probability of response* and the independent variable is that sample of total environmental stimuli present when the specified R-class occurs.

The *stimulus-sampling* theory may be illustrated by drawing upon the typical "conditioning" experiment. Let us call the entire ensemble of stimuli S and the conditioning stimulus S_c. The setting is one in which a buzzer is sounded and a shock follows. The "buzz" here is S_c and the relevant R-class contains all those behaviors reliably elicited by shock; for example, flexion of the shocked limb. Of course, S_c is only indefinitely described as a "buzz," since it also possesses certain frequency components, a certain amplitude (which varies as the animal is nearer or further with respect to the loud speaker) and still other characteristics not identified by the word "buzz." However, on any given trial, some finite number of elements of S_c will function as effective elements and will become conditioned to the R-class we have called limb-flexion. Let us denote as (x) those elements of S_c that become conditioned to the R-class, and let us call the average number of such elements present on any single trial (s_c). From trial to trial, a different number of (x)s will appear. We can express the *expected* number of such new elements occurring on any trial as:

$$\Delta x = (s_c)\frac{[S_c - (x)]}{S_c}.$$

To understand this equation better, assume that the total perceptible environment contains 100 unitary stimuli; that is, that $S_c = 100$. On any given trial, the *average* number of effective stimuli (s_c) is 10 and the number actually conditioned to the R-class is 5. Thus, $(x) = 5$. Then, the expected number of new (x)s to become conditioned to the R-class on another given trial is

$$\Delta x = 10 \times \frac{[100 - (5)]}{100} = 10 \times 0.95 = 9.5.$$

We see, then, that as the number of trials becomes large, it becomes ever more likely that *all* elements of S_c will gradually become conditioned to the R-class.

Instead of referring to the R-class, let us call limb-flexion F. We have already stated that the elements of S_c actually connected to F is (x). All other things being equal, the probability p that F will occur when S_c is present is simply,

$$p_F = \frac{x}{S_c}.$$

In the above example, this would yield a probability of 0.05, since S_c was given the value 100 and (x) was given the value 5. Since different elements of S_c show up from trial to trial and become (x)s, we see that that p_F will increase as a function of the number of trials; that is, S_c is constant, but (x) increases on a trial-by-trial basis.

There is much more (and a good deal more statistics) to Estes' theory, but this is sufficient to illustrate the theory's explanation of learning. Improvements in performance which result from "practice" are now seen to be the result of a probability process which ties elements of the R-class to elements of the total environment. Unlike Guthrie, Estes is willing to give "reinforcement" its due, but not to the point of having to explain "drives," "motives," and so on. In Estes' theory, a condition is reinforcing when it guarantees that successive trials will permit more and more of the total S_c to become (x)s.

The advantages of contiguity theories—and particularly one having the formal character of Estes'—are several and significant. As we shall see later in this chapter, the concept of reinforcement has a troubled past and a doubtful future to the extent that it is tied to presumed conditions of biological "need" or psychobiological "drive." The contiguity theorist avoids the problem of giving a biological explanation of learning largely by freeing his theory from such notions. That is, he does not ask associationism to add to its own burdens by taking on those of hedonism, the pleasure principle, homeostasis, and the like. Associationism is kept pure, and explanations are rendered in statistical and neutrally quantitative terms.

The disadvantages are also significant. Continguity theories offer plausible accounts of complex conceptual learning only by expanding the notion of S-*variables* to the point of tacitly assuming the very mental, the very psychological features of the organism which these reductionistic theories were designed to eliminate. The "insightful" learning displayed by the ape who joins two sticks together in order to reach an object placed at twice the length of a single stick calls upon the contiguity theorist to find something in S_c that corresponds to joined sticks, although the ape has never seen such equipment.

One of the chief liabilities of contiguity theories, although it is a liability that could be easily averted, is the failure to recognize the perceptual biases of all the developed organisms before learning has had a chance to take place. There are principles of perceptual organization, discussed in the previous chapter, which are operative in neonatal animals and which determine the efficacy of environmental stimuli. Some of these principles are relatively static; for example, spectral sensitivity as mediated by the pigment chemistry of the retinal cones. Others, however, are dynamic in that they are modifiable by experience and involve such psychologically significant processes as motion and shape perception, depth perception, and pattern recognition. Neither Guthrie's nor Estes' theory makes room for such native equipment and, as a result, both theories are saddled to a *tabula rasa* perspective on the newborn or the untrained animal. There is, however, nothing in either theory which requires this limitation. Taking Estes' theory as an example, we merely have to assign certain (x)s a high value prior to conditioning, leaving to research the responsibility of determining the value. This is a small arithmetic step, but a significant conceptual one. To adopt this strategy is, of course, to permit the intrusion of *teleological* elements into the theory, but these need be no more teleological than any explanation of behavior based upon *instinctive* patterns of behavior. Species have been shaped by millions of years of selection pressure and enter the world with a more or less developed set of dispositions to perceive and to respond. This is as established a fact in the life sciences as is the circulation of blood. Thus, only a metaphysical commitment to radical empiricism denies a theorist the right to incorporate such facts into his theory. There is simply no justification for treating environmental elements as all having the same probability of mating with response elements. Indeed, there is little justification for treating the relevant environment as elemental at all. We now know that in many cases the learning curves and measures of memory emerging from traditional studies of behavior can, as it were, be bred. That is, animals of the same species can be inbred to form strains whose members are more or less likely to reflect the functional relationships ordinarily found in studies of learning and memory.[22] Now that it makes sense to speak of the *heritability* of learning and memory, it makes less sense to embrace both with theories giving no a priori weight to specific response tendencies and stimulus patterns.

Setting these considerations aside, it is important to ac-

knowledge that other and rather common criticisms of contiguity theories are misdirected. For example, it is not the
case that the theories advanced by Guthrie and by Estes ignore or are unable to address such states or events as motivation and emotion. In both theories, these are assigned to
the overall pattern of stimulation forming the external and
the internal environments of the organism. In treating such
states and processes as *stimuli*, the contiguity theories permit them to be investigated experimentally, once the defenders of such states specify motivation and emotion with
sufficient precision and uniformity to allow these experiments. This, of course, is but a piece of the larger contiguity
system within which psychology can examine *only* stimuli,
responses, and the relations between them. On this account,
we do not have stimuli, responses, *and* motives (or emotions,
or attention, or goals), but only stimuli and responses.

What, then, is the fate of thought and awareness? In
adopting the contiguity models, must we abandon psychology's most venerable subject, the subject of consciousness itself? To answer this question, we must make a distinction
between the substantive and the metaphysical aspects of
such models. Guthrie and Estes are representative of that
behavioristic movement which has attempted to reduce all
of psychology to a study of stimulus-response (S-R) dependencies. The dependent variables in studies spawned by this
movement have been restricted principally to performances
in mazes, runways, Skinner boxes, and jumping stands, and
occasionally have included paired-associates verbal learning. Thus, the responses chosen have been those which lend
themselves to counting and to unambiguous specification.
Too often, the modest success permitted by such data has
tempted the metaphysical reductionist to make the claim
that *only* relations such as those uncovered by this research
need be included in a developed psychology. This, as it hap-

pens, is a false claim and was never a necessary one. It is not easy to think of ways of reducing thought to a form that would allow strict enumeration and unambiguous specification. But it is certainly plausible to judge thought to be a form of activity in which specifiable stimuli are operative. As we shall see in the next chapter, this is precisely what modern *cognitive* psychology is willing to assume. The bridge that now needs building is one that will unite the systematic features of contiguity theory with the enlarged conceptual domain of cognitive psychology.

Reinforcement

The concept of reinforcement is among the oldest in that literature devoted to the determinants of conduct. It is honored in such maxims as "spare the rod and spoil the child" and is the cornerstone of all utilitarian systems. We find the powers of reward and punishment extolled in Plato's *Republic*, in Aristotle's *Politics*, and in virtually every ethical system advanced in the modern age. Aside from these formal treatments, reinforcement theories have appeared latently in the actions of parents, teachers, animal-trainers, and pet owners since remote antiquity. And, in all developed associationistic psychologies except for contiguity theories, reinforcement is the alleged mechanism by which associations come to be formed and come to persist.

The scientific or quasi-scientific history of this ageless concept is much more recent, and may be said to have begun with E. L. Thorndike's *law of effect:*

Of several responses made to the same situation, those which are accompanied or closely followed by satisfaction to the animal will, other things being equal, be more firmly connected with the situation, so that, when it recurs, they will be more likely to recur; those which are accompanied or closely followed by discomfort to the animal will, other things being equal, have their connections with that situation weakened, so that, when it recurs, they will be less likely to recur. The greater the satisfaction or discomfort, the greater the strengthening or weakening of the bond.[23]

The only difference between Thorndike and all who preceded him in invoking versions of the "pleasure principle" is that Thorndike was in possession of experimental data. Note that I refer here to *experimental* data. The world is rife with facts, only some of which emerge from experimental inquiries. Surely those who subscribed to the pleasure principle before Thorndike's studies of cats based their adoption of this principle on *factual* (though not *experimental*) evidence. Thorndike himself rested his case not merely on the findings from the laboratory but from evidence arising from "the entire history of the management of human affairs."[24]

Since 1898, when Thorndike's "law" was published, the principle of reinforcement has undergone a number of surgical refinements all designed to eliminate mentalistic connotations. John B. Watson, otherwise a great admirer of Thorndike, was among the first to become suspicious of habits "implanted by kind fairies" and of explanations rooted in such notions as "satisfaction."[25] Those sharing this desire to dementalize the concept of reinforcement can be roughly divided into two groups. In the first, we find theorists who have attempted to reduce the concept to underlying biological processes associated with the physical needs of the organism. In the second, we discover a disinclination to theorize at any level, and a commitment to stand behind the facts as the laboratory generates them. The chief defense offered by members of the second group is the perennial failure suffered by members of the first group. As we shall see, both perspectives possess assets and liabilities. Because there is much variety within each group, it is not easy to choose apt labels for either. Yet, in the interest of economy, I will refer to the position taken by the first group as the *homeostatic* theory of reinforcement and that of the second group as the *statistical* theory of reinforcement. The full meaning of these designations will become clearer in the following discussion.

The most systematic and influential of the *homeostatic* theories is that first set forth by Clark Hull and subsequently modified by Kenneth Spence.[26] Theirs is a theory that fully respects the concept of scientific explanation presented in chapter 1; that is, the *hypothetico-deductive* model of explanation as developed by Hempel. Hull's is an elaborate theory, rich in technical terms and concepts and resistant to brief summaries. I will not attempt to summarize the entire Hullian system, but to review the Hullian perspective and to employ his notation and terminology only to the extent required by this aim.

Perhaps the most salient feature of Hullian theory is that it is *ecological* in the fullest sense. The theory attempts to explain—that is, to provide laws which cover—the continuing and complex interactions taking place between a biological system (the organism) and a physical system (the environment). It is clear from Hull's approach that what he intended, in the long run, was a *biophysics* of behavior which would reduce psychological processes to laws of a thermodynamical nature; laws describing energy-exchanges between *two* behaving systems, one of which happened to be "alive." Thus, the primary objective of the theory is to answer the question, "How does behavior sustain life"?

As an ecological theory, Hull's is necessarily biologically oriented in its basic assumptions, although entirely behavioristic in its data-base. The most fundamental assumptions are that survival depends upon behavior and that acquired behavior is governed by principles which, at base, are the laws of survival. This is the point of entry for the concept of *homeostasis*. What threatens life are those environmental extremes that fail to support the tissue-needs of the body. Behavior, like physiology itself, is one means by which the organism can resist, remove, or alter these extremes and thereby preserve a state of equilibrium; that is, homeostasis. At the most primitive level of existence, the organism is guided by the considerations of food, drink, procreation, and the avoidance of pain. Thus, food, liquid, sexual activity, and pain are *primary reinforcers* in that their effects upon behavior are independent of learning, practice, or the presence of any other stimuli. Such primary reinforces are either positive (S^+) or negative (S^-) depending on whether their presence conduces to homeostasis or disrupts it. The acquisition of S^+ and the removal of S^- are *reinforcing*.

It is through the principle of association that Hull moves from the concept of primary reinforcement to that of *secondary reinforcement*. If all the food an animal obtains is housed in a compartment containing a red light, and if food is never present in the compartment containing a green light, the animal will work to obtain the red light; that is, the red light will come to have effects on behavior like those produced by food. Here, the red light is said to be a *secondary reinforcer* (or *acquired* reinforcer) whose reinforcing properties depend upon prior associations with a primary reinforcer.

As the unit of length is, in one common system of measurement, the inch, so the unit of learning is, in Hull's system, the *hab* (*H*) which is the unit of *habit*. The term "habit" is especially apt, for Hull uses it to convey the idea of an ability to do X even though, at any given time, one might not be doing X. An example of this is bicycle riding. Many persons are able to ride bicycles—whether they are riding them now or not. Thus, they have developed the habit (skill) but may, at any given time, lack the opportunity or the motive to display this skill. In the course of acquisition, it was necessary for certain sensory events to become connected with specific motor events. The entire ensemble of these connections is, after all, what riding a bicycle is. The habit, then, is an assembly of connections between stimuli and responses. Hull's notation for this sort of connection is $_sH_R$, which stands for *habit strength*. The value or magnitude of $_sH_R$ is, in Hull's theory, a function of the number of reinforcements (N). In other words, if left turns (R_1) result in food twice as frequently as do right turns (R_2), then—all other conditions being equal—$_sH_{R1}$ will be twice as great as $_sH_{R2}$.

Yet, the animal trained under the foregoing conditions may not make any turns at all. It may not even run down the runway. If, for example, it has had constant access to food and water, it may spend its time sleeping in the START box. Thus, even though a given $_sH_R$ may be present at a high value, there may be no actual behavior emitted by the animal. Recall that homeostasis is the guiding principle of behavior. In the absence of biological needs, behavior—and particularly goal-directed behavior—can serve no biological function. The ability of a situation to evoke previously acquired behavior depends, therefore, not only on the behavior's habit strength $(_sH_R)$ but also on the presence of a relevant *drive* (D). According to Hull, the potential for evoking a response is jointly determined by the strength of the habit and the degree of drive:

$$_sH_R \times D = {_sE_R},$$

where $_sE_R$ is the *reaction potential*.

However, even the consideration of drive (D) is not enough to permit predictions of whether or not the behavior in question will occur. The animal may, for example, be physically exhausted—though hungry—and unable to stand, let alone run. In Hull's theory, fatigue plays a significant part. The hypothesis is that every response results in the formation of fatigue substances which tend to oppose continued expenditures of energy by the animal. The effect is one of *inhibition* of behavior, which Hull represents as I_R and which he calls *reactive inhibition*. To the extent that inhibitions, too, can be acquired, the theory makes provision for *conditioned inhibition* $(_sI_R)$ which conduces to fatigue in those settings reliably associated with the expenditure of energy. The *total* inhibition at any given time is the sum of reactive and conditioned inhibition:

$$\dot{I}_R = I_R + {}_sI_R.$$

On any given trial, then, the *net reaction potential* $(_s\overline{\overline{E}}_R)$ is the reaction potential less the total inhibition in the system:

$$_s\overline{\overline{E}}_R = {}_sE_R - \dot{I}_R.$$

It is also the case, as demonstrated experimentally, that animals will respond more forcefully and faithfully for larger rewards than for smaller ones, and less so for rewards that are delayed. Hullian theory incorporates both of these variables, treating magnitude of reward as *incentive* (K) and delay of reward as a kind of disincentive (J). All other factors kept constant, the reaction potential increases multiplicatively with K and decreases exponentially with J.

We can see in this sketch of the Hullian system that several variables operate in such a manner as to make the occurrence of a response more likely or forceful $(_sH_R, N, D, K)$ and that others make the occurrence less forceful or likely $(I_R, {}_sI_R, J)$. Note also that all the stimulus variables are amenable to the effects of *generalization*, as are all the response variables. Thus there is room for generalized drive, generalized incentive, generalized inhibition, etc. These facts give the theory a striking degree of flexibility in addressing even complex psychological processes such as conflict. The paradigmatic instances of conflict, within the Hullian system, can be expressed in the following notation:

(1) $_sH_{R1} = {}_sH_{R2}$. Here, two incompatible responses are incorporated into habit-strengths of equal magnitude. If all other variables are held constant, R_1 and R_2 (for example, a left turn and a right turn) are equally probable. Let us assume that the left turn will bring the hungry animal to food and the right turn will bring the same thirsty animal to water. Here we have the *double-approach* conflict.

(2) $D_1 = D_2$. Let us now assume that the degree of food deprivation just matches the degree of water deprivation. Now, the variable of *drive* establishes the conflict. Or, by taking D_1 as the drive associated with avoiding shock, and D_2 as that associated with the procurement of food, we have the paradigmatic instance of *approach-avoidance* conflict. The animal, to obtain food, must enter a compartment in which shock is administered.

(3) $_{S1}I_R = {}_{S2}I_R$. Here we have two instances of conditioned inhibition. Let us assume that in the one case, S_1, the stimulus is a blue light and that S_2 is a red light. Let us assume further that $_{S^+}H_R$ was established in the presence of a yellow light, S^+. This situation provides one means by which *discriminative responding* is established. Not only has yellow come to be the stimulus associated with reward, but red and blue have come to be associated with inhibition.

(4) $I_R = f(t)$. Reactive inhibition—which is a fatigue effect—diminishes with time, once the organism is removed from the effort-demanding context. It is well known that after a response has been conditioned and has then been restored by *extinction* to its initially low level, *spontaneous recovery* takes place. That is, if the animal is placed again in the experimental chamber a day after the first extinction session, the conditioned response appears again with somewhat less strength than it had on the last few conditioning trials, but with far greater strength than it had on the last

few extinction trials. Note how Hullian theory accounts for this. Reactive inhibition diminishes with time, but conditioned inhibition does not. Each extinction session produces both I_R and $_sI_R$, but the I_R dissipates during the rest interval. After the first extinction session, there is relatively little $_sI_R$ established, and the I_R weakens during the rest interval. Thus, spontaneous recovery is possible. However, as extinction sessions become more numerous, there is progressively more $_sI_R$ established until finally $_sI_R = _sE_R$, and no further conditioned responding occurs.

(5) $_s^+H_R$; $_s^0H_{R-}$. In the formation of any habit, there results what Hull called *generalized habit strength* ($_s\bar{H}_R$) such that the response will be emitted in the presence of stimuli physically similar to the conditioning stimulus. Let us recall that S^+ refers to stimuli associated with reward. Let me now introduce the notation S^0 to stand for stimuli associated with nonreward, and the notation R^- to stand for non responding. What these expressions illustrate are (a) the tendency to respond to a range of stimuli physically close to S^+ and (b) the tendency not to respond to a range of stimuli physically unlike S^+. We have, then both a *gradient of excitation* and a *gradient of inhibition* which, depending on the training procedures, may be overlapping. Now let us recall the phenomenon of *transposition* discussed in the previous chapter and earlier in this chapter. The Hull-Spence theory attempts to explain this phenomenon on the basis of overlapping gradients of excitation and inhibition. Figure 2 will help to clarify the point. Because of generalized habit strength for both responding (to S^+) and nonresponding (to S^0), there will be values along the left-hand portion of the excitation curve which are utterly unaffected by the gradient of inhibition. However, much of the right-hand portion of the excitation curve comes into the regions in which the gradient of inhibition is operative. We can chose values of S^+ and S^0 such that the animal will seem to be "transposing" when, in fact, all that is involved is the interplay of excitatory and inhibitory processes of a generalized nature. I will return to this expla-

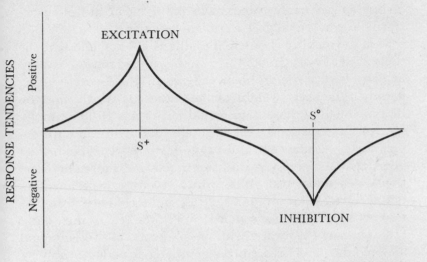

nation of transposition later and will discuss the insufficiency of the Hull-Spence approach to it.

The influence of the Hull-Spence theory on contemporary psychology has been considerable, if indirect. It has been some forty years since the earliest formulations and, at the present time, there is very little attention given to the actual formal properties of the theory. Put bluntly, we do not discover psychologists attempting to fit experimental findings to Hullian equations. The influence, therefore, must be looked for in different areas:—in how behavioral psychologists conceptualize learning and performance, in how psychology on the whole goes about explaining adaptive behavior, and in the latent assumptions that seem to guide research in various fields of psychology. In these respects, the Hullian theory has been profoundly influential. Not only are the relatively straightforward activities of experimental animals discussed in terms of "drive-reductions," "homeostasis," "incentive," and the like, but even complex aspects of human personality and social adjustment are often assessed in what, finally, is a *Hullian* manner.[27]

That the number of outright Hullians is small and that the theory itself now attracts little attention are facts not easy to explain. Part of the problem suffered by the theory is to be found in the sheer weight of the equations which must be manipulated by those who would perform a Hullian analysis. All the equations were orginally derived from data describing performance in runways and were based upon such dependent variables as running speed and muscular exertions—dependent variables which today's experimenters have shelved in favor of *rates* of responding.[28] Later formulations of the Hull-Spence model were adapted to such data, but by then the overwhelming majority of workers had adopted the purely descriptive approach defended so ably by B. F. Skinner. As we shall see, Skinner has been aloof to theorizing and, as his position gained adherents, systems such as the one advanced by Hull were early casualties. All told, then, some measure of the "failure" of Hullian psychology has nothing at all to do with discovered errors in the theory, but is based upon such global considerations as philosophies of science, theories of explanation, and aesthetic preferences.

If research itself has had anything to do with the gradual disappearance of Hullian psychology—and here I refer to the *formal* system developed by Hull and Spence—we might best recall the studies of nonnutritive reinforcement cited earlier in connection with Guthrie's contiguity theory. Indeed, the Hullian theory of drive reduction has, on the whole, come into very hard times over the past two decades. Hull's focus was on peripheral sources of "need"; for example, the nutritional requirements of muscles. But by the 1960s it was becoming apparent that any homeostatic theory of behavior would have to include central mechanisms of activation and drive reduction capable of by-passing peripheral cues for hunger, thirst and pain. Thus, the Hullian "drives," rooted as they were in the peripheral physiology of the organism, quickly became dated, though one is tempted to say that they also became prematurely dated. There is, we should recognize, nothing in the Hullian theory of drive that cannot be adapted to these more recent findings, but the point here is that the theory itself was peripheralistic at a time when homeostatic mechanisms were just about to be moved, bag and baggage, into the brain.

To these difficulties we must add the steady increase in the number of apparently primary reinforcers discovered by psychologists after Hull's theory had appeared. Monkeys, for example, will, without any prior training, work in order to gain visual access to human faces. Indeed, they will often forego food in order to catch glimpses of the real world.[29] On Hull's account, we now are forced to add the "curiosity drive" to those associated with food and procreation. Hull's theory does include a term for such instinctive tendencies. The term is $_sU_R$ and is designed to convey the notion of unlearned connections between stimuli and responses. But it was never dealt with in a systematic way. For Hull, such instincts were to be included as givens once research had established them as reliably present throughout the species. Yet, the temper of the times was against the multiplication of such "inborn" drives, and the fear was that behaviorism would become something of a "faculty psychology" if it were allowed to add another primary drive each time some animal was found to have a preference for some stimulus in the (apparent) absence of prior conditioning.

In a sense, Hullian behaviorism has disappeared only to return as a branch of physiological psychology. Neal Miller's experimental and theoretical efforts have been admittedly

Hullian, and Miller has shown how readily the Hullian approach can be assimilated by the facts and the perspective of the neural sciences.[30] Yet, as Miller and his colleagues and students have progressed in their work, their writings have moved further and further away from what is recognizably Hullian. Nonetheless, to the extent that contemporary behaviorism is ever explicitly physiological, the debts to Hull are real and are often acknowledged. Where contemporary behaviorism is purely descriptive and nontheoretical, however, Hull's influence is negligible.

Most of the specific phenomena that raise problems for Hull's theory tell equally against all associationistic theories and against Skinner's associationistic nontheory. Again, *transposition* is illustrative. What distinguishes the Hull-Spence approach to this phenomenon from other behavioristic approaches is not that Hull and Spence failed, but that they tried to deal with it. However, it now seems clear that the explanation based upon interactions between excitatory and inhibitory gradients is wrong. Studies have shown that, even when stimuli are widely separated along the physical continuum (as, for example, with sounds of varying intensities), organisms still display transpositional learning.[31] This is a sufficiently important point to warrant analysis.

Let us begin with a simple discrimination requiring a pigeon to peck in the presence of a light of 10 units of intensity, and not to peck in the presence of a light of 5 units of intensity. On the Hull-Spence account, a gradient of inhibition forms around the S^0, with maximum inhibition at 5 units. Some of this inhibition extends to the 10-unit value and even further, but most is concentrated in the region of intensities surrounding the value of the S^0. Similarly, most of the excitation is found in the region just around the 10-unit value, but with the gradient extending both to lower and to higher intensities.

The conditioned pigeon is now presented with another pair of stimuli. This time, one of the stimuli is the same 10-unit one which, during acquisition, served as the S^+. The second, however, is a 20-unit stimulus which was never present during aquisition. Traditionally, the view has been that, when the bird now responds preferentially to the 20-unit stimulus, the associationistic theory is refuted because (a) associations were only established with the 10-unit stimulus initially and (b) the 20-unit stimulus—now preferred by the animal—was never present during training. The Hull-Spence theory attempts to salvage the principle of association by proposing a gradient of inhibition that extends to the 10-unit stimulus, but not as far as the 20-unit stimulus. In other words, the inhibitory potential which reaches its peak at the 5-unit value is still effective at the 10-unit value, whereas there is virtually no inhibition at the 20-unit point on the continuum. Thus, when the 20-unit stimulus is offered, there is no inhibitory reduction of its efficacy, but there is some excitatory potential borrowed from the gradient of excitation developed during initial training. Thus, the animal pecks in the presence of the 20-unit light and tends not to peck in the presence of the former S^+.

The test of this hypothesis involves a choice of stimulus pairs whose members are widely separated along the relevant continuum. Suppose that, instead of choosing 10 and 20 in the test for transposition, we choose 90 and 95; that is, values that are both far removed from the values of the conditioning stimuli, but values quite close to each other. Here we have a condition in which no spread of inhibition or excitation should be expected. What we find, however, is that animals still choose the brighter of the two test stimuli. In brief, we are forced to conclude that the transposition effect cannot be explained on the basis of generalized excitation and inhibition of "associates."

How much importance one is willing to attach to such findings depends upon one's aims. Those who have argued that learning involves cognitive processes of a *relational* nature—processes to be discussed later in this chapter—have attached great importance to transpositional learning, seeing in it a refutation of associationism. That this may be an exaggerated use of the phenomenon is a possibility to be taken up at the end of this chapter. Now, however, let us turn to *statistical* theories of reinforcement as these are exemplified in the work of B. F. Skinner.

I have chosen to describe this approach as "statistical" even at the risk of novelty. And if this choice calls up the theories of Guthrie and Estes, so much the better. Guthrie and Estes avoid the problems endemic to theories of reinforcement by advancing associationistic laws neutral on the question of *mechanism,* and Skinner avoids the problems endemic to theories of reinforcement not by abandoning the concept but by abandoning theory itself.[32] We must be cautious, however, in describing Skinner's position as atheoretical. The form of theorizing to which Skinner has been opposed is aptly reviewed by Skinner himself. He is, he tells us, wary of "any explanation of an observed fact which appeals to events taking place somewhere else, at some other level of observation, described in different terms, and measured, if at all, in different dimensions."[33]

To say, then, that Skinner avoids the traditional difficulties associated with reinforcement theories by refusing to theorize must now be qualified. What Skinner has refused to do is *biologize* the concept of reinforcement. He has refused to "explain" what makes reinforcers reinforcing. He has resisted the temptation to invoke homeostatic notions, notions of "tissue-need," drives, wants, hungers, and the like. He is not opposed in principle to theories such as Hull's which are tied to experimental observations, although Hull's efforts specifically seem to be premature. What is worth saving in such a formulation is the commitment to *functional relationships* between measures of behavior and measures of the environment. Such explanations as science may provide are but these functional relationships. Their reliability, as experimentally determined, is all we can have in mind when referring to "laws." Accordingly, the laws of behavioral psychology are no more than that collection of reliable functional relationships resulting from the experimental analysis of behavior.

To every possible extent, definitions in the Skinnerian system are given an operationistic form. So-called "operational definitions" are those which exhaust the meaning of a term by specifying the procedures employed in observing and measuring the termed entity. Thus, "hunger" comes to be defined according to the number of hours since the last feeding, or in terms of the weight lost by the animal, or even in terms of how quickly the animal will run toward food. There is no reference to the animal's real or putative "feelings" of hunger. By these same operationistic standards, *reinforcement* is defined as any procedure which systematically alters the probability of a specified response. The stimulus experimentally isolated as the one associated with this altered probability is a *reinforcer*. Those stimuli whose removal increases the probability of responses just preceding the removal are *negative reinforcers*. Those whose availability increases the probability of preceding responses are *positive reinforcers*. Only the actual measurement of these probabilities permits us to treat a stimulus as a reinforcer. That is, there is no a priori classification of stimuli as reinforcing or nonreinforcing. Put another way, there is no deductive element in Skinner's system.

With remarkable consistency, Skinner has argued for the progressive movement of psychology away from the organism's subcutaneous world and into the organism's surrounding environment. As early as 1938, in his *Behavior of Organism*—and particularly in the closing chapter of that important text—Skinner attempted to divorce psychology from its historic partner, neurology. He has argued persuasively that the facts of behavior survive no matter what the facts of neurophysiology may prove to be, and that in important respects a developed science of neurophysiology actually must wait for developments in behavioral science. In any case, the psychologist need not quail in the face of biological evidence, or judge the value of his research in terms of its compatibility with biological data or theory. From the behavioral scientist's perspective, the organism may be safely judged as "empty," as a sort of "black box" which emits behavior under specifiable experimental conditions. The aim is to establish functional relationships between behavior and the environment. This can be achieved in the absence of any and all knowledge of the biological workings of the animal.

In Skinnerian psychology's externalization of laws, concepts such as motivation and emotion have also been moved into the environment. A "motive," if it has any operational meaning at all, must refer to some property of a stimulus by which that stimulus gains control over behavior. Similarly, an "emotion," operationally considered, turns out to be some environmental feature which faithfully elicits a constellation of responses we have learned to call "emotional." Again, a complete *behavioral* analysis, leading to functional laws, can be conducted without reference to the physiology of the brain, the passions of the animal, or the strivings for success and happiness. Nothing is added to the analysis and facts of behavior by the inclusion of concepts such as motivation, consciousness, and feeling, or for that matter by the inclusion of descriptions of neural discharges, biochemical events, or anatomical changes.

The appeal of this approach should be obvious even after so brief a sketch. Skinnerian psychology presents itself as an independent science, able to conduct its business without the approval of biology. The abiding issues of consciousness, will, purpose, and inner struggles are swept away by the stubborn commitment to confine the discipline to directly observable behavior. At the same time, this psychology foregoes none of the actual *behavior* traditionally associated with these issues. When we see Smith crossing the street and conversing with a friend, nothing is added to our observation by noting that Smith is "conscious." Indeed, all we could mean by such a claim is that Smith is *doing* something which those we call "unconscious" don't *do*.

In addition to its metaphysical cleanliness, Skinnerian psychology is appealing on the grounds of (apparent) generality. It has been brought to bear on a wide range of human endeavors and has been presented as an approach unembarrassed by even the most extraordinary human achievements. In *Verbal Behavior* Skinner has attempted to reduce language to an "operant analysis."[34] In *Beyond Freedom and Dignity* he has attempted the same reduction of civilization itself.[35] Whatever Skinnerian behaviorism may lack in formal elements, it is not modest in its reach.

But no matter how expansive the approach (or its defenders), the entire enterprise rests on the concept of reinforcement. Thus, the system stands or falls with the fate of this concept as determined experimentally and analytically. This is not to say, however, that the concept must remain static. There will be, I would think, neo-Skinnerian behaviorisms just as Skinner's is neo-Thorndikean. In this regard, I would note especially the work of David Premack on "reinforcement reversibility" where we discover that "for any pair of responses, the independently more probable one will reinforce the less probable one."[36]

Thus, the running behavior of an animal can be used to reinforce drinking, and vice versa. Some of this is anticipated in Skinner's notion of "self-reinforcement" but Premack's findings are convincing and suggestive. They are mentioned here, however, only to illustrate how the concept of reinforcement has already evolved and, therefore, how it may continue to evolve. Nevertheless, the central question will remain whether the full range of behavior conforms to the principles of reinforcement. If this question is, at any time, answerable experimentally, then the concept of reinforcement, no matter how it might evolve, must retain its essential Skinnerian features. Minimally, these are the following:

1. *Acquired behavior is a function of its consequences.* This is the most general and theoretically neutral form of Thorndike's "law of effect," and the form incorporated into Skinner's operational definition of reinforcement. It requires that the behavior in question occur, for without the behavior there is nothing to reinforce.

2. *Complex patterns of behavior are reducible to more elemental operants.* This is the argument against so-called emergent properties of behavior which can only be explained in terms of the "mediation" of some sort of "mental" activity. The statement requires that any ensemble of behavior be understood as a function of the organism's history of reinforcement; that there is nothing in the repertoire which cannot be tied to current or past "contingencies" of reinforcement.

If either (1) or (2) is false, Skinnerian behaviorism is false to the same extent. If (1) is false, then the determinants of behavior are not exhausted by the contingencies of reinforcement. If (2) is false, then a complete experimental analysis of behavior will be insufficient to unearth the variables underlying the bahavior itself. Tests of these propositions, both direct and indirect, are numerous and form the foundation of *relational* theories of behavior to which I now turn.

Relational Behaviorism

This is the appropriate place to discuss briefly the coherent senses in which one may be classified as a behaviorist. In the following paragraphs, I will review several of the more important studies that point to serious deficiencies in the propositions forming the backbone of Skinnerian behaviorism. Yet, most of these studies were completed by psychologists who would describe themselves at least as "behavioral scientists" if not as behaviorists. We must, therefore, make the distinction between *methodological* behaviorism and what I will here call *ontological* behaviorism. The methodological behaviorist is one who has selected measurable and observable behavior as the exclusive dependent variable in a scientific psychology. This choice, however, does not preclude theoretical inferences of a nonbehavioral nature; for example, inferences about underlying neural or even mental processes. The ontological behaviorist goes beyond this, and insists that behavior exhausts the domain of bona fide psychological entities. For him, there is not behavior *and* mental states or conditions; there is *only* behavior, and psychology's task is to convert traditional talk about minds, spirits, and the like to descriptions of behavior. Those whose research supports a form of *relational behaviorism* may all be called methodological behaviorists, but not always ontological behaviorists.

A substantial fraction of the research devoted to relational processes is indebted to the studies and writings of E. C. Tolman[37] and to the overall perspective of Gestalt psychology.

Tolman has always described himself as a "behaviorist"—
occasionally tolerating the ascription "cryptophenome-
nologist"—but there is little in his experiments or his influential essays that would pass for Skinnerian behaviorism.
Tolman and his students at Berkeley contributed seminal
findings to the behavioristic literature for forty years. Their
studies of *latent learning* are illustrative of the Tolmanian
approach to behavioral science. In the typical latent
learning study, animals are exposed to an environment
but are not rewarded for any behavior emitted in that environment. Subsequent tests of learning are conducted to determine if, in the absence of reward, the animals learned
anything about the environment. In one such study, animals
were strapped into little carts and were wheeled through a
maze! After a number of such journeys, the animals were
deprived of food and let loose in the maze, and records were
taken of the number of errors made on the way to the goal
box. When compared with an untraveled control group, the
animals that had been wheeled through the maze displayed
significant learning. In other studies, animals were fed to satiation before being placed in a maze, and were allowed to
roam freely in the maze on successive days, although no food
was placed in the goal box. After exposure of this sort, the
animals were deprived of food and again placed in the maze,
this time with food placed in the final (goal) compartment.
Again, these animals—that displayed no systematic change
in behavior during the *roaming* condition—came to perform
as well as a rewarded group after a single session. Thus,
while reward affected *performance*, it proved to be unnecessary for *learning*. The rats apparently were learning about
the maze merely as a result of moving around in it, even
though no response was reinforced directly.[38] Tolman's explanation of results of this kind employs the concept of *cognitive maps* to account for the animal's ability to improve by

mere exposure. According to this explanation, the roaming animal or the one wheeled through the maze is forming a "map" of the environment. The map itself is but a collection of associations among environmental stimuli. In this respect, Tolman's learning theory is a stimulus-stimulus (S-S) connectionism, rather than a stimulus-response (S-R) connectionism.*

Kindred experiments have been conducted by Harry F. Harlow and have been reported under the rubric "learning sets," which he characterizes as "the mechanism that changes the problem from an intellectual tribulation into an intellectual triviality."[39] What the learning set is, in Harlow's language, is *learning how to learn*, and the evidence for it is the systematic improvement in learning itself as the animal solves problems of a given genre. As the subject (monkey, rat, or child) makes correct discriminations, additional features of the stimuli are presented and these too must be discriminated. Thus, on one trial the correct choice may involve discriminating blue from yellow; on another, squares from circles. What is found is that the ease with which such discriminations are made is a function of the number of previous discriminations that have been made. The learner somehow develops a "set" or bias in confronting problems of a given type. These same effects are apparent in studies of *discrimination reversal*. Suppose, for example, that blue has been the S^+ on 50 trials and yellow has been S^0. On the 51st trial, this is reversed, and the animal must respond to yellow to receive a reward. What Harlow has shown is that the number of trials needed for the animal to perform the reverse discrimination is, itself, a function of the number of discrimination-reversal problems the animal has solved. After 100 such problems have been solved, the animal may

* Hence the term "sign-significate" or "sign-Gestalt" learning.

perform the discrimination reversal without any errors at all.

In discussing his findings, Harlow has remarked that if learning sets "appear independently of a gradual learning history, we have not found them in the primate order."[40] This comment is intended as a challenge to the Gestalt concept of "insight" and to related concepts which would have the organism forming "hypotheses" or otherwise engaging in mental as opposed to behavioral adjustments. Harlow, therefore, has not abandoned but supported behaviorism with his data. Yet, the data themselves do not require this interpretation. It remains to be shown that specific contingencies of reinforcement control discrimination reversal and permit essentially errorless performance after some hundred trials. And this is so particularly in light of Harlow's own insistence that learning sets cannot be explained on the basis of what occurs *within* a block of solution trials, but only in terms of what occurs across such blocks.[41] Moreover, these studies do not directly challenge the "insight" experiments conducted by Köhler since the Gestalt psychologists have not argued that "insight" is independent of experience, only that it cannot be explained by past experience. Köhler's ape, Sultan, initially had two sticks; a smaller one (A) which had to be inserted into a larger one (B) in order to reach food placed some distance from the cage. After Sultan joined A and B, by placing A into B, Köhler removed stick A and presented Sultan with stick C, the largest of the three. Without any errors or fumbling at all, Sultan now placed B into C. Thus, the stick which had been the receptacle was now the "active" one.[42] Köhler's explanation is not that Sultan's experiences with A and B were irrelevant to performance with B and C, but that a strict associationistic-reinforcement account of the findings is defective. Prior reinforcement would have had Sultan attempt to place C into B, for example, or would at least have required a sufficient number of "discrimination-reversal" trials for errors to accumulate.

When we leave the literature devoted to animal learning and confront that addressed to human *language*, the reinforcement model becomes even more problematic. The linguist Noam Chomsky has written on this in detail,[43] and only a few illustrations are required here. Research has shown, for example, that the age at which children engage in grammatical speech is roughly the same the world over, independent of the child-rearing practices of the parents. It is also known that the time it takes a child reared by mutes to acquire grammatical speech is a function of the *age* of the child. Thus, the amount of "reinforced practice" is determined by the level of maturity of the child. Then, too, there is the fact that children can respond appropriately to grammatical speech at an earlier age than that at which they can utter the same sentences. And, finally, there is the striking fact of language—that an adult can utter and comprehend an infinite number of grammatically correct and meaningful sentences in his native language. Together, these features of human language would seem to defy explanations based upon associationism and reinforcement. They seem, instead, to support a *nativistic* theory of language by which the rule-governed features of language are "hard-wired," as it were, in the human nervous system. We learn individual words, but language is more than a set of words. We may think of the performance of conversationalists as something like the performance of an adding machine in that the latter *adds* whatever is put into it, and the former organize in grammatically lawful ways whatever *words* are put into them. This, too, stands as a kind of *relational* theory of (linguistic) behavior in that the emphasis is upon internal processes by which inputs are regulated.

When we look across the phenomena of latent learning,

learning sets, insight, and language, we come to recognize the difficulty of maintaining allegiance to the two propositions on which Skinnerian behaviorism rests. No one doubts—and I should think that no one has ever doubted— the powerful role of reward and punishment in controlling behavior. Nor do any of the foregoing illustrations remove the *facts* of Skinnerian behaviorism. As Skinner has noted often, facts survive any construction we place on them. It is to the credit of Skinner and of those who have adopted his program that we now possess an immense catalogue of experimental findings describing the subtle and durable effects of "reinforcement contingencies" on adaptive behavior. This part of the overall contribution is as impressive as it is unimpeachable. But as Skinner himself has moved beyond the data, as he has advanced social and moral theories, as he has attempted to include under the umbrella of the law of effect the entire range of human activities, the Skinnerian system has repeatedly foundered and failed. There have been thoughtful defenses of his *Verbal Behavior* [44] but it now appears undeniable to all not wedded to the ism that the behavioristic explanation of language is simply wrong. There have also been attempts to reduce "insight" and "latent learning" to associational principles, but these too have strained the tethers of plausibility. What the data and reason itself permit us to say about the two fundamental propositions of behaviorism is that they are often true, but this is not the sort of claim upon which a developed science can prosper or depend.

None of this gainsays the significant contributions the behavioristic perspective has made to any number of fields. Modern psychopharmacology is simply unimaginable in the absence of Skinnerian techniques. Current forms of "behavior therapy" owe much to Skinner, as does the emerging field of educational technology. In these respects, behaviorism has blossomed as a kind of psychological *engineering*, even if it has failed to evolve into psychological *physics*. As had Watson, Skinner has been willing to rest behaviorism's case on its practical achievements, but the history of science offers all too many instances of theories working in practice but ultimately found to be fatally flawed.

What behaviorism offered psychology was an objectivity that promised to confer longed-for scientific status. However, this objectivity was won at a price. For many years, behaviorists looked upon genetics either as some kind of constant in their experiments, or as the hoary head of nativism returning to infect psychology with innate ideas, faculties, and those other vestiges of eighteenth-century mentalism. The effect of this was to convert behaviorism into a "white rat" psychology, able to say many things about a species which does not even exist outside the laboratory. Tied to this disregard for genetics has been indifference toward ethological methods and findings. Once the decision was made to bring behavior into the Skinner box, interest was quickly lost in the things animals had been doing for millions of years before behaviorism discovered them. The rich subject of instinctive behavior was avoided by those who otherwise described their perspective as Darwinian! As years became decades, and as the thick book of facts became thicker, it seemed that this now not-so-new "objective" psychology was as doomed as nineteenth-century armchair introspectionism. Granted it is a good idea to study experimentally human sensations, images, and feelings, when is enough enough? And, similarly, granted it is a good idea to study the effects of reinforcement on bar-pressing behavior, when will we have enough such data to know what we set out to know?

The problem here is not merely that behaviorism has neglected genetics, ethology, and the complex processes underlying such observed phenomena as insight and latent learning. The problem is that as a purely descriptive enterprise with official sanctions against biological and cognitive theorizing, it is not equiped even in principle to embrace such subjects and processes. When the contemporary Skinnerian psychologist admits the importance of heredity, or claims never to have doubted it, he still cannot take the more important next step and specify *how* Skinnerian behaviorism—as a system of psychology—formally incorporates this admittedly important variable. The impression conveyed by Skinner's own recent comments on all this is that genotypes do figure in behavior.[45] But how? They cannot be functions in the behavioristic equations, for Skinner offers no equations. Apparently, they are merely to be dealt with on an ad hoc basis, adding a few more pages of cumulative recordings. As long as this is so, Skinner's psychology is better described as scientifically *isolated* than as scientifically *independent*.

Summary

The behavioristic perspective has yielded a descriptive psychology grounded in measures of observable behavior. Varieties of this perspective can be distinguished on the basis of the role accorded to reinforcement, and the commitment made to the unearthing of biological substrates of behavior. Only Hull and Estes have advanced behavioristic *theories* of psychology. The more influential system proposed by Skinner is atheoretical and abiological. All systematic psychologies presented in this chapter deal effectively with a limited range of behavior, but none of them is able to enbrace the full range of behaviors emitted by organisms even in the otherwise impoverished Skinnerian environments. The behavioristic perspective has not yet paid more than lip-service to the sciences of ethology and genetics and, as a result, has not made conceptual or methodological contact with these sister disciplines. Additionally, such traditional topics of psychology as cognition, concept formation, personality, and mentation have been ignored, denied, or trivialized.* On the *reasons-causes* dichotomy, only Hull's theory is even explicit, seeking as it does to explain behavior in the *causal* language of the biological sciences. Guthrie, Estes, and Skinner limit "explanation" to statements of stimulus-response dependencies and offer so-called functional laws (correlations) in place of theoretical explanations. Thus, in the sense developed in the first chapter, there is no behavioristic *theory* of psychology except Hull's, and this one appears to have died on the vine. None of this has prevented spokesmen for behaviorism from extending their perspective to the social and moral arenas of life. However, since existing facts raise grave doubts about the adequacy of the few (two) propositions upon which the entire system rests, there would appear to be little reason to subject these larger implications to scrutiny. A theory of mechanics that cannot account for balls rolling down an inclined plane need not be studied for its merits as a cosmology. Even in very recent celebrations of behaviorism, we find the odd mixing of the notion of *lawfulness* with the very different entities we call physical *laws*. Thus:

If human actions did not repeat themselves, if the conditions under which people behaved and the phenomena of behavior themselves continually changed from one period in time to the next, the pursuit of "laws" of behavior would be futile. We might come to an understanding of human action, perhaps through the study of social and cultural history, but we could not develop scientific laws.[46]

* Except, of course, for Tolman's earlier work which ceased to be influential within behavioristic circles after the 1940s. It survives and prospers in cognitive psychology.

Weather patterns are "lawful" in that there are reliable antecedents of rain, snow, and thunder, but we do not now have "laws" of weather, for we do not now have a *theory* of weather. Moreover, in what significant respect do "human actions . . . repeat themselves"? And have not the "conditions under which people behaved" quite drastically changed "from one period of time to the next"? If the thrust of the above quotation is that scientific laws of behavior can only be discovered, if at all, under conditions in which human actions are tediously repeated and where the conditions of life display monotonous continuity, then, indeed, we are not likely to develop scientific laws. These laws, if they ever come, will take the form of universal propositions* from which the facts of behavior can be deduced. The closest behaviorism has come to such a covering law is the "law" of effect. However, this "law" is not only violated, but it has never been expressed in such a fashion as to allow deductions of other behavior studied under the very conditions in which the law of effect *is* confirmed; for example, in studies of the effects of partial reinforcement.

---

* In referring to propositions as "universal," I leave room for specifications of a statistical nature. Thus, "All non-reflexive behavior is determined by the history of reinforcement, but with an intrinsic variability of X% of the operant level" would qualify as a covering law. The "law of effect" is neither universal nor precise.

CHAPTER FOUR
PERCEPTION
MEMORY
AND
COGNITION

Perception and *cognition* are joined in this chapter because, as Ulric Neisser has recently noted, "perceiving is the basic cognitive activity out of which all others must emerge",[1] and also because developments in the fields of perception and cognition have by now made distinctions between the two seem arbitrary and misleading. Traditional treatments of perception as an essentially "sensory" affair and cognition as somehow "mental" never succeeded in divorcing the two. Perception, after all, entails a knowing subject if it is to refer to more than the response of afferent nerves to receptor activity. And cognition entails some objects, since it is not possible to ponder over *nothing*. Having said this, I must also add that the two words are not usefully employed as synonyms. General experience, ordinary language, and findings from the laboratory all indicate that there are close ties between perception and cognition, but that the processes involved are different. One commonly suggested difference is that perception involves a recognition of relationships among current stimuli, whereas cognition involves a recognition of relationships between past and present stimuli. On this construal, we can conceive of a *percipient* who is destitute of *memory*, but we cannot conceive of cognition in the absence of all memory. Stated another way, cognition is invariably a kind of *iterative* process, whereas perception need not be.

But at a finer level of analysis, we discover that perception has *recognition* as its primary object. Cognition, on the other hand, is most closely associated with *meaning*. Thus, perceptual outcomes are of a denotative nature; cognitive ones, of a connotative nature. Both perception and cognition pertain to our knowledge of the world and both, therefore, may be expressed in propositional form. In this regard, we might say that perception pertains to the *reference* of a proposition while cognition pertains to its *sense*. Propositions may have a sense without a reference:

The king of America is tall.

Since there is no king of America, the subject of the sentence refers to no one and to nothing, although the sentence itself is one out of which we can make sense. Indeed, were it otherwise, we would not know that it is wrong. There are also propositions containing referents but having no sense:

Three apples and two oranges are seven grapes.

All the nouns and modifiers in this sentence have existential referents, but the sentence as a whole is senseless. Let us look at the scribbling below:

Everyone is able to *perceive* this odd pattern, and even to copy it. Still, it is meaningless until we are told that it is the word "mine" with the reflection of the word given just below it. We now perceive the word where, before, we merely perceived the marks. Still, all that is involved here is a kind of recognition of relationships among the elements of the stimulus. That no comprehension is needed can be illustrated by selecting a different word:

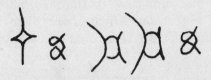

Here we form the Greek "gamma" using the Greek alphabet. Now that we know we are dealing with words and their reflections, we can tease out the upright from the inverted depiction. That is, we can *recognize* the pair of patterns. But with "gamma" there is no comprehension of the meaning of these patterns for one who does not know the Greek alphabet—even though there is still recognition. Even here, however, there is still a line dividing cognition and perception, since the percipient, equipped with a rule—for example, "stimuli are presented as if their reflections in a pool were also part of the presentation,"—is merely called upon to extract bona fide referents from an otherwise ambiguous array. It is obvious that, even in the case of "gamma," the percipient in possession of the rule can complete the task of recognition although he has never seen a Greek word or alphabetical character. No *memory* is required, except that of the rule itself. Nor is there a connotative element to be dealt with since "gamma" refers only to the third letter of the Greek alphabet; that is, it *denotes* that letter. In isolation, "gamma" refers to an entity but it has no meaning. What distinguishes the "gamma" case from the "mine" case is merely unfamiliarity with the symbols involved. Now, the point of all this is to demonstrate that cognition is not simply complex perception, but a process in which nonperceptual factors are invariably involved.

Let us now turn to an example of a different class of stimuli. Consider figure 3. The first drawing *means* that the smoking of cigarettes is forbidden; the second, that vehicles must come to a full stop; the third, that force is proportional to the product of mass and acceleration. Normal percipients arriving from a planet on which there have never been cigarettes, stop signs, or physics equations would be able to

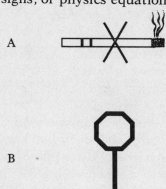

A

B

C   F = M x A

recognize, draw, and otherwise *perceive* these stimuli, but would have absolutely no conception of the meaning of any of them, or even that there was a meaning. Yet, adult citizens educated in the English-speaking world are immediately aware of the fact that (a) is a blanket injunction against smoking, that (b) is a general rule of the road, and that (c) is a fundamental law of mechanics. They know, for example, that the "X" placed across the cigarette has a meaning entirely different from the meaning of "x" as it appears in (c). Thus, they know the *connotations* of these symbols and know these only through a relationship between the physical features of the symbols and a memory of rules and principles learned in the past.

Here, then, is an illustration of "cognition" as it will be

treated in this chapter. For our purposes, "perception" will refer to the person's knowledge of things. "Cognition" will refer to the person's knowledge of the meaning of things. As we shall see, the latter turns out to be a knowledge of *rules* governing the permissible relations among things. Accordingly, there can be no "incorrect" cognition for the same reason that there can be no "informed ignorance." Instances involving reports of what are known to be impermissible relations (e.g., $5 + 4 = 12$) will be treated as evidence of noncognitive reports. This is an unorthodox position requiring some justification, and all the more so as it has direct bearing on the critical review of contemporary theories of cognition forming the bulk of the present chapter.

The fact that distinctions among such terms as "cognition," "perception," "learning," "memory," and "attention" are often difficult to make with any precision does not grant blanket semantic immunity to those who employ these terms. There may be (and are) disagreements among theorists, but the given theorist is obliged to provide an unambiguous statement of what he means by, for example, *cognition*. Of course, declaring an obligation is no guarantee that it will be honored. As it happens, none of the leading theorists whose efforts are most closely associated with cognitive psychology has actually offered such a statement. The definitions provided are generally ostensive; the theorist points to a collection of studies, methods, and findings and states, *this is cognitive psychology*. As one major spokesman has stated,

A new field called *cognitive psychology* has come into being. It studies perception, memory, attention, pattern recognition, problem solving, the psychology of language, cognitive development, and a host of other problems . . .[2]

In their influential text, Lindsay and Norman present the subject as the study of "information processing" in kinship with the computer sciences.[3] Many other examples are available and all of them are of this very general character. Yet, an analysis of the theories guiding research in the field leads to a recognition of what is at least implicitly adopted as a definition of cognition. The theories either study or take for granted covert (nonbehavioral) events of a mental or neural nature by which perceptual data are organized around fixed principles. Thus, "cognitive development" is the specialty addressed to the time-course associated with the appearance of these fixed principles. "Information processing" turns out to be the experimental examination of the organism's capacity to detect, store, and conceptualize environmental occurrences and to perform these functions in problematic situations. And "the psychology of language," as it appears in the literature of cognitive psychology, becomes the study of those fixed principles underlying the recognition of words and meanings, and the construction of rule-governed (grammatical) symbolic chains.

These aspects of cognitive psychology give it an independent identity vis-à-vis "learning," "memory," "attention," and the like. First, cognitive research and theory are conspicuously *not* stimulus-bound. Research on perception investigates discriminative reactions to specifiable features of a physical stimulus. Research on learning often does the same, but emphasizes the effects of reward and motivation. But cognitive research and theory, although borrowing from the methods and the data of these related fields, explore the underlying *logic* of perception and learning. At the root, then, it is a *rational* psychology with experimental branches. As a developing psychology, it is not required to possess all the rules operating in the realms of human information processing, language, problem solving, and perception. But the assumption that there are such rules is an unmistakable feature of cognitive psychology, and the feature that most readily permits distinctions to be drawn between it and, for example, behavioral psychology. Now, to the extent that this is so, it follows that the person or organism in a "cognitive" setting either has (obeys, follows, displays) the rule in question or does not. To the extent that a "wrong rule" is obeyed, the subject fails, or else the very concept of a rule becomes a rope of sand. We do not say, for example, that Smith is following the *wrong* rules of chess, but that Smith is not following the rules of chess—which is to say that Smith is not *playing* chess. Similarly, we do not describe the murderer as one who follows the rule of law incorrectly, but as one who violates the rule of law; otherwise, we would be obliged to respect the murderer's "sense of duty." Accordingly, it makes little sense to speak of an experimental subject as having "the wrong cognition" regarding task X. Rather, to the extent that the completion of task X requires possession of rule 1, and to the extent that the subject lacks rule 1 and therefore fails task X, the subject has no cognition at all in regard to task X. Not having the rule, he hasn't the *meaning* of the task, for "meaning" is rule-governed. Put in the form of a bromide, the relationship may be expressed thus: No rule, no meaning; no meaning, no reason; no reason, no cognition. The subject, in relation to task X, might just as well be the extraterrestrial being who confronts the stop sign. He *perceives* that it is a hexagon, that it is red, and that it is connected to a post. He can draw it, recall it, and make another like it. But he simply does not know what it *means*, even though he may know everything about it physically. We do not say that the Martian has a "faulty cognition" about stop signs, but that he hasn't a clue as to what a stop sign is.

We find a parallel to this in scientific explanations which are, to be sure, "cognitions" of a special sort. Scientific explanation is based upon a universal ("covering") law from which specific occurrences are deducible. One of the Hempel-

ian requirements imposed upon such laws is that they be
true; and this for the indisputable reason that *an incorrect
law explains nothing.* Ptolemaic astronomy, we now know,
did not provide a poor or weak explanation of the earth's
unchanging location in the heavens, because a theory disconfirmed by the facts only "explains" that which is not the
case. Again, it explains nothing. Cognitions, too, are laws
which permit the cognizer to incorporate particular instances into a universal scheme, and thereby explain the
problem (or percept) to himself. He either succeeds (by ap-
plying the appropriate law) or he explains nothing. If cognitive psychology has a topic unique to itself, that topic is
nothing less than the laws of thought. If there are no such
laws, there can be no cognitive psychology. If there are such
laws, Smith either possesses them or he doesn't and, if he
doesn't, he is not "cognizing."

That there are laws of thought was established long before
psychologists became interested in the matter, for what is
the formal logic of Aristotle if not "laws of thought"? A textbook example will serve us well:

Major Premise	ALL MEN ARE MORTAL.
Minor Premise	SOCRATES IS A MAN.
Conclusion	SOCRATES IS MORTAL.

Nothing is altered when specific referents are removed from
the syllogism:

All xs are bs.
c is an x.
c is a b.

If we were to ask an experimental subject the question,

"If all xs are bs, and if c is an x,
is c also a b?"

and if this reply were anything other than "yes," or "of course," we would not say that his comprehension of the syllogism was weak or in error, but that he lacked all comprehension of the syllogism. We would declare that he could not *reason* syllogistically. The reference (extension) of universal propositions is, by definition, boundless. In this respect, specific denotata are utterly irrelevant. In fact, the observer or subject who requires such denotata demonstrates a failure of comprehension. We have every right to conclude that his cognitive abilities do not include syllogistic reasoning in just the same way that we have the right, were he to fail every problem in addition, to conclude that he has no comprehension of the rules of addition.

I have gone on at length here because the analysis I am proposing creates difficulties of some consequence for many cognitive theories, and for all that are based upon the performance of individuals in laboratory settings in which the manipulation of objects is involved. Piaget's seminal studies of *conservation* will help to illustrate this point.[4] The young child is faced with two glass jars or urns of different shape. One is long and thin, the other short and wide. The former is filled with marbles or beads, and the latter is empty. When the contents of one are poured into the other, the child is asked questions designed to extract his sense of what, if anything, has happened to the number of beads. These are now very famous studies, the results have been replicated often, and in general most children fail to "conserve" before a certain age, and most unfailingly "conserve" at an older age. Research of this sort is designed to assess cognitive development and to study the genesis of conceptual thought. What the conservation problem requires for solution is the recognition that *number* is conserved throughout any and every purely spatial distribution of the constituents. But it is precisely because the principle of conservation is a principle—a law of thought—that possession of it is *necessarily* independent of specific material demonstrations. If one knows the law (has the concept), empirical evidence is gratuitous. If one lacks the concept, empirical evidence will yield only estimations of probability. In this respect, once the Piagetian psychologist finds it necessary to show the child *anything* concrete, there is prima facie evidence that the child lacks the concept. If he must look at the column of beads, he simply doesn't know what is going on. The principle of conservation is, itself, not the gift of experience but a deduction from still higher covering laws. Indeed, conservation is generally *disconfirmed* in experience. When a tall column of ink is poured into a fatter beaker, some of the ink remains on the walls of the original beaker; some of it evaporates in transit; some rests on the lip of the thin beaker. The careful "empiric" will insist that the volume of ink is *not* conserved as it is moved from one place to another.

Note that it will not do to declare that the child is *testing* the law of conservation, for to "test" a law is to doubt it, and to doubt it is to know what it asserts. However, to know what it asserts is, among other things, not to need a physical depiction of it. To say that Smith "conserves"—if, by this, we mean that Smith has a conception of the principle of conservation—is to say that Smith knows that the conservation of number is *necessarily true in all cases*. The laws of science are universal propositions which attach necessity to particular outcomes. If we knew, for example, that Smith lacked the concept of *necessity*, we would know, ipso facto, that he could not have the concept of numerical conservation. The latter is syllogistically required by a general rule of thought, and is itself a principle from which lower-order principles are deducible. On the account I have proposed, the Piagetian subject can only be said to have the *concept* of conservation if he solves the problem without looking. One glimpse and he fails!

It must be emphasized that nothing said here is intended to vitiate the conclusions based upon Piagetian research. The child who solves a given "conservation" problem solves nearly all such problems; the one who fails, tends to fail all such problems; the one who fails and is then trained on a given problem displays virtually no generalization to other problems of the same genre. These findings from the laboratory are interesting on any number of counts but, if the analysis I have proposed here is correct, they are not relevant to the matter of cognition or its ontogenesis. A principle such as that of conservation is a universal proposition whose validity is inextricably tied either (a) to a formal theory of the universe and its constituents or (b) to an unimpeachable law of thought underlying the propositions we articulate do deal with the facts of experience. The key phrase here is "we articulate," for it sets cognition apart from mere generalizations. If we arrived at the concept of the conservation of number by *counting* the balls each time they were placed in a different urn, we could only assign a certain probability to the "likelihood" of the number remaining the same on the next test. At the very foundation of conservationist thought is, of course, the principle that entities are continuous in time and *therefore* in space—no matter what the space. This is not necessarily how things "look," but how they must *be* if only to allow us to have the concept of a continuous *personal identity* throughout the seasons and geographies of life. But propositions of this sort, whether they refer to balls in an urn or to one's own self, are symbolic, not empirical. Angular momentum is conserved if and only if a certain system of theoretical physics is correct. Experimental data are relevant to tests of the theory but only disconfirming tests really count. The ultimate status of the theory—assuming no experimental disconfirmation—is determined by its logical coherence and explanatory parsimoniousness.

I am not suggesting here that the child, if he is properly said to have the "concept of conservation," must know the laws of physics. Rather, I am arguing that this concept, and all other concepts, are of a logical-verbal nature such that the manipulation of balls, jars, urns, and the like is entirely beside the point. The child who knows he is "Billy," and that he was the same "Billy" yesterday, has *a* concept of conservation: the conservation of "self" over time and space. If he were to ponder whether he is still Billy when he is in a crouch or in a tree we would know that he simply had no idea of what it means to be Billy or anyone else—or anything else. That his knowledge of self is not the result of experience is obvious, since a succession of experiences can only take place if there is a continuous self *having* them.

It is clear, then, that from Billy's perspective, Billy remains Billy as a result of a concept of conservation, and that this concept cannot be gained from experience. Perceptual knowledge never rises higher than the level of probability, whereas one's self-identity (pathology aside) is known certainly. In the case of self-identity, it is also clear that one's having memory will not succeed as an explanation, since memory logically entails a continuing personal identity. Only Billy has Billy's memories, at least in the way that Billy has them; that is, by acquaintance and not by description. Thus, we have a concept, the concept of personal identity, and we see that it cannot be forged by experience or by memory but is, itself, the logically required precondition for there to be experience or memory. Moreover, this concept of a continuing *self* is conservationistic and is cut from the same cloth as all other identity relations. In the language of Kant, such concepts are "analytic" in that their denial involves a contradiction; something true of no perception and of no memory. "I am not the same person I was yesterday" is contradictory in the logical sense, whatever literary or psychoanalytic force such a claim may have. Only "I" could possibly know "the person I was yesterday" with certainty. Should I happen to forget all that ever happened in my life until one minute ago, I would still have the concept of *self*, but could not provide any of the details of the life of that self. Thus, the concept survives even in the absence of memory. The amnesiac knows *that* he is, though he doesn't know *who* he is. He has the concept of "self" but not that of retroactive self-identity.

If we extend this analysis of self-identity, which is a form of conservationistic thought, to the Piagetian problem of conservation, we will begin to penetrate the subtle incompatibility between the object of the investigation and the form the investigation takes. What such studies seek to establish is the age at which persons attain conceptual thought, and more particularly the age at which the concept of *conservation* becomes part of the child's cognitive equipment. In the usual setting, the child is called upon to indicate whether there are now more or fewer or the same number of beads or balls once these items have been removed to a different receptacle. But what does it mean to ask "More?" or "Less?" or "The same?" except in relation to some standard? And how can there be a *standard* except through a principle of conservation? That is, just to ask about an "it" is to take for granted the continuation of "it" over some span of time. I submit that the question is intelligible only if there is conservationistic thought available to the auditor, and unintelligible otherwise. Indeed, the very notion of *number* proceeds from conservationistic concepts as do the notions of amount, size, and shape. Judgment itself entails the operation of a conservationistic principle, and it can and does proceed in the absence of perceptual referents or items in memory. What is required, of course, is some means by which those in possession of a concept can make their comprehension public. Since concepts are no more than the management of propositions, the only possible sign of conceptual thought will, itself, be of a propositional nature. In a sense, the entire enterprise is a Wittgensteinian "word-game." Perception may offer models or instances—as may memory—but the process is purely symbolic. And it is precisely because neither perception nor memory has any direct bearing upon conceptual thought that the actions of children confronted with beads and beakers are of doubtful relevance.

Some of these distinctions between perception and cognition were appreciated centuries ago as, for example, in the works of Descartes. It was Descartes who (following the example of St. Augustine) noted that we can have a *conception* of a thousand-sided figure (a chiliagon) but we cannot have a mental image of it. The Cartesian distinction between conception and imagination is similar to the distinction I have offered between cognition and perception. The Cartesian "concept" is an intellectual construct based upon our knowledge of principles. The Cartesian "image" is a perceptual entity reconstructed by memory and tied to particular stimuli. We can have conceptions of that which we have never seen— for example, chiliagons—and, of course, we can have the image of that of which we have no conception. The role of experience is to provide the data from which we extract principles so that, among other reasons, we no longer need experience itself in order to predict other occurrences.

With this background, it is possible to provide definitions of "cognition" and "cognitive process":

1. Cognition is the possession of valid rules of deduction and inference.

2. A cognitive process is the application of such rules in a manner coherently related to a given problem.

We now turn to theories of cognition prevalent in contemporary psychology, beginning with those that are actually theories of perception but that possess something of a cognitive dimension.

Features, Fields, and Gestalten

Perceptual theories of a quasi-cognitive stripe have already been discussed to some extent in chapter 2 in connection with Gestalt psychology and Pribram's holographic model. In the present context, let us ignore the physiological aspects of these theories and focus upon their cognitive elements. What is common to field, Gestalt, holographic, and feature-analysis theories of perception[5] is the assumption of essentially fixed *rules* of organization of the external world as it is received or "processed" by the mechanisms of perception. This is as true of the Gestalt theorists who have always leaned in the direction of physiological explanations as it is, for example, of the "field" theorist Kurt Lewin, who was forever skeptical of physiological explanations.[6] The only bona fide cognitive element in all such theories is precisely this assumption of *rules* of organization. The actual nature of the rules and the mechanisms underlying their operation are matters of continuing controversy. Köhler, as we noted in chapter 2, proposed electrical field-effects as the means by which the organization of percepts is achieved. The work of Hubel and Wiesel, cited in the same chapter, has been interpreted in favor of neuronal "feature detectors" by which pools of cortical cells are able to extract specific and salient properties from an array of stimuli. Pribram's theory calls for something like the electrophysiological equivalent of a holographic reconstruction of stimuli. Uttal has shown that a computer program involving autocorrelational analysis provides results quite in keeping with human pattern perception.[7] Each of these theoretical possibilities can claim support from experimental findings and each has difficulty with other experimental findings. It is also worth noting that none of them is utterly incompatible with the others, and that the human nervous system is sufficiently elaborate both structurally and functionally to be able to house the mechanisms asserted by these theories—and then some.

In addition to emphasizing the rule-governed nature of perception, cognitive theories—as contrasted with behavioristic and physicalistic theories—treat perception as a *transaction* rather than as a *reaction* or response. The percipient is assumed to be something of a participant in his own perceptual experiences. His participation takes the form of attention to certain details and inattention to others. Moreover, his needs, goals, and expectancies are all recognized as determinants of the perceptual outcome. Then, too, a cognitive theory of perception is invariably a *contextual* theory in that it acknowledges the overall psychological "space" within which perceptions occur; not merely the physical space within which the physical objects of perception are located.

It almost goes without saying that these aspects of cognitive theories of perception are faultless at a common-sense level. Daily experience teaches that we are more likely to see what we look for; that in a cheerful setting we tend to interpret ambiguous information positively; that the overall condition of our lives can profoundly affect the manner in which we perceive the world. These inferences from life have been augmented by any number of scientific demonstrations and experimental findings. The contextual effects on perception can be graphically shown by the well-known Müller-Lyer illusion (figure 4). When lines A and B, which are equal in length, are placed within outward-pointing and inward-

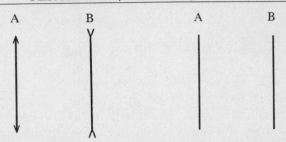

A   B   A   B

pointing arrows, the perceived length of the line depends upon the direction of the arrow. In this illustration, B appears longer than A.

Projective tests such as the Rorschach and the Thematic Apperception Test (TAT) provide vivid evidence of the role of one's overall "life space" in shaping one's perceptions. Stimuli that are ambiguous (e.g., the Rorschach inkblots) or neutral (e.g., the scenes depicted in the TAT) will be judged as containing all sorts of events, implications, plots, and possibilities, depending upon the general mental disposition of the percipient.

Then there is that vast and growing literature devoted to human "information processing"[8] which has established the powerful effects of memory, meaning, attention, motivation, and expectation on the perception of both simple and complex stimuli. A list of some of the more suggestive findings will be sufficient to convey the thrust of information-processing approaches:

1. Single words, imbedded in noise so that they can only be heard half the time, become reliably heard when presented in a meaningful and grammatical sequence.[9]

2. Subjects presented with two different messages—one delivered to the left ear and the other to the right—will "hear" only the message in the channel they are told to listen to, and may even fail to detect changes in the gender of the speaker delivering messages to the nonattended channel.[10]

3. Under the conditions cited in (2), brain responses to sig-

nals delivered to the nonattended channel are greatly diminished, and often totally absent.[11]

4. Subjects given a single and brief presentation of a stimulus—such as a word, a letter of the alphabet, or a symbol—and then required immediately to count backwards by 3s, will fail to recall the stimulus if they are tested for retention more than 20 or 30 seconds after the presentation. The backward counting is designed to prevent rehearsal, and in the absence of such rehearsal human short-term memory is found to be limited to less than a half a minute.[12]

5. Subjects given a brief exposure to an array of stimuli (e.g., six or seven letters or numbers) will often be able to "recall" one of them when its location is circled or marked just after the brief exposure. Thus in the array: a   m   t   d   j   w   h   c   the subject may be able to "recall" only one or two after a very brief exposure. If, however, within 10 or 20 milliseconds after the exposure, one of the eight locations is circled—say, the fourth location, the subject is very likely to report the correct letter (d).[13]

Hundreds of such findings have been generated in the past decade and any number of recent texts may be consulted for reviews of the literature.[14] What is common to most of these studies is the attempt to identify a *process* able to account for the findings. Now, the term "process" shares the ambiguities we found in connection with "system," "cognition," and "perception." To overcome the problem, cognitive theorists have begun to employ the language and data of the neural sciences, but on the whole this tendency has only aggravated the difficulties. Neurophysiological data do not lend themselves to cognitive translations, nor do the findings from studies of cognition translate easily into neural functions. Typically, the "neurologized" cognitive "process" is merely the replacement of one hypothesis with another. When we refer to the complex sequence of events by which ingested food is converted to nutrients and to waste as "digestion," we mean no more by the term than this sequence of events. To say, for example, that "the stomach digests food" is no more than to acknowledge that the stomach happens to be the place and happens to contain the known agents associated with the breakdown of food into nutrients and waste. But when we say that "cognition" occurs "in the brain," we are making a fundamentally different claim. First, we are not able to translate "cognition" into the same sort of statements employed when defining "digestion." Second, not only is problem solving different from digestion, but it is unlike anything now known about neural events. Thus, while some of the ambiguity might be relieved were there a causal connection established between cognition and brain events, there is no such connection now available and there is, therefore, no less ambiguity in the neurologized formulations than in the purely psychological ones.

A second feature of information-processing approaches shared by most current studies is the attempt to identify *stages* of processing. I will not libel any of the more influential workers in this area by reducing the search for stages to little more than a restatement of the findings themselves. The subject who fails to recall a letter or word 10 seconds after it was flashed in a tachistoscope—and about 10 seconds after the subject begins to count backwards by 3s—is said to have failed to place the "information" in something called "short-term storage." And the explanation for this is that something called "short-term storage" must not be interfered with during "processing" if its "contents" are to be "deposited" in "long-term stores." Explanations of this sort are judged to gain credibility when it is discovered that certain neurological disturbances or surgical interventions produce short-term amnesias in patients or experimental animals. The problem, of course, is that amnestic syndromes are usually accompanied by alterations in motivation or attention or even levels of consciousness. There is simply no comparability between brief studies of healthy undergraduates looking into tachistoscopes and clinical examinations of patients with severe insults to the nervous system. When we turn to the putatively relevant studies of animals, and especially those studies of retrograde amnesia produced by electroconvulsive shock, matters become even more vexed. There is great divergence among the reported intervals over which these shocks produce amnestic consequences. It would, of course, be hazardous to take the *average* of reported values. The weight of evidence, however, clearly indicates a "cortical consolidation time" far greater than the 15 to 30 seconds usually reported in studies of human short-term memory. That time is required for recently perceived material to be stored or rehearsed in such a way as to be accessible to the subject at some later time is not in dispute. All the evidence points to some form of preliminary reception which is tentative, and a more permanent form of reception. We need not quibble about the choice of terms; "short-term" and "long-term" are as serviceable as any of the more obvious alternatives. There is, however, some difficulty associated with the term "memory" in this connection. When the subject fails to report "d" in the array cited in (5) above, and later does report it when a ring is placed over the position "d" had occupied in the array, we are hard pressed to speak of "memory" and "recall" as if there were no *perceptual* event to concern us. It would be contradictory to speak of the recall of that which was never perceived in the first place, unless by "remembering" we mean something different from the revival of an earlier experience. Turning to perception, we find numerous cases in which the *report* of a stimulus is determined by many factors, not the least of which is the report-measure we select. Stimuli which are backward-masked by more intense stimuli coming a fraction of a second later offer a useful illustration. If the subject is *asked* whether he saw the first stimulus—or is asked how many stimuli he saw—we learn that the first of the two was not "seen." If, however, the subject is required to press a key as soon as he sees anything, we learn that his reaction time is just as fast when the first stimulus is presented alone as it is when a second "masking" flash is presented with it.[15] One explanation for effects of this kind is that reaction time is mediated by neural mechanisms different from those associated with perception + awareness.[16] The point, however, is that the position we are able to take on the question of what the subject has "processed" will depend in large measure on the response indicator used in our studies: verbal report, reaction time, pupillary reflexes, electroetinograms, estimates of confidence.

As the whole of the literature is canvassed, we find not so much a two-stage memory "process," but a multitimed— perhaps even a continuously variable—ensemble of receptive and registrational functions. Some interference and/or retrieval effects occur in the 50 to 200 millisecond range; others in the one-second range; still others in the range of fractions of a minute. Thus, the number of stages may depend more on our ingenuity as experimenters than on any fixed feature of human information processing. The visual mechanisms give us access to the complexities of the case. Taking the number of retinal rods and cones at something on the order of 130 million, and assuming that each can respond photochemically and can then regenerate photochemically in something on the order of 1 millisecond, we have a mechanism capable of making 130 billion yes–no decisions in a second; that is, 13×10^{10} bits. If we now take 100 milliseconds as the fastest motor response to a visual stimulus, we have a maximum output capability of 10 bits in the same second. Clearly, in terms of the output capacities of organisms, it would be pointless were all the peripherally sensed information to be processed all the time. Some sort of filtering is in order, and this filtering can be achieved in more than one way.

The easiest method of filtering, from the point of view of design, is in the choice of physical materials. Just as a loudspeaker is made of materials which resonate primarily over the musical range of frequencies, so too biological receptors are "tuned" by virtue of their physical composition. The lens of the eye, for example, has greatly reduced transmissivity in the ultraviolet region of the spectrum, and the ocular fluids are relatively opaque to wavelengths in the infrared region of the spectrum. But these physical limitations can yield only a fixed filter, and it is obvious that what we reject of incoming signals involves more than their physical characteristics. For a selective and variable filter, we must have something that is dynamic and adaptive. There are, for example, neurons in the visual system of the monkey which respond most efficiently when the stimulus presented to the eyes has the shape of a monkey's hand.[17] This sort of "feature analyzer" is illustrative of a selective filter, although a somewhat primitive one. Neurons of this sort would confer obvious advantages on the species, so it is not surprising to discover that such innately tuned processors are common among the advanced species. But a truly adaptive filter is one whose processing varies as a function of prior stimulations. In psychological terms, we would say that it is a filter whose characteristics are altered by learning and memory. The two types of filter—the innate and relatively fixed one, and the more flexible one—are not mutually exclusive. Both can be found among all the advanced species. In both cases, what we discover is a bias in the perceptual (and often in the neurophysiological) reports favoring particular stimulus features, patterns, or Gestalten. Because of this, the expression "information processing" is too indefinite. What, after all, is the "information" in a stimulus to which the organism is insensitive? No matter how many bits have been transmitted, if the organism is incapable of receiving the signal, it is utterly uninformative from the organism's point of view. And, if the perceptual apparatus of the organism is especially adapted to certain kinds of stimuli (e.g., hand-shaped figures), such stimuli will be far more informative than those to which there has been no special adaptation.

Gestalt approaches to perception have generally been desultory in the matter of exact measurement and specification of the physical characteristics of stimuli. This is understandable, however, in light of the Gestalt orientation which challenges attempts to understand perception on the basis of *local* effects. It makes little sense, for example, to worry about the exact number of millilamberts in a visual flash, and the precise angular size of the flash on the retina, if the theory under consideration is a field theory which emphasizes the role of the entire perceptual mechanism. I do not mean to suggest that Gestalt research is sloppy; only that its aims have been such as to lessen the need for the sort of care ordinarily exercised in basic psychophysical research. On the other side, we find those in the information-processing school exercising some care in the specification and control of the physical parameters of stimulation, but generally indifferent to the matter of perceptual predispositions. The stimuli chosen are by-and-large neutral with respect to the native biases of the percipient. Visual stimuli tend to be circles or points of light; auditory ones are confined to pure tones or bursts of noise. In this, the information-processing theorist is operating out of a traditional psychophysical context—which is all to the good—but may be measuring

aspects of the system which are not typical of the processing
that takes place when ecologically significant stimuli are involved. I might illustrate this point with a trivial example.
We know that infant ducks will pursue cardboard silhouettes shaped roughly like adult ducks. Early in life, during
the "critical period," the ducklings can be *imprinted* to such
simulations such that, later in life, the ducks will actually
prefer the silhouettes to real ducks when the time for mating
occurs. Here we have a very powerful stimulus able to
engage complex patterns of behavior. Now, suppose we
knew nothing of imprinting, critical periods, or the effects of
initial experiences on the subsequent behavior of adult
ducks. Suppose, further, that we proceeded to study the absolute and difference thresholds of ducks in the presence of
circular patches of light; backward-masking functions in the
duck; visual reaction time under conditions of hunger and
thirst; the duck's ability to respond discriminatively to two
rapidly presented stimuli. I would venture to say that all the
data gathered under these conditions of stimulation would
not permit us to predict reaction time, masking effects, discriminative responding, and the like in the settings in which
the stimulus is the imprinted one; that is, the cardboard sil-
houette. An analogous problem presents itself when we confine our studies of human information processing to settings
in which stimuli are ecologically neutral or undefined. What
would be useful is the combination of the Gestalt perspective in the selection of stimuli and the psychophysical perspective in the selection of methods and measurements. That
the information-processing approach, when employed by the
cognitive psychologist, is not stimulus-bound—that is, is not
strictly psychophysical—is less an asset than a liability
unless the stimuli chosen are of demonstrable psychological
significance. There is no need to do with letters of the alphabet or numerical characters what the psychophysicists have
been doing with spots of light for the past century.

The usual complaint brought against Gestalt and field theories of perception is that they are more committed to phenomena than to functional relationships. The experimental psychologist is accustomed to data obtained under precisely defined conditions permitting expressions of the sort, $R = f(S)$. Thus, the Gestalt principles of "goodness" or *Prägnanz* or "grouping" seem to be will-o'-the-wisp. The insistence that perception is "of the whole" and that peripheral, local effects of stimuli are insufficient to account for the facts is difficult to incorporate into a program of research devoted to establishing fundamental psychophysical relationships. Similarly, the psychologist used to thinking of memory in strict associational terms wonders why the Gestaltist must invoke field effects to explain our ability to recognize stimuli we have seen before. Yet, the facts of perception and those of learning and memory often seem to call for the sort of explanation advanced by Köhler and his disciples, and are not as readily explicable in peripheralistic or associationistic terms. We have already seen sketches of stimulus configurations which give rise to more than one percept even though the stimulus remains constant. To these may be added the hundreds of visual illusions whose effects simply cannot be accounted for in terms of receptor-neural processes.

When we examine that form of memory known as *recognition*, in which a current percept is identified with an earlier one, we again find some justification for the Gestalt notion of fields of (neural) activity. On the assumption that such recognition is mediated by processes occurring in the brain, and on the added assumption that very few experiences are exact copies of each other., it is clear that the problem of matching current stimuli with prior ones is formidable. Were we restricted to a point-for-point matching operation, every recognition task would be painfully difficult, and recognition itself would display none of the spontaneity and clarity we know it to have. But once we assume that each percept is somehow coded "as a whole" and that its *perceptual* (as opposed to its merely physical) residue is structural (and not a collection of neural "points"), we then are less surprised by the accuracy and the swiftness—the effortlessness—of recognition. If, for example, we have been given this address:1237 37th Street, and as we cruise about in search of it we see *Twelve Thirty-Seven*, we know (recognize) immediately that this is the place for which we have been searching. The translation from the numerical to the literal code does not involve psychophysical discriminations but symbolic ones, suggesting that the original learning and the current recognition are also of a symbolic form. Similarly, we have never "seen" railroad tracks such as those depicted in figure 5, but we immediately recognize the sketch to be that of railroad tracks. Again, it would seem that the actual representation of such stimuli is of a structural nature, and that subsequent recognition involves the

matching of structures, not the matching of specific stimulus "elements."[18] That Köhler's proposed brain "currents" have not been confirmed in any rigorous fashion tells against the neurological aspects of his theory, but has no bearing upon the phenomena themselves, or upon the failure of elementaristic theories to account for them.

Memory and Forgetting

The second prong on which contemporary theories of cognition rest is that of memory. Together with perception, memory provides the stuff of which cognitions are made, although as I have argued cognition is not reducible to perception and memory and is surely not synonymous with them. Theories of memory have a long history although this has not produced much by way of variety. Aristotle was one of the first to propose a form of "trace" theory which has proved to be a popular option ever since. We find it adopted by such otherwise divergent theorists as Pavlov and Köhler. In modern times, the "trace" has given way to the "icon", and the persistence of traces to "iconic storage," but these terminological nuances leave the original notion largely untouched. It is worth recalling that Aristotle's theory of memory was bound up with his theory of perception, for even today notions such as iconic storage are wed—if unwittingly—to a particular kind of theory of perception; one I will call the "copy theory." As I noted in the second chapter, this theory has heavy liabilities. When it is set forth dogmatically and explicitly, it is wrong; when it is not patently false, it is generally unintelligible. The external world does not paint pictures on the brain. The recollection of a melody is not a copy of the melody, nor is it even acoustical. The sense in which we "picture" a face is clearly different from the sense in which we revive a tune or recall being cold or having a toothache. Thus, even if we were willing to accept a copy theory of visual memory, we would not be able to extend it to other sense-modalities.

Concepts such as "trace," "icon," and "image" are misleading on several counts. Aside from the fact that they are of doubtful validity when generalized beyond visual recall, they suggest a feature which even visual memories tend not to have: that of *reconstruction*. Even when we attempt to oppose the tendency, it is typically the case that our visual "images" are contextually impoverished whereas our actual perceptions are not. When we picture uncle Harry we call up a face but nothing surrounding the face. The borders of our images are black, as if we were looking at a slide of the subject in a darkened room. Then, too, such images are strikingly immobile even when we attempt to picture visual motion. Try, for example, to recall (to picture) the last concert you attended. Recall also the music and attempt to match the actions of the conductor to the revised melodies. If I am not mistaken, it will be impossible to picture sustained action by the conductor, although the melody will proceed continuously. What is likely is that the conductor will be pictured in a choppy series of stills, creating perhaps the sense of movement, but not a depiction of movement.

Against this claim may be opposed studies of so-called mental rotation which require the subject to turn an image through 180 degrees "in his mind."[19] The term is a misleading one in that what is rotated is no more mental than any other percept. Let us call the phenomenon in question "image-rotation" and perform the experiment ourselves. We close our eyes, think of a coffee cup tied by string to the ceiling and slowly spun around. Now let us try to maintain the image of this continuous angular motion. Again, what appears are a number of stills, and the jerkiness in the movement cannot be overcome. Thus, even visual "icons" fail to reflect important features of visual perception, and it is only within the visual sense that the concept of memory as a copy has been at all plausible.

The conceptual oddities of the copy theory can be evaded to some extent by exchanging the notion of a copy for that of a code, but here the advantages are only apparent. When we recall a melody, we do not recall anything that seems like a "code" of the melody, but the melody itself. Of course, it is trivially true that the original percept was also "coded" in the sense that the mechanical vibrations did not directly enter the brain. Be that as it may, the original percept was *auditory*, the revived melody is *not*, and the revived melody is still, somehow, a faithful reproduction.

When we turn from sense memory to verbal memory the problems with the trace theory become insurmountable. It has been known for a half-century that the degradation of recall occurring over time is determined principally by the kind of activity that is interpolated between original learning and later tests of retention; that is, that time qua time is not a major determinant.[20] Thus, explanations of forgetting on the basis of the "decay" of "traces" are unsuccessful at least in these contexts. Instead, *interference* theories have been proposed[21] which seek to account for forgetting in terms of destructive interactions between current and past learning or percepts. The major variables shown to effect the degree of interference are (a) the semantic similarity between original and current items, (b) the physical similarity between past and current percepts, (c) the degree of mastery developed in original learning, (d) the amount of material committed to memory during the interpolation period, and (e) the position of the item to be recalled when a sequence of such items was initially learned. In studies of short-term memory—where effects occur over a period of seconds—interference is greatest when the rehearsal period is filled with material acoustically similar to the item that must be remembered. As a general rule, acoustic interference is greatest for short-term memory, and semantic interference is greatest for long-term memory. Thus, in a long-term memory task, the word "feline" would interfere more with the recall of "cat" than would the word "bat."[22]

Perhaps the first question leaping out of such accounts has to do with just what is being interfered with, but this is not a question likely to be answered until we have a coherent theory of learning itself. It is not enough to say that it is not a trace, or to say that it is an icon or representation, or a code. Statements of this sort are no more rigorous than one which would simply repeat the findings; for example, "It is 'cat' that is being interfered with." As Lindsay and Norman have said: "Just how information is represented within the data structures of human memory remains a mystery."[23] And as long as this is the case, such notions as copies, traces, and icons are not theoretical but analogical. Those schooled in the terminology will have no difficulty in composing lengthy statements which *seem* to be theoretical. I will try my own hand at it, although I must admit that I have not really developed the knack:

The external world is represented within the data structure of the human nervous system as a code. Sensory events are initially registered in the form of neuroelectric pulse-codes and persist within reverberating neural circuits. Successive presentations of the same stimulus enhance the signal-to-noise ratio within a given circuit. Presentations of similar— but different—stimuli enlarge the size of the circuit by including more of the available functional units anatomically associated with the basic circuit. The function of the circuits is an iterative one, with each complete cycle of repetition producing relatively permanent alterations in the RNA chemistry of the participating neurons. The ultimate representation, then, is a chemical one in that a relatively permanent biochemical *system* is fashioned out of the recurrent experiences of the organism. For every discriminable feature of the experienced environment, there is a biochemical code. "Recall," therefore, is but the reactivation biochemically of those neural circuits initially engaged by the earlier experiences. As the neural circuits lead to the formation of a biochemical system, so too the biochemical system can trigger neuroelectric activity in the associated circuit. So-called *interference* effects in memory are nothing more than confused codes, not conceptually different from confusions occurring in, for example, telegraphy or, for that matter, spelling.

Now, I offer this not as a theory—for it is not one—but as something of a parody on the sorts of explanations routinely encountered in the psychological literature. All the trendy terms are carefully chosen and strung together: RNA, circuits, system, codes, iterative, functional units, data structure. And yet, the statement taken as a whole is a piece of invention, a bit of scientistic fluff. The anatomy is missing. The physiology is simply unknown at the required level. The proposed links between electrical events and biochemical ones are nowhere to be found. The only "code" we have is the relatively simple one by which the intensity of a stimulus is converted into a greater rate of impulse initiation in sensory fibers. "Data structure" begs the question, since we have no idea that there are even "data" in the brain. (Note the easy slide from having data *from* the brain to statements about data *in* the brain.) It is far from clear, on purely conceptual grounds, that the brain even has memories, although it may be the case that memories are stored in the brain. What is clear is that *we* have memories and that, since we have to put them somewhere, we may put them in the brain. But this no more means that the brain has memories than a

ticket to the opera, kept in my desk drawer, means that my
desk drawer is going to the opera.

Cognitive Theories

I have tried to make the case throughout this chapter that
cognition is not simply magnified or multiplied perception,
nor is it perception plus memory and learning. My thesis is
that, properly understood, cognition is the management of
propositions, and that these propositions—though often containing empirical contents—are not necessarily tied to experience or memory. It is often intimated in the literature of
cognitive psychology that the principles of organization
which seem to underlie perception are the same as those underlying cognition. Thus, when it is discovered that infants
seem to possess Gestaltlike perceptual predispositions[24] we
are asked to believe that these somehow are the primordia of
cognitive processes.

A moment's reflection will convince all but the committed
that cognition and perception are not expressions of the
same underlying principles of organization. We have in the
psychology of perception a large chapter devoted to *illusions*. But there could be no such chapter were it the case
that cognition and perception are governed by the *same*
principles of organization. Instead, if the principles of organization are the same, then the two processes must be the
same when the same stimuli are involved. My point is that
the only basis we have on which to argue that *this* is illusory
and *that* is not is the basis of epistemology; that is, cognition. It is in this respect that cognition and perception stand
in something of an adversary relationship. Cognitive processes serve as the means by which the errors and illusions
of sense are corrected; the means by which veridical perceptions are *known* to be veridical. The position defended here

is somewhat different from Jerome Bruner's, according to which perception is devoted to the testing of hypotheses.[25] I would agree that perception involves the gathering of data relevant to the testing of hypotheses, but the test itself is a cognitive affair. The outcome of a perception, as I have suggested, is of a propositional nature: *That is an orange.* We have here a factual claim whose truth depends upon a correspondence between the perceived physical properties of *this* orange and the exhaustive list of predicates attached to the class-term, ORANGE. Thus,

$$\text{All } x\text{s are } y\text{s};$$
$$k \text{ is an } x:$$
$$k \text{ is a } y—$$

where x stands for the ensemble: orange color, round, fruit, pungent, etc. We advance hypotheses to account for facts, and we conduct tests to weigh the merits of hypotheses. The facts are the gift of experience—of perception—and it is through cognitive processes that we locate these facts within a hypothetical context which here I will call "what we know." That subsequent perceptions provide the additional facts needed to test "what we know" is, of course, true, but the perceptions themselves cannot constitute the ultimate test of the aptness of the hypothetical context, for it is these very perceptions which fill it. The test must come from beyond the domain of factual knowledge and is, therefore, quite literally a *metaphysical* test. It is what cognition is all about, and it is fundamentally different from perception, memory, attention, or motivation. It is what, in a more innocent period, was called *thought.* To say, then, with Neisser, that cognition is "all the processes by which the sensory input is transformed, reduced, elaborated, stored, recovered, and used."[26] is, in my view, both misleading and insufficient. It is misleading because it limits cognition to labors performed upon perceptions, whereas the highest reach of cognition involves abstractions for which there may be no sensory or even real-world equivalent. And it is insufficient because it does not include what would appear to be the raison d'etre of cognition, the *testing* of "sensory input" for its truth-value.

In some respects, what I am proposing draws inspiration from the much maligned "faculty" psychologies of the eighteenth and early nineteenth centuries. I recognize how little is actually explained by treating cognition in terms of a capacity (or "faculty") for logical thought. But in every systematic account of the events and laws of nature, a point is reached beyond which further analysis is either impossible, impractical, or impracticable. Every scientific discipline and every philosophical system has a number of primitive terms and concepts which must be taken for granted and which defy any further reduction. This is true not only of such exclusively deductive systems as geometry, but of physics and chemistry as well. In psychology, it may one day be possible to identify neural functions without which logical operations are not possible. But even if we were in possession of this information, it would not permit us to conclude that logical operations are only these functions; that is, that logical operations and neural functions are strictly identical. Clearly, most of the logical work done by persons is also done by any number of machines which have no "neural" component whatever. Thus, neurophysiology may constitute a sufficient condition for operations of a certain kind, but surely not a necessary condition. Moreover, whatever the status of this future science may be in these regards, it is unlikely that a neurophysiological description will be any more "objective" or suggestive than those propositional descriptions available right now. It is far easier to say "Smith does not recognize transitivity in framing his judgments" than to say what Smith's neurons are doing. I strongly suspect it will remain easier for many, many seasons.

The "faculty" psychologies of Thomas Reid, Dugald Stewart and others—including Gall and the phrenologists—were defended principally along the lines I have just drawn. The caterpillar crawls across hundreds of leaves until it reaches one suited to its needs. We call this behavior, with appropriate reservations, "instinctive," and are willing to say that the little animal has a "faculty" for finding suitable nourishment. A rigorous behaviorism would have us abandon such talk and learn to live with the fact that our "faculty" is just this *finding of food*. The term "faculty," it is urged, adds nothing to the observable behavior. It attempts to float an explanation in what are finally mystical waters. On the behavioristic account, we should be searching for those environmental events that come to control such behavior as crawling. If we do so, we will soon discover that leaf *x* reliably causes the caterpillar to stop in its tracks and eat.

The problems with this approach are now legendary. We do, after all, want to know what it is about this or that feature of the environment that gives it the power it is said to have. That is, we want to know *why* the caterpillar stops at *this* leaf and not at others. The behavior itself explains nothing in just the sense that no fact explains anything. The fact is what needs the explanation, not what provides it. If we look to biology for the desired explanation, we are likely to receive a Darwinian summary of selection pressures, the pruning of the species' genome, and the successive increase in the proportion of caterpillars able to locate this particularly nurturing leaf. At a more microscopic level, biology may teach us that the caterpillar has unique receptors serving both vision and olfaction such that *this* leaf triggers an innate assembly of neurons intimately associated with consummatory behavior. *But this is all Reid, Stewart, and the others ever meant by a faculty!* We may quibble over the specific ones they proposed, but even the most *au courant* of our theoretical psychologies is heavily laced with faculty concepts. I submit that, at the end of their conceptual tethers, notions such as "cognitive maps" (Tolman), "schemata" (Piaget; Kagan; Neisser), *Gestalten* (Köhler), and "fields" (Lewin) are indistinguishable from the eighteenth-century "faculties," except to the extent that the newer notions are often more ambiguous.

According to Neisser, *schemata* are internal structures comprising a portion of the perceptual cycle and relatively specific to the objects of perception.[27] They are *like* the formats used in computer programming, but they are also *like* the "plans" proposed by Miller, Galanter, and Pribram.[28] Indeed, the schemata are not only at the base of the plans underlying perception but also the means by which actions are organized.[29] And if all this is not enough, note that

. . . we are probably born with schemata sensitive to expressions of emotion and intention; the schemata of speech perception may develop out of such beginnings.[30]

According to Kagan, who has discovered tendencies in infants by which perception is predisposed to regular as opposed to "scrambled" stimuli, the schemata are mental images or pictures developed *by* experience but prior to it.[31] For Piaget, the schemata are cognitive frameworks governing the approach to problem solving and the manner in which information is assimilated.[32]

If we compare Neisser's, Kagan's, and Piaget's use of schemata with the eighteenth-century notion of "faculties," we find only negligible discrepancies. Kagan and Neisser and, to a lesser extent, Piaget are more explicit in acknowledging the part played by learning and by maturation, but none of the older faculty psychologists was indifferent to such considerations. In their innocence, they generally took a normal, nurturing environment for granted, and then asked why it was that animals and persons displayed relatively invariant tendencies under specified conditions. Their answer, and one we have been all taught to suspect, is that such tendencies came from "the mint of nature"; that the animal in question was *so constituted* that it nursed its young, foraged for food, ran from light, or flew southward in November. Gall, of course, pressed on to propose that all such "constitutional" predispositions were (somehow) in the brain, but most of the faculty psychologists were willing to settle for an essentially ecological account and not speculate on the matter of mechanism. In recognizing that some strains of dog were "naturally" good hunters, they did not thereby argue against training or learning or experience. They simply took the facts where they found them, and reasoned that some strains of dog were therefore better candidates for training because of a *native* inclination. Is this not what a *schema* is?

What is troubling about the concept of schemata as used by cognitive psychologists is not that it is something of a return to faculty psychology—for, in fact, we have only abandoned this tradition in name—but that it isn't a *cognitive* concept at all. It is a *perceptual* concept. This becomes most clear when we see the use to which it is put by those who propose theories of language acquisition and speech. Neisser's treatment is again illustrative.[33] The emphasis here is on the *reference* of words whereby the child comes to identify objects with those sounds (names) with which they are most frequently associated. Soon, a schema is developed—this time an *anticipatory* schema—such that the child's perception of the object is tied to its name, and such that this kind of expectation extends to all objects. With each new item introduced into his environment, the child anticipates a name for it, and assimilates the name to the thing. But none of this, as I see it, has any bearing upon what is unique about human language—its nonobjective, propositional, and connotative functions. Consider, for example, the task of teaching a child what a gift is. Note I do not mean only a "present"—which is something received on a particular date—but a *gift* which may be proffered at any time and for no apparent reason. Or consider the task of teaching a child what it means to *steal:*

> MOTHER: Johnny said you stole his toy.
> CHILD: He said he didn't want it anymore.
> MOTHER: But did he say you could have it?
> CHILD: He said he was going to throw it away.

Note the words "stole," "want," "could," and "throw" in this exchange. They are inextricably bound up with intentions, possibilities, values, and the like, and are not reducible to specific referents or to specific actions. Nor is the lesson in question reducible to a moral maxim, "Stealing is taking what belongs to another," for the relation "belonging" is, itself, connotative. For the child to know that the toy "belonged" to Johnny, he would have to know what it means to *own* something in contrast with simply *having* it. In so many words, he would have to comprehend what are called "rights," but these too cannot be defined ostensively; that is, we cannot point to a right.

It is doubtlessly true that the words children learn to use in such a way as to name things correctly are learned after the manner proposed by Neisser. I would refer to such learning (and to such language) as *denotational* and would propose that such learning requires nothing by way of *cognitive* function. Thus, I see no reason why it should not be possible to teach chimpanzees—or, for that matter, pigeons—to employ such symbols (names for things and for actions) in a coherent fashion. Symbols of an *intensional* nature, however, are quite another matter and are at the very core of the function of human language. Were we not concerned with meanings, there would be no advantage to human language over more primitive gestural languages. But if we are, indeed, social animals, and if the idea of human society is coextensive with the ideas of justice, duty, moral judgment, and political rights and obligations, then our language must be suited to the teaching of such concepts, and the concepts, of course, can only be taught to those able to transcend the realm of the particular. It can only be taught to beings possessing the "faculties," as it were, by which mere things can stand for universal propositions. If it is more reassuring to speak of these capacities as "schemata," so be it. But the schemata able to assimilate certain specific actions as instances of *stealing*, certain specific items as instances of *gifts*, and certain opportunities for action as instances of *rights*, will not be part of what Neisser calls a "cycle of perception."

The cognitive theory which has most directly addressed issues of this sort is that advanced by Lawrence Kohlberg.[34] Kohlberg has studied moral development in terms of the genesis of moral reasoning, and has observed that, other factors being roughly equal, the stages of maturation bring with them progressively higher stages of moral judgment. The testing format in Kohlberg's research is a story in which a conflict exists between actions and the child's sense of right and wrong. One of the more familiar stories involves a man whose wife is gravely ill. There is only one pharmacist in the region. He has the medicine which will save the woman's life, but he has set a price on the drug which is far beyond the husband's means. The husband steals the medication and returns to save his wife's life. Note that the story can be adjusted to meet the nuances of age, culture, and locale. Having heard the story, the auditor is asked such questions as,

Did the husband do the right thing?
If so, why?
If not, why?
If he is caught, should the husband be punished?
If so, what should be the punishment?

Kohlberg has gathered responses to these and morally equivalent stories from subjects in various cultures and at different ages. The research is not without problems and the findings have not gone unchallenged. Nonetheless, it is clear that the responses can be partitioned into distinctly different conceptual categories. For example, those who judge the husband's conduct to be wrong "because mommy says you should never steal" are basing their judgment on grounds different from those invoked by those who say that "society cannot exist without laws, and the husband—no matter what the purely personal stakes—must obey these laws." And both of these responses are grounded in principles alien to the view that "life rights invariably take precedence over mere property rights and, therefore, what the husband did was morally obligatory." Note, however, that none of these responses is intelligible at a purely *perceptual* level. What Kohlberg has studied is the *logic* of moral reasoning. Once he knows the major (moral) premise of the person responding, he knows the solution (judgment) that will be reached regarding nearly any (moral) problem. Perception will tell us who is the husband, who is the pharmacist, and which bottle contains the medicine. It will never tell us about property rights, life rights, the rule of law, or society's good on the whole. As long as cognitive psychology discounts such meanings, and confines the study of meaning to the use of denotational language, it will simply rediscover the dictionary, as it were, and not those "laws of thought" which are its proper subject.

To some extent there are signs of a growing appreciation of these considerations. In the 1930s, Woodworth and Sells explored experimentally the use of syllogistic reasoning by those without any special training in logic.[35] Interest in this approach was revived by Mary Henle's excellent essay in 1962,[36] and over the past several years a number of interesting studies have appeared.[37] What is usually investigated is the actual application of syllogistic reasoning to problems presented in a more or less formal, logical way. As Henle has noted, when subjects are not led astray by ambiguities in the questions or the methods, they display nearly faultless logic as they go about framing conclusions on the basis of the premises presented by the experimenter. When errors (invalid conclusions) occur, it is often the result of a tendency on the subject's part to treat the syllogistic *is* not as a symbol for inclusion, but as a symbol for identity. A major premise of the sort "All apples are fruit" simply asserts that each and every element x is included in the class A, where x stands for apple and A for fruit. This, of course, is quite different from an assertion of identity; for example, the Morning Star *is* the Evening Star. However, if the subject treats the syllogistic *is* as an $=$, he will incorrectly conclude that, for example, if all apples are fruit, then all fruits are apples. To what extent the performance of subjects would be perfect in the absence of such otherwise trivial errors is an open question, but it is encouraging to witness progress in this area. Still, this is only a small and, to a certain degree, peripheral aspect of what I have been proposing throughout this chapter. In arguing that cognition is, by its very nature, propositional and that the study of it is, therefore, but the study of "the laws of thought," I have not so much urged research into the human use of formal logic as research into the logic of problem solving. That this latter logic must be compatible with—and even stand as a mirror for—propositional logic is not disputed. However, a person often applies unerringly a formal law or principle which, on direct examination, he does not seem to comprehend fully.

I referred earlier to the child's concept of personal identity as an illustration of conservationistic thought. I suspect that children have a fully developed concept of an enduring *self* long before they are able to solve or weigh arguments in which identity relationships figure centrally. Initially, they may have the concept of contingent identity whereby the person on the telephone, for example, happens to be "Mommy." Thus, if "Mommy" is X and "the person on the telephone" is Y, then $X = Y$ *contingently*. It is surely not necessarily the case that the person on the telephone be "Mommy," but since in this instance it is the case, the child—if he has any conception of identity relationships— will impute precisely the same predicates to "Mommy" as those he is willing to impute to "the person (now) on the telephone."

The leap from contingent identities to necessary identities is a great one. With the former, the child need only recognize that the same item (person, object,) goes under different names; for example, "Morning Star," "Evening Star"; "Billy," "son." Indeed, it is entirely possible that initially even his self-identity is of a contingent sort since children, with their striking imaginations, seem quite ready to adopt the identities of any number of real and fictional characters. A recognition of *necessity*, however, is not achieved merely or even usually through naming and substitution, but through propositional analyses. And formally, of course, such necessity only exists propositionally. There are no necessities in the material world except those invented by our propositions. *What is necessary is necessary on a given hypothesis,* and the child who comprehends necessity must, ipso facto, be the child able to frame hypotheses.

Evidence for this may be most easily gleaned from the games children play and, more specifically, from the rules they set forth as a condition for the game. The batter, for example, is "out" when he has failed to hit "safely" and this is *necessarily* true, unless he (a) has "walked," (b) has been hit by the pitch, or (c) has been interfered with by an opposing player. Note that children playing baseball will argue about whether a given pitch was a ball or a strike; about whether the ball landed in fair or foul territory; whether the runner arrived at the base before or after the ball. All such disputes are disputes about *facts;* that is, about perception. But the child who knows the rules of baseball never argues over whether his side should continue to bat after the third out. Thus, to examine what children at play are prone to dispute and what they are ready to take as law is one means of assessing their conception of *necessity.* Note, too, that the same children who know that the third out *necessarily* retires the side may be utterly unable to define the word "necessarily" or to use it correctly in a problem of formal logic. Discrepancies between what might be called *functional* logic and *formal* logic are likely to be reducible experimentally to the sorts of variables discussed by Henle. Where the formal logic is flawless, the evidence for bona fide cognition is unimpeachable. Where there is evidence for functional logic but not formal logic, the factors of education and experimental "noise" are most likely responsible. Where there is evidence for neither functional nor formal logic, there is no cognition of the problem (symbol, game, event, proposition) at hand. This, it seems to me, is a defensible basis upon which to establish the independence of cognitive research and theory; an independence rich with opportunity.

Prevailing approaches to the study of cognition are hampered by the tendency to combine perception, memory, attention, and conceptualization under the single category of "cognition." The uniqueness of the cognitive point of view is based on the respect for the rule-governed nature of perception, memory, and thought but the inability to establish distinctions among these processes gives cognitive psychology a tentative, even an aimless quality.

The proposal set forth in this chapter is that cognition qua cognition be regarded as an essentially propositional process which is "objectless." Although perception provides much of the data *about which* inferences are made, inference itself requires no existent. And, in the realm of deduction, data of any sort are entirely gratuitous. In defense of this proposal distinctions have been drawn between perception and memory on the one hand, and cognition on the other. The historical and, to some extent, current influence of Gestalt psychology and field theories have been briefly discussed, primarily in support of the claim that we do not have developed theories of cognition; only pretheoretical models of perception and memory. Even these, however, are shown to suffer from conceptual and empirical difficulties.

Intelligence

The habit of isolating "tests and measurements" or "psychometrics" from the mainstream of cognitive research can be attributed to historical factors as well as to methods endemic to the respective disciplines. Binet, Galton, Stern, and other pioneers in the psychometric tradition generally took the principles of human cognition and perception for granted and then proceeded to construct instruments for determining individual differences.[38] Binet was the product of a French tradition in psychology which tended to be suspicious of the Wundtian–Fechnerian psychology of Germany; a psychology aloof to the facts of clinical neurology, aloof to the value of hypnosis as a research tool; aloof to the operation of unconscious mental processes. As early as 1899, Stella Emily Sharp, in her searching review of "mental measurements," was able to detect significant differences between the two traditions.[39] Although American psychology soon moved away from the perception-oriented approach of the Leipzig school and toward Binet's cognitive approach, psychometrics had already taken on an identity of its own. Two world wars created immense opportunities for those psychologists working in the field of mental measurement, as did the steady growth of special schools, public education for the masses, and the emergence of ultraspecialized occupations. Thus, the combination of history and opportunity tended to remove psychometrics from the growing disciplines within what we now take to be cognitive psychology.

The separation between these two fields was never necessary and is certainly no longer defensible. Those engaged in test construction and validation and those who frame theories of human intelligence on the basis of such tests have, quite understandably, relied upon statistical rather than experimental methods. Those, on the other hand, who have adopted the methods of the laboratory in search of underlying cognitive "structures" have, it would seem, found little of merit in the psychometrician's "mere correlations." The plain fact, of course, is that both groups are studying the same organism, are often tapping the same mental operations, and are attempting to solve the same problems. In cognitive psychology, the genesis of given forms of thought ("cognitive structures") is examined by exposing children of different ages to problems requiring specifiable strategies. The mental test which presents a hierarchy of difficulty for children and adults is, after all, performing the same function, or is at least justified in the same terms.

That both specialties are, to a significant extent, pursuing the same goal—a coherent theory of human mentation—and that both have pursued this goal with vigor and imagination cannot be said to have brought us much closer to a genuine *system* able to explain human intelligence. It becomes more obvious with each passing season that the traditional I.Q. test is a means of locating averageness and that the predictions made possible by it are of the most prosaic sort. We have studied the "gifted" for more than a half-century and are now only in a position to say that children who do very well on standard tests often do well in subsequent literary, scientific, or scholarly pursuits. The tests generally yield wholesome correlations with grades earned in primary and secondary school, and even decent correlations with academic performance in higher education. What they do not predict, however, is *eminence* which, it would seem, is what we would all like to know about in advance.* There is enough similarity between the kinds of tasks presented by such tests and those which fill the ordinary academic curriculum that the correlations, though high, are scarcely surprising. That the tests are not "culture-free" is a fact that has for too long provided a wheel on which more than one ideological ax has been ground. Intelligence, itself, is not "culture-free"—but this of course does not make any assertion either way about its *heritability*. Early experience is known to have profound effects upon most variables we ordinarily accept as psychological. The magnitude of these very effects is probably determined to an important degree by genetically related factors.[40]

---

* Eminence is here contrasted with achievement. Terman's high scorers have achieved much, but the relative *merits* of their achievements are another matter.

The strengths of the psychometric approach are precisely the weaknesses of the experimental approach, and vice versa. Psychometrists are eager to establish the validity of their measures. They express this concern in a search for real-life correlates of test performance. Too often, however, the case is settled by scores earned on the tests, and little attention is given to the manner in which the child went about solving the problem. Cognitive psychologists are eager to unearth the child's strategy—his cognitive "schemata"—but too often disregard the relationship between performance in a given experiment and performance in life in general. Then, too, there is such a riot of problems and methods that it is simply impossible to combine findings from more than a few cognitive studies. Considerable progress could be achieved by the development of *batteries* of cognitive tests administered to large numbers of subjects who have also been assessed in the nonexperimental reaches of life. As of now, however, there is hardly a courtship between these two disciplines. Both show the effects of this unnatural isolation.

Summary

The methods and general approach of cognitive psychologists make it difficult to partition their findings and theories into distinct categories of perception, memory, and cognition. This cannot be justified on the grounds that cognition includes or depends upon perception and memory, for even this claim requires that the several processes be discriminable. What does seem to set cognitive research and theory apart from perception and memory is the implicit assumption that cognitive processes are rule-governed. It is argued in this chapter that this assumption can be made more explicit and can be expanded; that cognition, proper, is fundamentally propositional; that its "contents" need not be percepts; that the process it represents is essentially "objectless." On this analysis, such notions as Gestalten and fields are cognitive only to the extent that they can be extricated from the study of perception.

There is no full-fledged theory of cognition, nor is there a general recognition of the natural bonds between cognitive psychology and psychometrics. The cognitive researchers tend to employ problems of an ad hoc nature, thereby making it difficult to integrate findings from different laboratories. The findings themselves are often indistinguishable from traditional (and neotraditional) studies of perception and memory. Attempts to relate these findings to the actual or hypothetical features of human brain function are frequent but strained and unconvincing.

CHAPTER FIVE

PERSONALITY MOTIVATION AND THE PSYCHOANALYTIC PERSPECTIVE

A school or system of psychology can be comprehended to a great extent in terms of the position it takes on the concept of *self*, for this concept is often at the heart of such enduring issues as free will vs. determinism, nature vs. nurture, empiricism vs. rationalism, materialism vs. idealism, behaviorism vs. humanism. A psychology prepared to address the concept of self necessarily must include consciousness, awareness, and purpose in its theories, since self is inextricably tied to these. Even a theory of *unconscious* motivation must take consciousness and, therefore, self for granted, since the concept of unconscious motivation entails consciousness. Moreover, such traditional topics as personality and motivation take place within a larger scientific or cultural context bounded by theories of self, even when such theories are only implicit. The psychology of personality is, after all, a psychology devoted to accounting for the attributes of psychologically distinguishable *persons*. The self on this account becomes the entity, agent, or subject to which these attributes are attached. And, no matter how stripped of self are our theories of animal motivation, the psychology of human motivation—behaviorism aside—tacitly accepts the self as at least the repository of motivating states of affairs or as the source of those goals, aims, and ends which motivation strives to achieve. It is appropriate, then, to begin this chapter with a brief discussion of the concept of self as it has been treated historically.

Explicit theories of self are relatively recent in intellectual history, but the idea appears at least latently in any number of ancient works and practices. Find a body of laws which hold individuals personally responsible for their actions—a body of laws permitting distinctions among accident, negligence, and intent—and you have evidence of the concept of self. (Note, then, that it is entirely consistent for B. F. Skinner to promote the slogan "No praise, no blame"[1] as part of his general defense of behaviorism. To *blame* Smith is to confer self-awareness and intentionality on him, and to make him thereby more of a psychological "organism" than modern behaviorism allows.) The same implication attaches to views of insanity as a form of possession, for if actions are committed by a body possessed, then the normal actions must have been committed by a self *dispossessed*. Magic and ritual-healing are as old as the record of man, and even the oldest evidence points to a belief in possession.[2] Similarly, the oldest written laws, including Hammurabi's famous Code, take for granted that some actions are intended and, accordingly, that the actor is *personally* responsible.

Evidence of this sort is inferential but, I should think, unarguable. By the time man became formally analytical, that is by the time of the founding of philosophy, talk of self was common. In one of the earliest recorded philosophical maxims we are given the injunction to "Know thyself." In the Platonic Dialogues we often confront questions of the sort, "Is Socrates the same when standing and when seated?" Here we have a question aimed at discovering the essential Socrates, the *self* that is Socrates. How the Socratics answered this question is very well known, but a sketch of their analysis will not be out of place here. Socratic epistemology is *idealistic*, in the philosophical sense, in that it accepts as "true" only those enduring and immutable principles (Forms) which transcend both matter and sense. Sense-knowledge can be of particulars only, whereas the Forms are universal. Thus, the latter are not accessible to the senses. As universals, the Forms are also (necessarily) immaterial and, therefore, indestructible. So too, then, must be that aspect of us able to have commerce with and knowledge of the Forms. This is the immortal *soul*, the essential *self*. For centuries, this Socratic conception of self as essence (*ousia*) survived in the adapted form given it by the early Christian philosophers. Each person received his own soul and it was this which would ultimately be judged. Man as a spiritual being—man in the indestructible sense—is the *soul* of man. If one is "possessed" by spirits or demons, it can only be the soul that is so possessed for, in the natural state, it is the soul that governs the affairs of the body. The body is, in the words of St. Augustine, the tool of the soul.*

In the modern period the earliest critiques of this millennial verity were assembled by the British empiricists, particularly Locke and Hume. Neither of them set out to overturn the traditional concept of self, but both were forced to address the issue by the very terms of their epistemologies. Locke rejected the Cartesian theory of innate ideas[3] and substituted a rather modest empiricism to account for the "furniture" of the mind. He presented *experience* as the means by which we come to think and know of *things*, although he granted both an *intuitive* knowledge of God and a *demonstrative* knowledge of the concepts found in logic, mathematics, and moral reasoning. Given his willingness to include in-

---

* Here echoing Aristotle and anticipating Aquinas.

tuitive and demonstrative modes of knowing in his epistemology, Locke could have skirted the issue of self by relegating it to the category of those things which we know by intuition. Instead, he attempted to account for it experientially. For Locke, the self was constructed out of our consciousness of a continuing personal identity and was, therefore, the gift of memory.[4] I know I am the person who wrote the preceding chapters of this book because I *recall* having written them. Had I no memories of any kind, I could not possibly have a knowledge of my self.

Hume's theory is even more radically empiricistic, though the defense is somewhat subtler than Locke's.[5] In a famous passage, Hume asks what it is he discovers when he searches for himself:

For my part, when I enter most intimately into what I call *myself*, I always stumble on some particular perception or other, of heat or cold, light or shade, love or hatred, pain or pleasure. I never can catch *myself* at any time without a perception, and never can observe any thing but the perception. When my perceptions are remov'd for any time, as by sound sleep; so long am I insensible of *myself*, and may truly be said not to exist.[6]

The difficulties invited by such accounts of self were quickly recognized by Hume's less celebrated contemporary, Thomas Reid.[7] With a combination of mockery and analysis, Reid dismissed the sense theory of self, noting that one could no more debate with a man who doubted his own existence than with one who thought he was made of glass. To Reid, the memory theory seemed just as ludicrous but with the added liability of logical incoherence. Imagine, said Reid, a brave officer who recalls being the young boy once punished for stealing fruit from the orchard. Imagine, further, that the brave officer, years hence, is a decorated general reflecting on his military experiences. The general recalls being the brave officer, but does not remember being the boy punished for stealing from the orchard. On Locke's account, the general is the brave officer; the brave officer is the young boy; but the general and the young boy are not the same person. Thus, the transitivity of the relationship is shattered, and with it the very identity that constitutes the concept of self.[8] Reid did not solve the problem of self but placed it in the realm of irreducible concepts. We *begin* with self, we do not look for it. Indeed, who or what can be the subject of the search if not the self, itself? Reid's position, then, was close to the historical one. He took self to have existential status, but to be an immaterial, irreducible substance.

There are important comparisons to make between Hume's and Reid's psychological philosophies, but only recently have scholars displayed renewed interest in Reid. Hume's influence on modern psychology and on science in general has been immense. The general wariness within the psychological and scientific communities to speak of *causes* is illustrative. Following Hume, the modernist is likely to defend the view that, properly speaking, all we mean by a cause is the regular conjunction between two events, with one of these two always coming *after* the other. Causality, then, is essentially a cognitive affair and not one safely imputed to nature, itself. It is not appropriate in the present context to examine the complexities of current philosophical analyses of causation, but I should point out that Hume's skeptical position survives in psychology in two forms; first, the prevailing diffidence in the use of causal language, and second, the prevailing confidence that a purely descriptive psychology is not only defensible but quite consistent with the best scientific thinking.

Reid was at pains not only to demonstrate that the Humean notion of causation was preposterous, but that, even if it were acceptable as an account of natural events, it could not be extended to the realm of human action. Regarding merely material things, noted Reid, it makes no sense to speak of a cause without simultaneously acknowledging its effect. The very concept of a physical cause entails an effect for, where there is no outcome, there could be no cause to identify. Yet, in human affairs, it makes quite proper sense to say that, for example, Smith has the *power* to bring certain things about, even if Smith does not now exercise his power. When Smith does something, we grant that he is the "cause" of it—meaning in Reid's terms that he had the power to do it, and he did it. There is, then, an asymmetry between physical causation and human implementation such that the two cannot be collapsed into one process. We do not say that one billiard ball has it within its "power" to move another, for to say so is to contend also that the billiard ball has it within its "power" *not* to move the one it strikes. This difference between a cause and a power was one basis upon which Reid distinguished between acts of *will* and purely physical transactions.[9]

Besides being inapplicable to human actions, Hume's account of physical causation struck Reid as woefully flawed. Hume had argued that causes were not demonstrably external to the percipient, but constructions of the mind forged out of perceived regularities. Thus, *any* event will be judged to be the cause of another if it always precedes it. Reid's rejection of this thesis was grounded in two facts: first, that many pairs of events which satisfy Hume's criteria are not judged to be causally related; second, that many events which are judged to be causally related do not satisfy Hume's criteria. Probably no two events have been as reliably correlated as day and night, and yet no one, as far as we can tell, has ever thought of day as *causing* night. Then, too, examine the instance of opening a jar. We do not come to think of ourselves as "causing" the lid to come off because, regularly in the past, the lid has come off when we have twisted it. We *know* the first time we have any effect on any-thing that we are the cause of it. This is not to say that we do not improve our skills with practice and thereby become more efficient in the work we do. It is to say only that, from the actor's point of view, the sensed causal connection be-tween his actions and the outcomes of his actions is immedi-ate.[10]

The foregoing remarks on Locke, Hume, and Reid are in-tended to introduce the discussion of modern psychology's approach to personality and motivation, and to establish a useful context for an examination of the psychoanalytic point of view. Reid's substance theory of self and his distinc-tion between causes and powers are honored in modern psy-chology not only by humanistic schools but also, if only tacitly, by all theories of personality and motivation which take for granted a conscious, active, intending, and willful being. The Lockean–Humean theory of self, rooted in ex-periential determinants, and the Humean theory of causality find modern expression in associationistic and behavioristic formulations of personality and motivation. As we shall see, psychoanalytic theories employ the language of the former but the explanatory principles of the latter—often combin-ing what is especially defective in both.

Personality

Psychology's failure to provide a generally accepted and pre-cise definition of personality has not stood as an obstacle to research or speculation. The subject of personality probably claims more pages of text than any other in theoretical psy-chology, not to mention psychiatry. At least since the time of the Hippocratic physicians, the so-called disordered person-ality has been discussed in biological terms. In the second century A.D., Galen defended a *humoural* theory of personality which proved to be authoritative until well into the eighteenth century. In fact, a fair amount of contemporary speculation differs from Galen's · only in the choice of biochemicals. Galen proposed that personality was determined by either (a) a superabundance of blood, leading to a *sanguine* personality, (b) a disproportionate amount of "yellow bile," yielding a *choleric* disposition, (c) relatively more "black bile," conducing to melancholic states, or (d) an excess of "phlegm," giving rise to *phlegmatic* individuals. We may consult an Elizabethan, however, for the most direct statement of what the humoural theory of personality asserts. According to Ben Jonson, a humour is to be understood thus:

> Some one peculiar quality
> Doth so possess a man, that it doth draw
> All his affects, his spirits, and his powers,
> In their confluctions, all to run one way.[11]

Today's theorist is more likely to substitute "trait" for "humour," but the notion has remained essentially the same for the last seventeen centuries—and more counting ancient Greek authorities. It is a notion designed to account for the striking persistence of certain characteristics in the face of varied and varying environments, and under what are often very great pressures to change. When we come to know someone well, to observe him in a variety of circumstances, to witness his approach to personal problems and social demands, we are prepared to say something about his "personality." And, more often than not, what we are willing to say is based upon our estimation that "some one peculiar quality doth so possess" him that his actions are predictable.

Having offered a grudging defense of "faculties" in the previous chapter, I will not tarry to discuss the similarity between the concept of a personality "trait" and a mental "faculty." The nouns we choose would be utterly irrelevant if it were not for the tendency to think, each time we adopt a new word, that we have arrived at a new understanding. What words such as "trait," "faculty," and "capacity" seek to convey is the presence of something independent of learning or even general experience. If a century of research has done nothing else, however, it has produced a healthy skepticism in psychologists toward explanations based upon "traits," "faculties," "instincts," and the like. That the environment has effects is sufficient proof that there is *something* to be affected. After several decades of behavioristically induced neglect, genetics is again gaining the attention of psychologists, but the older and grimly mechanical hereditarianism of the 1920s and 1930s has been abandoned. When we learn now that a given trait is highly *heritable*, we no longer throw up our arms despairing of any hope of doing anything about it. To say that X is highly heritable is to say that genetic factors account for a significant fraction of the total *variance* displayed by the trait in the measured population. We know that the heritability of X is not its *average* value; that the average value can be altered no matter how high the heritability is; that computed heritability is not a number etched in stone. It is a figure arrived at by examining a sample of individuals within a constricted range of environmental variations. As it happens, certain features of personality, as these are revealed by standard tests, do display high heritability.[12] A century ago, this fact would fortify even the scientifically tutored in the conviction that "the apple does not fall far from the tree," or some other ageless maxim supporting rigid, hereditary determinism.

The apple, of course, never falls so far from the tree as to become a peach, and for precisely the same reason—for the same genetic-physiological reason—that a Japanese husband and wife are not likely to produce blond offspring with freckles. In acquiring a richer understanding of the continuous interaction between genotypes and their environments, we have not abandoned the concept of trait, just as modern population-genetics has not required the abandonment of the concept of race. A breeding population isolated for sustained periods and thus engaged in inbreeding will, in time, contain gene frequencies discriminably different from those of the species as a whole. The term strain, like the term race, refers to the frequency with which certain genes occur in a once-isolated breeding pool as compared with the frequency with which the same genes occur in the species as a whole. These are statistical terms, however, and are inapplicable to individual members unless appropriate qualifications are made. We are entitled to call Smith an Eskimo as long as we recognize that the ascription refers to *traits* he has in common with Eskimos: parentage, geographic location and distribution, specific blood groups, shape of the ocular orbits, and others. These phenotypic commonalities are judged as reflections of genotypic commonalities such that it is more correct to locate Smith's genes in the Eskimo pool than in, for example, the Bantu pool. And this is precisely the case when we speak of *personality traits*. They refer to statistical distributions, to populations, and what we are entitled to say about *Smith's* personality is that it falls more fully in one population of traits than another. On some dimensions, a *given* Eskimo may be more similar to the Bantu than to the average of the Eskimo population. On some dimensions, *this* "introvert" may be more similar to "extroverts" than to other "introverts."

In defending the concept of a trait, one does not commit oneself to any particular theory of traits or list of putatively valid traits. The literature yields a range of possibilities, from C. G. Jung's introversion, extroversion, and ambiversion[13] to W. T. Norman's "2,800 personality trait descriptors."[14] Any phenotype can serve as a trait. The significant question therefore has to do with the grounds upon which a trait is to serve as a trait of *personality*. Why, for example, are we inclined to include "affectionate" in a list of personality traits, but not "tall"? Why is "meekness" an apparently apt description of personality, but not "intelligence"? Both intelligence and tallness are, after all, relatively enduring features of the individual; both display high heritability; both have a bearing on one's approach to society, on one's "self-image," and on the regard in which one is held by others.

The traits which theorists are willing to include in their accounts of personality depend upon a larger theoretical commitment to a particular philosophy of mind, to a particular *metaphysics*. In the tradition of Galen, some theorists have assumed a causal relationship between the biological constitution of the individual and one's overall approach to and perception of the world. W. H. Sheldon, for example, has argued that the human physique falls into three more or less distinct categories: the endomorphic, the mesomorphic, and the ectomorphic. Endomorphs have relatively underdeveloped bones and striated muscles, have soft bodies, and are rotund. Mesomorphs are muscular, hard-boned, strong, and less vulnerable to injury. Ectomorphs are thin and somewhat delicate, lightly muscled, and rather frail. The personalities which, according to Sheldon, accompany these somatotypes are indicated in chart 1.[15]

There are nontrivial correlations between somatotype and measures of personality, but it is far from clear that these correlations arise from a biologically causal nexus. A very portly entertainer was fond of explaining his joviality in terms of the fat man's inability to fight or run! Strong and

Chart 1

ENDOMORPHS	MESOMORPHS	ECTOMORPHS
somewhat gluttonous	bold and active	restrained in motion
slaves to comfort	aggressive	tense and inhibited
sociable	competitive	seek solitude
dependent	self-expressive	poor sleepers
tolerant	physically vigorous	introspective
complacent	confident	introverted
Viscerotonic	**Somatotonic**	**Cerebrotonic**

muscular individuals may be aggressive and assertive merely because nothing in their childhood opposed these characteristics; that is, weaker playmates failed to have a civilizing influence.

Sheldon is a representative of an entire school of thought on the question of personality. His correlations are among the more significant, and his proposals, if anything, have been framed more carefully and specifically than is customary in that "type-theory" literature drawing on the biological sciences for support. The problem is not really that not enough is known about the biology or biochemistry of personality, but that no one can say what would have to be known for such theories to be either confirmed or refuted. At base, the problem is a conceptual one. If we accept Sheldon's descriptions of personality—tolerance, affection, assertiveness, competitiveness, inhibition, dependency—we might ask two questions: What sort of biochemical event or physiological process could *cause* these characteristics, and how is the biochemistry tied to those features of the *social* environment known to have profound effects upon the expression of all social behavior? We know from the efforts of N. Tinbergen that the stickleback responds in stereotypical fashion to anything resembling the red abdomen of its mate, and that such a stimulus appeals directly to what are called "innate releasing mechanisms."[16] But it would strain the shoulders of credibility to suggest that, for example, the news that one had failed a test "triggers" a similar "mechanism" such that the endomorph now looks for affection and the mesomorph now smashes his hat.

Biological theories of personality have, for the past century, sought support from Darwinism, but today's attempts are no more convincing than the older and more innocent ones. Darwin discussed the role of facial expression and posture in maintaining stable relationships among members of a species and in maintaining a line of defense against other species. He thought he had found among the lower orders of animal life the primordium of such human characteristics as laughter, intimidation, defiance, flirtation, and surrender.[17] Yet, from the very founding of evolutionary theory, eminent scientists—including Alfred Russell Wallace, the codiscoverer of "Darwinian" theory—had serious reservations about the applicability of such observations to social, moral, and rational man.[18] The emerging discipline of sociobiology is an attempt to complete Darwin's program for psychology, but the old reservations have lost none of their cogency. Moreover, there seems to be a tendency to confuse or ignore features of evolutionism in an attempt to defend an almost mechanical explanation of how certain characteristics appear in a species and across species. These must be discussed if we are to appreciate some of the deeper problems besetting biological theories of personality.

To say that a given trait has *evolved* is not to say that it has become larger, rounder, bluer, or heavier. And to say that a given trait, observed among the members of species *A*, has an analogous form in species *B* is not to say either that the *functions* are the same or that the underlying *mecha-nisms* are the same. On the neo-Darwinian account* traits, like species, are forged out of the interaction between geno-types and environments. The effect of this interaction is to make certain gene combinations more likely (more success-ful) and others more scarce. The mode of genetic transmis-sion is *discrete* such that new combinations do not necessar-ily produce more or less of a characteristic, but (more typically) produce qualitatively different forms of the char-acter in question. The arm of the primate is not simply or even relevantly "bigger" than the fin of the fish, but is a qualitatively different structure. It functions differently in an environment whose pressures are different from those confronted by fish. Primates use their arms for locomotion, as fish use their fins for locomotion, but this serving of a sim-ilar function is not evidence that the appendages themselves function similarly. An ax and a circular saw can both *func-tion* to cut down a tree, but they do not function according to the same principles. Too often, particularly in "sociobio-logical" circles, there is a tendency to confuse *serving a func-tion* with the *principles of function*. Even greater is the ten-dency to assume that a qualitative similarity must exist between any two traits when it can be shown or plausibly inferred that one evolved from the other. This is part of the associationist's fallacy, discussed in chapter 3, which would have the concert pianist's performance include all the errors made during the learning of the piece. That we arrive at a certain level or state by way of stages does not mean that the new level or state *contains* these stages.

---

* Darwin's efforts proceeded in the absence of the facts and principles of modern genetics. Darwin and most of his contemporaries were Lamarck-ians, subscribing to the view that acquired traits were passed on to succeed-ing generations. By *neo*Darwinian theory, I mean Darwinism corrected by modern genetics.

Combined with the associationist's fallacy is the behaviorist's fallacy by which indistinguishable *behaviors* are thought to entail indistinguishable causes (or aims) of the behaviors. Birds "feather their nests," and mothers prepare cribs for their young. Both offer evidence of "maternal" behavior only if we know that (a) both are mothers, (b) both have offspring, and (c) both are *aware* of the needs of the offspring. We would not refer to the wind as "maternal" if it happened to cause a collection of leaves and twigs to accumulate in the vicinity of young robins. Once we eliminate the ingredient of intentionality such attributions as "maternal," "aggressive," and "loving" become meaningless. But it is simply not possible to infer safely from mere behavior that any intention is behind it. Thus, every assertion of evolutionary analogues of intention is a form of question-begging. The monkey that takes an orange from a neighbor cannot be said to be *stealing* unless we have also demonstrated that the monkey has the concept of property rights. The general caveat has been expressed well by a leading sociobiologist, R. A. Hinde:

The behavioural gap between animals and man is in fact enormous. In their level of cognitive functioning, in the degree of foresight and awareness of which they are capable, in their ability to reflect on their own behaviour, all animals are markedly inferior to man. . . . The application of concepts derived from the study of relatively simple animals to the immeasurably more complex human case is rendered even more hazardous if those concepts tend to simplify even the animal case from the start.[19]

The point here is that a biological theory of personality, to the extent that it is based on Darwinian considerations, takes for granted the very evidence one would need to assess the generality of evolutionary theory. The variety of human personality, like the richness of human language, is one of the obstacles Darwinian theory must overcome, and is surely not a required deduction from that theory. We must avoid complacency when we discover that monkeys or cats can be bred for "emotionality," or that they can be rendered docile by a surgical procedure, or that they display "neurosis" in conflict situations. The bearing these findings have on *human* emotionality, docility, and neurosis cannot be *assumed* on evolutionary grounds, for the very theory of evolution is, finally, what is at issue. To summarize:

1. A behavioristic approach to personality is limited by the fact that behavior, qua behavior, permits little by way of valid inference to those underlying motives and feelings generally considered to be aspects of human personality.

2. Biological approaches, to the extent that they are grounded in neo-Darwinian (biogenetic) considerations, are troubled by the lingering inability of evolutionary theory to provide plausible accounts of many distinctly human activities; by the fact that personality, itself, is one test of the theory; and by the fact that even this theory does not require the qualitative uniformities often searched for by psychologists operating out of this tradition.

3. Type-theories, therefore, which are either tacitly or explicitly hereditarian, have no more general theory under which to place the subordinate theory of personality. That there is a genetic foundation of physiological processes is indubitable. Less obvious is the physiological foundation of personality. The conceptual connections would have to come from a general, neurological theory of learning, memory, and emotion, but we have already noted that there is no such theory.

Type-theories, of course, do not have to be wed to the biological sciences or to evolutionary theory. Cattell, for example, has presented a factor-analytic model of personality which summarizes the fewest traits that must be included to account for the manner in which persons are described by their intimate friends. As a result of statistical analyses, Cattell has uncovered what he calls surface traits—35 in number—by which persons reveal their personalities to others. These are *public* characteristics and are labeled as "responsive," "sentimental," "frank," "genial"; or, "aloof," "hostile," "secretive," etc. These public traits, on Cattell's account, are grounded in source traits, of which there are 16, lumped under the headings Dominance and Submission.

  H. J. Eysenck has developed a trait-theory through factor-analytic methods also, and has been able to include many ascriptions under the three broad categories, Neuroticism–Stability, Introversion–Extroversion, and Psychoticism. The circle (figure 6) is adapted from Eysenck (1964).[20] There are, as Eysenck acknowledges, quietly active persons, persons

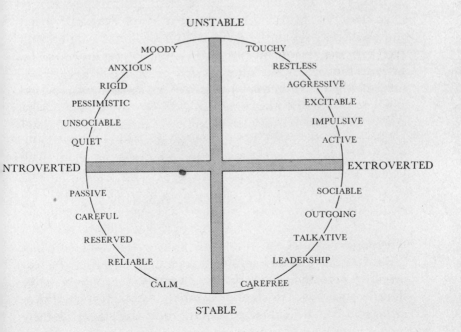

who are rigid and aggressive, persons who are both outgoing and thoughtful. In fact, most persons at various times in their lives will display all the traits presented in the circle. Unlike Jonson's humours, it is rare that a trait of personality will "so possess a man" that "all his affects, his spirits, and his powers (will) . . . run one way." Such a person would be, according to contemporary wisdom, a *neurotic* of the obsessional variety.

Although a strictly behavioristic approach to personality is something of a contradiction, there are *environmentalistic* approaches which emphasize the part played by social learning in the forming of the adult personality. These approaches may be considered under the category "trait-theory" to the extent that they allow the *learned* dispositions to become veritable fixtures in the life of the individual. Let us recognize that the concept of trait refers to relatively fixed features of the individual but it is not necessarily tied to heredity as the only means by which they become fixed. Moreover, as I have noted, genetic "glue" is not indissoluble. Indeed, the metaphor "glue" is a poor one, for heredity establishes what is better thought of as an elastic reaction range within which the organism and the environment must come to terms. History is filled with instances of radical transformations in character; religious conversions, new-found courage on the fields of battle, the turning over of new leaves, metamorphoses caused by great and grave traumas. The "new man" in such circumstances may remain the "new man" all the days of his life, and it is quite proper to describe his new features as traits even though he was not born with them.

Short of trauma and sudden conversion, however, the features of personality which have tended to support trait-theories are those which are extremely resistant to modification once the individual passes through the stages of early childhood. Albert Bandura has shown how effective social models can be in altering the child's attitudes and conduct toward people and things.²¹ But there is no convincing evidence to suggest that the adult personality is so malleable. Even conversions have the character of New Year's resolutions about them; hence the common apology, "The spirit is willing, but the flesh is weak."

If theories of personality are of a woolly and often question-begging nature, theories of the *abnormal* personality cannot hope to be on any firmer ground. Here, too, the shadow of Darwinism is ubiquitous, for we learn time and again that to be "abnormal" is *to fail to adapt to the demands of the environment*. As a catch-phrase, there is much to recommend this, but on close examination it is theoretically impoverished. The two nouns in the phrase are undefined, and the two verbs are little more than expressions of a certain point of view. No discipline has ever used a word without precisely defining it as frequently as psychology has used the word "environment." On the matter of failure, this, like beauty, tends to be in the eyes of the beholder. Many runners "fail" to run a four-minute mile, but most of the human race fails to run a seven-minute mile. The salient feature of saints and heroes is that, to one or another extent, they did not do what the environment seemed to demand. This, of course, is also and lamentably true of madmen, but it does not mean that saints and heroes are mad or that madmen are either saints or heroes.

From the clinician's perspective, one has "failed" when he judges his own life as a failure, even though (or especially if) others would judge him to be successful. Yet, the clinician is also prepared to deal with public failures who recognize their deficiencies and with public failures who do not. There is, however, nothing in the *theories* of personality which would allow us to discriminate among these three categories of failure: the public success who is a personal failure, the public failure who is a personal failure, and the public failure who is a personal success. What the theories assert typically is that "normal" dispositions, feelings, and actions fall within a roughly defined range, and that those falling outside this range are (if only statistically) *abnormal*. The arbitrariness of all this has created problems of a therapeutic, legal, and ethical nature. The source of these problems, of course, is the absence of a bona fide theory of personality able to accommodate hereditary factors, social learning, and the demand-characteristics of psychologically relevant environments.

Motivation

Kurt Lewin (1890–1947) could have been given a central position in either of the previous two chapters, but his work is most appropriately considered in the context of motivation. His own intellectual development occurred during the flowering of Gestalt psychology, but his *field theory* is not a version of Gestalt or a lineal descendent. Even Köhler admitted ignorance of just "how Lewin's important work is related to Gestalt psychology,"[22] and Lewin, it should be recalled, had been Wertheimer's student at Berlin.

Lewin's aim was to bring to psychology the scientific methods and perspective of Galileo; to analyze causal relations and build scientific constructs.[23] He envisaged his program as a departure from (what he called) the Aristotelian legacy. According to Aristotle, motion is to be understood as the inherent property of things. The post-Galilean perspective, however, asserts that "the existence of a physical vector always depends upon the mutual relations of several physical facts, especially upon the relation of the object to its environment."[24] A science of behavior, then, becomes a search for the functional relations between features of the person and features of the environment. The emphasis here is upon psychologically significant features of the environment; the total ensemble of natural events which affect conduct at a given time. This ensemble is what Lewin called the *life space*. A scientific psychology must be able to provide theoretical accounts of the determinants of movement within this life space. Chief among these is *motivation*, which Lewin conceived of as a vector. The psychological *forces* operating on the individual vary in strength, in direction, and in the time of their application; properties shared by physical (mathematical) vectors. There are, of course, conflicting forces operating in the life space. Behavior in such cases reflects the *resultant* of the participating vectors.

Movement through the life space is toward some regions and away from others. The attracting and repelling features of the environment are called *valences* in Lewin's theory and these are either positive (+) or negative (−). What the person seeks to achieve is a goal. The distance between himself and the goal is not merely physical, but also psychological. A horse, for example, will tend to run more and more quickly as proximity to the stable increases—a fact which, in Hull's theory, is an expression of the *anticipatory goal-gradient*. Psychological and physical distances are correlated but are not identical.

The variables of force, vector, and valence are combined in Lewin's theory thus: force is directly proportional to valence and inversely proportional to psychological distance. It was Lewin who popularized the expression $\text{B} = f(P, E)$ in psychological circles. It is primarily in the P term that we find his theory of motivation. He proposed that the primary motivating variable was some condition of *tension* in the person; a tension produced by *needs*. These tensions determine the amount of valence associated with any goal, for what makes it a goal is its ability to relieve the tension; that is, to reduce the need. The concept of tension, however, is not exhausted by mere biological needs for food, shelter, and procreation. There are psychological needs, as well, such as the need to complete undertaken projects or tasks. Situations which make the relaxation of tension in one "tension system" depend upon maintaining or increasing the strength of another "tension system" are the wellspring of all conflicts. It was Lewin who developed the approach-approach, approach-avoidance, avoidance-avoidance model of conflict which still dominates psychological discourse. Conflict arises when forces are sufficiently equal to render goal-directed behaviors incompatible with one another. Often the only solution is that of "leaving the field" which, on Lewin's account, is one of the salient characteristics of mental illness.

Much of this will remind readers of Hull's theory of learning reviewed in the third chapter. Like Lewin, Hull attempted to construct a formal theory, mathematically articulated, and based upon the general character of theories in physics and biology. Lewin's emphasis, however, was on human behavior and is decidedly more "psychological." Hull committed himself to associationistic principles which simply will not explain entire realms of behavior, and to biological notions which time has not treated well. Lewin, on the other hand, provided a more abstract theory. He carefully refrained from taking a stand on specific physiological mechanisms or principles. There is no equivalent in Hullian theory for the Lewinian P in $B = f(P,E)$. For that matter, there is really no Hullian equivalent of E, since the Lewinian E is as much a psychological environment as a physical one.

At the same time, Lewin's theory is heavily burdened by many of the liabilities noted in connection with Hull's. The theory is plausible within a Lewinian "field," but there are few connections established by the theory between this field and the actual life spaces in which we find ourselves. The touches of realism which give Lewin's theory much of its appeal—for example, defining goals and needs in psychological rather than biological fashion—are actually theoretical limitations and deficiencies, unless the theory explains precisely how these goals land needs come about. Behind all the equations and topological notation, Lewin's theory has a somewhat folksy quality. It teaches us that we shun settings in which we have failed; that our aversion is even greater when the task we have failed is an easy one; that we work to eliminate tension; that our perceived distance to a goal is not simply a linear function of the physical distance; that in the face of apparently (or actually) irresolvable conflicts, we often simply walk away; that when one goal is unreachable—or reachable at a prohibitive price—we often move toward one having "substitute valence." This, I submit, is all very true but it does not explain *why* our behaviors and motives are the way they are. The theory wisely shuns amateurish physiology, but replaces it with a set of equations whose terms are so general as to defy either verification or falsification. We may illustrate this with the equation for "substitute value":[25]

$$SV\ (G^2\ \text{for}\ G^1) > 0,\ \text{if}\ t(G^1) = F\left(\frac{1}{\text{cons}(G^2)}\right)$$

where

SV = substitute value
C^1 = initial goal
G^2 = substitute or alternative goal
$t(G^1)$ = the tension relieved by goal 1
$\text{cons}(G^2)$ = "consumption" of G^2.

Now in English: The substitute value of, say, saccharine for sugar, is greater than zero if our need for (tension due to the absence of) sugar is reduced or relieved by the consumption of the saccharine. What this amounts to is the claim that the substitute value of a stimulus is its substitute value. It is, I suggest, an ornamented tautology.

It is in large measure because psychological theories of the Lewinian type can be criticized in this way that behaviorists since the time of Watson have attempted to provide non-mentalistic accounts of motivation. If one paragraph could summarize the entire effort, it may well be this one, taken from E. C. Tolman:

Organisms of given heredities, given kinds and amounts of previous training, and given maturities are immersed in environments and are driven by conditions of physiological disequilibrium. And because of these environments and these disequilibria, they behave. Mental processes are but intervening variables. . . .[26]

There are several interesting and revelatory aspects of this paragraph. Let us note first that it is rare to the point of invisibility for us to find anywhere in the behavioristic literature a study in which the heredities, kinds and amounts of previous training, and levels of maturation have been systematically manipulated and analyzed for their respective contributions to behavior. Thus, Tolman's claim is clearly not an empirical claim, nor for that matter is it a theoretical claim in any rigorous sense. It is, in fact, a directive if it is not simply a hope. Second, the expression, "mental processes are but intervening variables," is nearly droll in the context, since every mentalistic hypothesis advanced since the time of the Socratics has held no more than this. To say that mental processes are intervening variables that mediate environmental events and behavior—while taking heredity, maturity, and past learning into account—is to say that our behavior is efficiently caused by our mental processes! Let us translate Tolman's statement into the less charged language of physiology:

Organisms of given heredities (etc.) are immersed in environments containing fats, proteins, and carbohydrates. Survival depends upon making these substances available to the body. Digestion is but the intervening variable between food in the environment and the physical well-being of the organism.

A neutral witness reading the foregoing would conclude that digestion is the sine qua non of survival, and would surely wonder why the qualifying and deprecating "but" was included in the passage. It gives the sentence the same sort of ring as "Oxygen is *but* the essential requirement for metabolism," or "Regarding the general's strategy, it resulted in nothing *but* victory."

Setting this odd locution aside, let us agree that the depiction of real persons as "organisms . . . driven by conditions of physiological disequilibrium" lacks even the rudiments of *face* validity as an account of human motivation. Even starved monkeys seem to take more pleasure in looking out at a busy environment than in working for banana pellets.[27] And if we are to explain this in terms of a "curiosity drive," we might just as well accept the layman's theories of life. Ever since Woodworth coined the term,[28] "drive" has enjoyed a growing family; one called upon to do all the work once done by "free will." When a monkey eschews the chance to obtain food, and elects to work at a latch that will give a clear view of other monkeys or people, we gain no more by dubbing the effect a "curiosity drive" than we did when we used to say, "The monkey wanted to see the people—monkeys like that sort of thing."

The original expectation was that *homeostasis* would serve as the linchpin for a developed theory of motivation. Taking hunger, thirst, pain avoidance, and sexual stimulation as the *primary* drives, it was hoped that conditioning theory or some version of associationism would permit the construction of lists of *acquired* drives, culminating in the sorts of states that energize and direct complex human activities. If this program had succeeded, the facts of *personal* motivation still would not be fully explained, however, since an account of what makes us *want* something is not, ipso facto, an account of the *wanting*. It is only an account of the *something*. That is, from the actor's point of view motivation is a sense of desire and resolve, coupled with the belief that actions of a given kind will be successful. To show that Smith's "reinforcement history" caused his choice of peach ice cream over vanilla is to say nothing whatever about Smith's *desire*. But the point at issue is the program itself, and all the evidence conduces to the judgment that it has failed. Instinctive behavior flourishes throughout phylogeny and has all the appearances of *motivated* behavior. That it serves the function of survival of the species cannot be relevant to the motivation of the organisms engaged in it, unless we are willing to impute a knowledge of Darwinian theory to them. Either way, the range of behaviors and the variety of environmental conditions calling forth these behaviors are both too great to be explained in terms of drives. Otherwise, we will have to contend with twig-lifting drives, hole-digging drives, dam-building drives, and feather-fanning drives.

When we move from instinct to human social behavior, the drive model of motivation is flagrantly defective. Studies of obedience,[29] of the behavior of bystanders,[30] of simulated prisons,[31] all point to the alarming ease with which behavioral patterns cultivated over the course of a lifetime may be surrendered to the "demand" characteristics of an authoritarian setting. Neither heredity nor "reinforcement history" accounts for such transformations and, although a fair degree of "physiological disequilibrium" is probably created by such experiences, it seems scarcely likely that the data can be explained in homeostatic terms. Zimbardo's "prisoners" were at liberty to leave the experiment simply by declaring that their participation had come to an end. Yet, they remained in their cells, submitted to the often brutal actions of their "guards," and soon adopted the mentality of real prisoners bereft of hope. What is the "motive" for such behavior? What "drive" is reduced by submission to such conditions? What "homeostatic mechanism" is served under these conditions? I do not raise these questions in the belief that they are unanswerable, but to suggest that traditional drive-reduction theories of motivation do not offer plausible answers, at least to the extent that these theories are causally connected to biological mechanisms or the person's prior training.

These and related considerations have led spokesmen for the behavioristic perspective to distinguish between the *empirical* law of effect and what we might call the biological or *hypothetical* law of effect.[32] The distinction seeks to confine talk of the law to descriptions and generalizations about observable behavior. Thus, the empirical law asserts no more than that animals emit certain responses with a higher probability when these responses have been reinforced. No position is taken on the underlying mechanisms of reinforcement, and nothing is conjectured about what makes a stimulus reinforcing. Thus stripped of its biological and Darwinian supports, the law is no more than a restatement of a number of experimental findings. But even in this antiseptic state, the law appears to have rather diminished injunctive powers. Gordon Allport was one of the first in a long line of critics to point out that human conduct often does not conform to the law either in its purely descriptive dress or in its theoretical form.[33] A most interesting discussion of Allport's criticism and its relationship to achievement motivation can be found in Atkinson.[34] Allport observed that human beings do not reliably reflect reinforcement effects in their behavior. A person playing horseshoes, for example, does not faithfully return to the spot on which he enjoyed his last success. In this and similar games, the player sets challenges for himself such that success, if anything, is a signal to behave *differently*. The task regularly calling forth such behavior is one in which the person is, to use Allport's term, "ego-involved." To predict his behavior, one must know something about his level of aspiration, the value of success in this circumstance, his overall attitude toward achievement, and his expectation—that is, the *subjective* likelihood—that he will, in fact, succeed. It is not enough, however, to say that these are "merely" variables which determine what is "reinforcing," for the variables in question are *personality* variables which entail a knowing, striving, and planning person.

Atkinson,[35] McClelland,[36] and their students have attempted to incorporate these principles into a theory of human motivation which strives to preserve what is most useful in traditional *S–R* theories but which also avoids the pitfalls of these same theories. In Atkinson's formulation, the subject (indeed, the animal kingdom at large) is taken to be *active* by nature. No external stimulus is needed as a goad to behavior. To this extent, motivation is taken as a given, but it has, of course, external references. Given that there is a general *motivational* state (M), it is then proposed that what is usually called the reinforcement history will determine the individual's *expectation* (E) of reward. Finally, the goal in question can vary in its *incentive* value (I). The *tendency* (T) to behave persists as long as the goal is not reached, and this tendency is a *general* one (T_G) in that it will attach itself to alternative or substitute goals when the primary one is unavailable. As a first approximation,

$$T = (M \times E \times I) + T_G.$$

Specific states of motivation (M) such as the achievement motive and the affiliation motive are taken to be integral features of the personality. The theory, therefore, explicitly accepts individual differences and is, to this extent, a type-theory of motivation. There are also Lewinian and Hullian elements in the theory, in that multiple tendencies are able to stand in adversary relation, thus creating conflicts which are resolved in favor of the stronger tendencies.

The theory of achievement motivation is illustrative of attempts to reconcile the facts of human nature to the methods and findings of the animal laboratory. It is not an antiexperimental model, less an antiscientific one. Like Lewin, the advocates of this theory judge it to be very much in the tradition of Galileo's science. The aim is to obtain precise measures of what, for now, must remain rather loosely defined concepts: personality, incentive, tendency, need for affiliation, need for achievement. Not until this precision is won will it be possible to assess the theory in critical terms. In one respect, this means that we will not be able to say much about it until there is a generally accepted theory of personality, itself, suggesting that the theory of achievement motivation will have quite some time to evolve.

The Psychoanalytic Perspective

The study of personality and motivation and the psychoanalytic perspective have at least this in common: they are attempts to answer questions about why persons feel and act the way they do, and to answer these questions by subsuming them under a general theory. Of all such attempts, certainly none is more famous than Freud's.

It is customary in beginning an essay on Freudian psychology to repeat Freud's own conviction that man has been assaulted by three great truths, each of them leading to a revolutionary change in man's idea of himself: First, there was the Copernican revolution which, it is averred, displaced the earth from the center of the heavens and thereby belied the ageless premise that God so favored us as to put our home at the very focus of His creation. Then along came Darwin with a theory directly opposed to our belief in special creation; a theory that anchored us firmly to the very same continuum on which the entirety of animal life is found. Finally, psychoanalytic theory established that the most profound sources of our conduct, beliefs, motives, and feelings are *irrational* and largely *unconscious;* and, accordingly, that our prized autonomy is chimerical. Perhaps a few words are in order about two of these three "revolutions" before examining the claims of that which is said to have given rise to the third one.

As Copernicus himself was careful to note, the theory that the earth moves around a stationary sun had been advanced in most of the ages of intellectual energy. In ancient times, Aristarchus had proposed as much. Aristotle weighed the proposal and then cautiously rejected it. (If the earth were in motion, there should be a steady wind blowing in the direction opposite that of the motion.) Several predecessors of Copernicanism, among them members of the clergy, can be found between the twelfth and the fifteenth centuries. Indeed, all western predecessors, not to mention Copernicus himself, were devout Christians. *None* of them saw a direct link between the hypothesized motion of the earth and the principles of religious belief.

Let us also remember that, to this day, the citizens of the world arise in the morning and retire in the evening as avowed Ptolemaicists. The educated ones happen to *know* that the earth moves, but all of them *see* the sun rise and set; none of them *sees* the earth rise and set. From the perspective of the percipient, it really makes no difference.

It makes equivalently no difference to the theologian or his flock. Galileo's difficulties with the Inquisition were largely the result of his literary flair, his hounding of the "Aristotelians," and his general (and, as we now know, sound) insistence that theological science and physical science proceed from different premises, make use of different facts, and evolve through the application of different methods. It is true that in his *Letters on Sunspots* (1613) he caused something of a scandal by his almost casual acceptance of Copernicanism over Scripture. Yet he was allowed to publish an analysis of the Ptolemaic and the Copernican views (1624) as long as he pledged to be "impartial." It might be more correct to say that Galileo's attacks on the authority of Aristotle had more to do with official opposition to his Copernicanism than did his Copernicanism itself. Moreover, with all this set aside, there is simply no evidence whatever for the claim that Copernicanism had "revolutionary" effects on the general, religious sentiments adrift in the world. For the typical believer, we might suspect, the God that made the heavens should have no difficulty giving *this* little ball a push.

Thomas Browne, in his *Religio Medici*, spoke more aptly of the human condition when he concluded his essay thus: "there is no happiness under (or, as Copernicus will have it, *above*) the Sun. . . . All is vanity and vexation of Spirit." Browne, we see, judges the "revolution" as worthy of a parenthetical and wry remark, and as having essentially nothing to do with the larger matter of man's life on earth. And these words came from one of the most astute scientific minds of Elizabethan civilization. Is it likely that average folk thought of the issues more carefully or with a greater sense of urgency?

The Darwinian "revolution" also came (and went, it would appear) with no larger audience. A good deal of romantic fiction has been written around the "persecution" of the Darwinists; the "struggle" of the great biologist; the ironclad resolve of the establishment to oppose evolutionary theory chapter and verse. Those willing to put down such accounts long enough to ascertain the facts will be repaid by reading reviews of *Origin of Species* in the leading journals of Darwin's day.[37] Since the eighteenth century, philosophers and naturalists had generally adopted an evolutionary perspective. Cuvier took evolutionary theory for granted. Even the clergy found ways of adjusting Scripture to the emerging view. Darwin, of course, was already a highly respected figure in British science. Reviewers of his massive tome generally expressed this respect profusely. The psychological and moral implications of the theory were only hinted at in the book of 1859, and were not developed until a decade later in *The Descent of Man.* The fundamental proposition, that man is an animal, was judged by some reviewers as such a commonplace as not even to call for comment. The rather different proposition, that man is *merely* an animal, was found to be unsupported by Darwin's facts, and was opposed by the cofounder of the theory, Alfred Wallace, on factual grounds; for example, the inability of the concept of selection to account for such human endeavors as mathematics, music, and language.

Darwin*ism* is, certainly, something quite different from Darwin's theory of evolution. The ism is an ethics, a metaphysics, an implicit theory of politics. Darwin had nothing directly to do with these grandiose extensions of his natural science and, in the end, even T. H. Huxley worried that the wrong implications were being drawn.[38] Then, too, once the ism began to catch on, competing isms were summoned to defend themselves; hence, the absurd Scopes trial and related expressions of orthodox zeal. Modern citizens, as best as I can tell, do not seem to carry the burden of pedigree imposed by this theory, and do not show signs of having lived through the sort of revolution Freud thought had taken place. To some extent, people are interested in their roots and are pleased to discover a magistrate or fiddler in their ancestry; embarrassed to learn that there were also two arsonists and a chicken thief. But by and large the business of life is too diverting, the press of conscience and aspiration too heavy for most men and women to wait until science has voted on their remote lineage.

Those most likely to have sustained commerce with evolutionary theory are those who have already come to terms with scriptural stories. The person who believes that God made the universe seldom gets caught up in details. The person who does not share this belief will not find unequivocal support in fossil records. It would appear to be the case that the modern citizen is somewhat more materialistic in his desires, situationistic in his ethics, and agnostic in his theology than his cousins of a century ago or two centuries ago. The sources of this transformation predate Darwin by many years. We are, as it were, still coming out of the Middle Ages, still attempting to celebrate the wisdom and prowess of the Plain Man, still testing the merits of the *idea of progress* over and against the fundamentally different and Hellenic *idea of harmony*. Darwin's theory is as much the effect of this evolution of perspective as it is one of the more recent defenses of it. It is hardly the cause. That there has been a profound change in the sensed relationships among man and state, the individual and the institutions of traditional authority, the members of different classes, etc., is beyond dispute. It is not clear, however, that this change speaks to something fundamental in human nature; that it goes any deeper than opportunism and those other petty vices which make us so interesting to historians. But viewed against the turbulent centuries of revolution and reform, *Origin of Species*—whatever its scientific worth—was a ripple in an ocean.

Psychoanalytic theory, which is after all the central topic at hand, has surely affected the modern vocabulary, and has had some effect on the manner in which the educated classes talk about themselves. It has been something of a new way of justifying old vices. During the 1930s and 1940s, particularly in the United States, it was all the rage in urban settings. Terms such as Oedipal complex, repression, sublimation, and the Pleasure Principle were bandied about the way today's conversationalist speaks of consciousness raising, biofeedback, and transcendental meditation. There is always a market for this sort of thing and it deserves as much attention as any other spectacle. Yet, the fact that many may write about consciousness-raising does not mean that something is actually being raised, or even that the writer and his readers have the slightest notion of what is being said. Thousands sit daily in the lotus position as thousands, twenty years ago, attempted to keep hula hoops from falling around the ankles. In both cases, practitioners report favorable results, and only a crank would dispute the claim. Note also that what is at issue is not the truth of psychoanalytic theory, but the insistence that it has caused a "revolution" in man's sense of himself. The theory may be valid, practically useful, confirmed by any number of predictions, supported by any number of facts and still be unknown or doubted by the overwhelming majority of persons presumed to be influenced ("covered") by it. Metabolic physiology is regulated in part by the Krebs cycle, but very few have even heard of the Krebs cycle, and fewer could say anything correct about it. As a cultural phenomenon, psychoanalytic theory can scarcely be said to have had revolutionary consequences, if for no other reason than the ignorance of the vast majority of the members of the culture vis-à-vis the theory itself. What can be said of the theory—true also of Copernicanism and the theory of evolution—is that it has inspired debate and controversy in the circles of reflection. Like Copernicus and Darwin, Freud was anticipated by many in all the ages of thought; anticipated in the theory of dream symbolism, in the theory of dreams as wish fulfillments, in the theory of *active* forgetting, in the theory of repressed hostility, in the theory of unconscious motivation. Also like Copernicus and Darwin, Freud treated these ideas with originality. His account was more thorough, and his recognition of the implications was clearer than that of his precedessors. His theory is a landmark in the history of psychological discourse, and this remains true no matter what the ultimate status of the theory proves to be. We learn from the mistakes of great thinkers, sometimes more than we learn from the truths they unearth.

There is no psychoanalytic *theory;* there are formulations of personality based upon psychoanalytic hypotheses. The *theory* continues to evolve. But it does not evolve in the way that, for example, evolutionary theory did. In the latter case, advances in genetics and molecular biology made it possible to fill gaps unavoidably present in Darwin's original formulations. The accomplishments of science made it possible to replace Lamarckian with Mendelian modes of hereditary transmission. The bridge has yet to be crossed that now separates Darwinian processes from the double helix, but in principle it should be possible to translate the broad ethological laws of evolutionary theory into the emerging laws of sub-microscopic physiology.

One test of the scientific status of a theory, but by no means the crucial test, is the extent to which it is accessible to the enriching and modifying effects of discoveries in science at large. Evolutionary theory passes this test; Freudian theory fails it. Seventy-five years have elapsed since Freud's thought was made public. He published his *Studies in Hysteria* (with Joseph Breuer) in 1895. Five years later *The*

Interpretation of Dreams appeared; the following year, his *Psychopathology of Everyday Life*. *The Introductory Lectures on Psychoanalysis* were printed in 1917. Over this span, there have been extraordinary accomplishments in what would seem to be sister disciplines: neurology and neurophysiology, neurochemistry, the experimental analysis of behavior, psychometrics, sociometrics, archeology. Yet none of the most important developments in any of these fields has displaced, installed, or even significantly altered the psychoanalytic perspective as bequeathed by Freud. The so-called neo-Freudian schools, led by Otto Rank, Karen Horney, Carl G. Jung, and Alfred Adler did not arise out of the ashes of Freudian psychology. In no demonstrable sense can these schools even claim to be improvements over the orthodox Freudian renditions. Rather, they are just *other* attempts, drawing inspiration from Freud's views, and offering alternatives to what the later theorist judged to be a deficiency or gap in the Freudian account. Thus, psychoanalytic theory is evolving in the sense that fiction has been evolving since, say, Fielding; the sense in which modern art has been evolving since the pre-Raphaelites; but not the sense in which mechanics has evolved since Galileo or optics since Kepler.

The point here is not that psychoanalytic theory is not "scientific"—for who seriously claims that it is?—but that it is not *systematic* in the way that a developed system of thought must be if later scholars are to make *more* of it. Freudian theory is neither formal and analytical in the scientific sense nor descriptive and taxonomic in the disciplinary sense. Paraphrasing a statement Flourens made about Gall's phrenology, one might say that the founders of psychoanalytic psychology dreamed up a set of hypotheses and then dreamed up a set of facts to go with the hypotheses.[39] But this makes the hypotheses no less interesting, and it is to them that I turn.

At the heart of psychoanalytic theories is the notion of unconscious motivation. Thanks to the immense contribution of Henri Ellenberger[40] one is now able to refer to a single text for those eager to explore the history of the discovery of the unconscious. Here it is enough to say that clinical findings which had been accumulating for nearly a century, coupled with the striking effects of hypnosis on a wide range of hysterical symptoms, had convinced many that there were some psychological disturbances that could not be explained either in neurological terms or in terms of the patient's will or guile. It was already commonly recognized by clinicians that such disturbances often bore a thematic relation to events in the patient's life; that the symptoms often appeared soon after a psychologically traumatic episode; that the course of recovery was often marked by the appearance of apparently unrelated symptoms. This was as true of neurotic paralyses as it was of such disorders as multiple personality. Clever means had already been developed for discovering simple fraud such that, by the time Freud began his practice, malingering was not a serious problem.

Before the first of Freud's publications, there was also a growing record of interest in and speculation on *sexual* pathologies and the sexual origins of psychopathological conditions. Havelock Ellis and R. von Krafft-Ebing had directed attention to such phenomena. Their works were part of Freud's theoretical development. Additionally, *conservationism* was something of a fixture in late-nineteenth-century science largely as a result of Helmholtz' *On the Conservation of Energy*. But the notion itself was an old one, and its relevance to biological science had been discussed with penetration early in the nineteenth century by Pierre Cabanis.[41] It would be a misattribution to claim that Freud invented the idea that psychological energies are "conserved" by expressing themselves in the physical affairs of life, but it is certainly proper to say that no one before Freud had developed the idea of psychophysical *conversion* to the same degree.

If *conservationism* was at center stage in physics, evolutionary theory was the new light in biology. As I have noted, the intellectual foundations of the theory were old by the beginning of the nineteenth century so, had there never been a Darwin, anyone receiving the scientific education to which Freud was exposed would have been an odd student had he *not* thought of personal and cultural development in evolutionary terms. The leading medical writers from 1800 on were often explicitly evolutionistic in their orientations: Cuvier, Cabanis, Magendie.

These several tendencies all came together in Freud's conceptualization of *psychological* man: an animal whose mental apparatus emerged from the primitive roots of the lower orders; an animal whose mission is to survive as an individual and as a species, and whose survival is inextricably tied to sexual arousal and conquest; a machine of sorts in which the flux and flow of energies seek equilibrium and cannot be eliminated as long as life goes on; a machine, too, in which pressures diverted from one region unfailingly surface elsewhere in the system; but a *developing* machine each of whose "stages" brings new demands and new means with which to meet them. The instinctual past is ever present in this creature now steeped in high culture. The old voices still speak, even if heard only at unconscious levels—levels in which survival itself is rooted. If one law dominates it is that of the "pleasure principle," which gives a hedonistic impulse even to the most selfless of our actions. Man seeks gratification; seeks to avoid pain; seeks to express the ageless urges of his species.

Man, however, is not *merely* this cauldron of primitive energy. He is also a supremely *educable* animal whose species has fashioned those institutions and procedures which are the mark of civilization and which, finally, conduce to the prosperity of the species as a whole, no matter what constraints they impose upon each member. Within each individual therefore a life-long tension is established; a tension between the primitive urges of animal-man (the *id*) and the social obligations of civilized man, the man of *conscience* (the *superego*). The unsteady peace between these opposing forces is the daily, public, and consciously known *self*, the *ego*.

The clearest picture we have of man before the superego is, of course, man in the state of infancy. Prior to the heavy weight of civilization, the id reigns unchecked. The infant's hourly mission is nothing less than the pursuit of happiness which, at this stage of development, is no more than stimulation of a certain sort. In the earliest stage of psychosexual development, maximum pleasure is available through those events associated with sucking and nourishment; this is the *oral* stage. Soon, the pleasures of elimination gain priority in part through natural maturation but also as a result of the fact that, for the first time, the child's actions can control the psychological environment. It is in this *anal* stage that actual transactions occur between the parent-teacher and the trainable child. This stage gradually dissolves as the *phallic* stage waxes. Gratification through genital stimulation and genital self-stimulation becomes a primary source of pleasure, but one on which the species as a whole cannot rely for survival. The business of sexual "education" is one of translating gratification through self-stimulation into the *genital* gratification associated with procreation. Thus, the adult personality is one that finds its sexual pleasures in the procreative act. Alternative forms of gratification are, quite literally, *regressive* and are signs of arrested development.

The psychosexual development of the child is only partly

"natural" in that the forces of maturation are not left to themselves. The adult world, and principally the parents—and more particularly, the mother—stand ready to help development along! In the character of a hedonistic being, the child's search for gratification is indiscriminate by civilized standards. That he comes to identify his own mother as the source of gratification is the simple consequence of past experience at the nipple. But every house has only one master, and the child soon learns that his father rules and reigns. The longing for mother then produces the fear of castration at the hands of the father. The child, through this *Oedipal* saga, must come to channel his desires in nonthreatening directions, which means that he must come to choose another as the source of his gratifications. Here we have but an early instance of the need to *repress* certain feelings and dispositions, and the need to find suitable outlets for these repressed energies; that is, the need for substitute gratifications which is answered by the process of *sublimation*. At every turn, it is the self, the ego, which must be defended, and any number of ego-defense mechanisms prove to be serviceable: *regression* to a less threatening stage; *compensation*, by which a less threatening alternative course is elected; *denial* of the urges themselves. It is when these defenses fail that the symptoms of neurosis appear, but these symptoms too are forms of defense; as it were, the last line of defense. The woman who longs to run off with her lover but who cannot face the fact of abandoning her invalid father arrives at the clinic complaining of growing paralysis of the lower extremities; a paralysis that finally renders her immobile. Here we have the psychological solution to a war between competing needs. The psychological energies are converted into physical maladies, and the maladies settle the problem. But, of course, they don't. The course of treatment must then "reeducate" the patient by having her relive the conflict; to pass through once more that combination of feelings and decisions standing at the core of the disorder; but to pass through it this time with conscious access to the causes of the feelings and discovery of the true explanation for the decisions. These will invariably be found in the "remnants" of childhood traumas and unresolved tensions. To a greater or lesser degree they will be expressions of what are fundamentally sexual problems.

The evidence for Freudian theory was culled from a variety of contexts. The content of dreams was judged by Freud to be the royal road to the unconscious, but the responses of patients in tests of free association also produced what was thought to be confirmatory data. Acts of forgetting, "slips" of the tongue and even humor were included by Freud in his assessment of the psychopathological tendencies of everyday life. We cannot recall where we have left the invitation to a party which we really prefer to avoid. Our colleague proposes something to which we are opposed and we refer to his resolution as a "revolution." In a dream, the patient who (unconsciously) resents the love showered on younger siblings is found opening a pen and permitting the animals to escape, or is attacked by small creatures, or is suddenly shrunk in size. Lest consciousness have to deal directly with facts forced by repression into the recesses of the unconscious, the elements of the dream appear in symbolic form and are guarded by a dream "censor." Were it not for its symbolic disguise, the repressed material would make sleep itself impossible. The true character of the symbols can be unearthed hypnotically, but this information is of value only to the therapist, not to the patient. In Freud's experience, only a conscious reliving of the crucial experiences of life could free the patient from the grip of the past. To serve the function of derepressor, the therapist himself becomes the object of hate or love or conflict through the process of *transference.* He is now the target toward which the libidinal energy can be directed.

Among the disciples and coarchitects of psychoanalytic theory, Adler and Jung were most influential. Their departures from Freudian psychology were numerous but not always fundamental. In both Adlerian and Jungian psychology, the *irrational* determinants of action remain central. Adler laid more stress on the mechanism of *compensation* than did Freud, and was persuaded that neurotic disorders were disproportionately tied to feelings of inadequacy which had their origins in organ inferiority.[42] The adult personality is then dominated by the need to compensate, by the quest for superiority. The guiding principle is the "self-ideal," a goal fashioned by the mind and one to which the person's entire being is surrendered. Adler's departure, then, is in the direction of social influence and in the rejection of sexual forces as the only or even the most powerful ones. Adler's is something of a liberalized Freudianism, but not to the point of adopting a common-sense or rationalistic position on the determinants of personality.

Jung is, of course, the most difficult theorist to summarize, if only because of the many shifts in his thinking over the course of his long life. His theories were even more "Darwinian" than Freud's, emphasizing the hereditary migration of primal "archetypes" and the phylogenetic transmission of unconscious energies down through the ages. Each person, on the Jungian account, is equipped with the "collective unconscious" of humanity—of life at large—such that various ages and cultures will reinvent and relive the lessons, symbols, and yearnings of the species as a whole.[43] His type-theory of introverts and extroverts has already been noted, but let us recall Jung's own qualification: that "Every individual is an exception to the rule."[44] Where Freud located the source of neurosis in the sexual conflicts of childhood now raging in the unconscious record of the patient's own life, Jung argued that the source is in attempts to revive or in obsessions with primal, archetypical symbols in our collective unconscious; in the neurotic desire to find gratification at the ancestral well, instead of coming to terms with the current, individual life we must live. Adler's therapy, sociologically inspired, drew attention to the need for a *life-plan*.[45] Jung's—to the extent that there is a specifiable Jungian therapy—aimed to lead the patient in the direction of his innate inclinations, stopping periodically to teach the patient how his mental archetypes continue to express their message in his fears, hopes, and frustrations. The Freudian tension is one between the pleasure principle and the reality principle; between id and superego; between the unresolved conflicts of psychosexual development and the demands of the world on the adult personality. The Adlerian tension is between the individual's self-image and related needs on the one hand, and the opportunities available to him in the real world on the other; between his "life ideal" and his perceived life; between the search and the life-plan. And the Jungian tension is between the archetypical forces operating in the subconscious of modern man, and modern man's actual distance from these; between the primitive needs and goals established by the very nature of the species, and the gratifications available to its most modern member. The Freudian libido is an essentially sexual force; the Adlerian one, something of a social force; the Jungian one, nothing less than the life-force itself, the *elan vital*.

The skeptic examining these passages would be tempted to ask, "Can any of this even be *wrong?*" while the disciple will say, "How foolish that we never thought of it before!" Feelings run high in these areas, and did from the outset. Both Adler and Jung each became persona non grata among Freud and his constant circle, and both were moved to found their own societies. Most accounts of the Freudian, Adlerian, and Jungian movements credit Freud's for being more systematic than Adler's or Jung's, but I would suggest that the systematic character of Freudian theory is largely literary. At first blush, Freud's claims seem to be tied to specific observations of an objective nature, but on further examination the relevant data are as hypothetical and interpretive as the hypotheses they are said to support. The patient who has difficulty establishing heterosexual relationships may, in fact, also have a great fear of his (her) father. This fear may express itself in dreams in which a "father-figure" menaces the dreamer. So much for the facts. There is, however, nothing in these facts relating the fear to a fear of castration; relating the current problem of adjustment to this lingering fear of father; relating the dream, itself, to the anxiety experienced in the waking state. To establish the first of these it is necessary to accept Freud's classification of dream-symbols according to their sexual significance—but this begs the entire question, since the classification assumes the validity of the theory! Indeed, there is the traditional Freudian distinction between the *manifest* and the *latent* content of dreams, and the Freudian proviso that it is the latter that counts. The latter, as it happens, is what the *interpretation* unearths, but the interpretation is everywhere beholden to the theory itself while simultaneously serving as the means by which the theory is to be tested. What the theory does not offer are the grounds on which its defenders would abandon it; the grounds of falsification. It explains everything and nothing. The innocent critic who cannot recall ever having sexual feelings toward his mother learns that, *of course* he cannot recall such feelings: He has *repressed* them. Yet the criminal records will reveal cases of children actually killing a parent and not repressing that act; and the record of life yields countless instances in which the most horrific of imaginable actions press all too heavily on the thoughts of the perpetrators. The theory speaks of repression, but it does not identify the psychological features of an experience or thought which will reliably result in repression. It does not permit us to predict which of the ego's defenses will be marshalled in specified situations. It does not allow us to distinguish with anything bordering on precision even what constitutes neurosis. In making us all sick to one or another degree, it makes us all healthy—all somehow the same—until matters go so far that one of us is a threat to life and limb and to kid and kin.

It is not uncommon for those who protest against such speculation to be told that only when one has "gone through analysis" is one able to measure the essential truth of the theory behind it. If this were indeed the case, we would have prima facie evidence that we are not dealing with a theory or system at all. And if it were the case, we would at least have the right to expect that a transcription of the proceedings, recorded from a number of sessions, would establish some connection between theory and practice. There is no evidence to suggest that such a connection exists. Freud's literary talents and energies need no defense, nor does his struggle to explain what must be the most complex set of phenomena in the universe. That his effort amounts only to something of an autobiography—a *Confessions*—makes it no less laudable or instructive. What it cannot be said to be, however, as long as the terms theory and system have definite meanings, is a *theory* of man, a *system* of psychology. It is a view of man; one fashioned out of the suffering of a small number of middle-class Austrian women alive at the close of the last century. And as a view of man it is somewhat tied to time and place in the way that Shakespeare's is not. The psychoanalytic canvas, it would seem, was simply not large enough and the painter's brush, if anything, was far too broad. In its largest projection, the psychoanalytic view is a kind of religious view with God and Satan replaced by nameless forces. Perhaps this is why the psychoanalytic perspective wins converts even among those who have never read a line of its bible. But as we shall see in the next chapter, some of the conversions are short-lived.

Summary

The psychology of personality has been dominated by "trait" theories which have recently incorporated elements of social learning theory. By and large, the formulations are descriptive rather than explanatory and are reminiscent of the older "faculty" psychologies of the eighteenth century. The concept of "trait" is not sufficiently refined to serve as a useful theoretical construct, nor is it compatible with what seems to be the flexible and dynamic course followed by personality in the course of life.

Theories of motivation have evolved from the drive-reduction model of Hull and others to include more psychological determinants of motivation; that is, needs for achievement, affiliation, etc. However, the gain in realism and face-validity has been at the expense of precision both in definitions and in measurement.

Psychoanalytic theories, as exemplified in the works of Freud, Adler, and Jung, are neither developed theories nor even systematic accounts of the determinants of behavior and feeling. The psychoanalytic approach to explanation is tautologous when it is explicit, and biographical when it is merely suggestive. The theories set forth by the founders of the movement have a distinctly religious quality in the appeal they make to the reader in the sense that one's willingness to accept the theories depends largely on an act of faith. Seventy-five years of scientific progress have left these theories essentially untouched, indicating that the connection between them and science itself is only apparent.

CHAPTER SIX
THE "THIRD FORCE": PHENOMENOLOGICAL AND HUMANISTIC PSYCHOLOGIES

This may be the sketchiest chapter in the book since it concerns itself with forms of psychological speculation that are both more recent and less articulated than those to which previous chapters have been addressed. Though less defined—and, to some extent, *because* less defined—the phenomenological and humanistic perspectives have been adopted by increasing numbers of psychologists, and by that part of the general public constrained to choose a system of psychology as something of a guide to life.

The expression "third force"[1] has been chosen as a means of conveying a radical departure from what have been the greatest forces in modern psychology: behaviorism and psychoanalytic theory. What the third force opposes in these traditional formulations is, on the one hand, the mechanistic and reductionistic commitments of behaviorism, and, on the other, the irrational and brooding elements of Freudian and neo-Freudian theories. The third force explicitly rejects attempts to comprehend psychological man either in physical terms or in terms of unconscious motivations. In these respects, the third force is more a throwback to eighteenth- and nineteenth-century psychologies than a new "force," but from the perspective of its defenders it is not merely a restatement of classical humanism. Unlike the older humanisms, the third force offers itself as *scientific*. It insists, however, that the mechanistic conception of science is one of the habits of the modern mind it is devoted to correcting. The relationship between the humanistic and the phenomenological elements of the third force is that of outlook and method. By adopting the phenomenological method of comprehending the world, it is argued, we are driven to an essentially humanistic position on human psychology.

The third force has many spokesmen and they are not entirely of one mind on the meaning of even those terms that would appear to be central to the approach. Some of these terms; for example "existential," "phenomenological," "humanistic," are not employed in a manner consistent either with historical or recent philosophical usage. The principal obstacle, then, to a critical analysis of the movement is the combination of disagreements within the movement and the penchant for nuances in the language used to present the ideas of the movement. If there is a common tie joining the majority of third force spokesmen, it is the European intellectual tradition begun in the 1930s and 1940s; a tradition whose own origins are to be found in the writings of Hegel, Marx, and Brentano. In noting this, I do not suggest particularly strong ties among these three. Rather, each represents a movement away from Kant and away from the entire rationalistic superstructure of Enlightenment thought. The break with this tradition would spawn a veritable jungle of new orientations, personal philosophies, ethical systems, and philosophical psychologies, giving rise to a "continental" perspective fashioned by such otherwise divergent thinkers as Edmund Husserl, Martin Heidegger, Søren Kierkegaard, Maurice Merleau-Ponty, Jean-Paul Sartre. The extent to which this new Continental movement is, in fact, an escape from the *spirit* of Enlightenment rationalism is not a proper subject here. Nor will I attempt even a very light sketch of the central ideas of those who have led the more recent developments. Instead, I will briefly review several of the significant issues judged to be left unsettled as the present century began, and then move on to the relationship between the attempts to settle these and the emerging third force psychology.

It is appropriate to begin with Kant, although it is not easy to locate him within any of the competing schools of thought prevailing in his own time. There is one sense in which he is the archetypical rationalist; another in which he is an unblushing idealist; yet a third in which he is the very culmination of traditional empiricism. By one set of lights, his *Critique of Pure Reason* is the definitive refutation of Hume's skeptical epistemology; by another, it is a work that completes Hume's program.

The "dogmatic slumber" from which Kant said he was awakened by Hume is one that overtakes us all in the daily affairs of life, and even in the more analytical pursuits of science and philosophy. While in this slumber, we take for granted that our experiences are experiences of *something;* that the *something,* within tolerable limits, is just what it appears to be; that events in our perceptible environment are *caused;* that the universe is managed by a system of eternal and knowable laws; that the moral maxims which guide civilized life are grounded in the impeccable dictates of reason and are obeyed at least by the thinking parts of our humanity. Hume's *Treatise* convincingly asserts that each of these propositions is, at best, indefensible and, at worst, provably false. The mind, on Hume's account, possesses sensations and is able to reflect on these. Nothing in direct experience proves there are causes in nature. The *belief* in causation is the product of experiences in which events reliably covaried and conformed to the principle of succession; that is, one always followed and one always preceded the other. As for moral reasoning, it either takes the facts of experience as its subject, or it is literally nonsense. But moral reasoning aside, what makes us behave the way we do are our *feelings*, and especially those associated with pain and pleasuure. In human affairs, the passions rule and the intellect follows. All we know of the world and ever will know is what we can experience, and what we can learn by reflecting on these experiences. So-called *ultimate* truths—the putative gifts of deductive analysis—are merely *verbal* truths.

Kant determined that Hume's epistemological skepticism can be reduced to the claim that there are no *synthetic* propositions that are true a priori. He distinguished between *synthetic* and *analytic* propositions thus: A proposition is *analytic* if its denial constitutes a contradiction. The proposition, "All unmarried men are bachelors," is analytic in that its denial is a violation of the very meaning of "unmarried." The signal feature of an analytic proposition is that the predicate *includes* the subject either by being a synonym of it or by being its logical entailment. With *synthetic* propositions, no contradiction results from their denial, and the predicate-term does not include the meaning of the subject-term. The proposition, "All unmarried men are poor," is illustrative. The meaning of poverty does not include being unmarried, and there is nothing contradictory about the claim, "All unmarried men are not poor." According to this classification, Hume's assertion is that no synthetic proposition can be established as true a priori; that is, prior to experience. Only the truth of analytic propositions can be ascertained a priori. The truth of synthetic propositions can be ascertained only a posteriori. On still another construction, we may say that synthetic propositions, when true, are not *necessarily* true, whereas analytic propositions are.

Kant's monumental achievement goes well beyond the reach of this chapter, but a few remarks are in order on the manner in which the *Critique of Pure Reason* deals with this aspect of Hume's philosophy. What Kant must establish, if Hume is to be refuted, is that there is at least one synthetic proposition whose truth is independent of experience. Kant chose Hume's discussion of *causation* as an acid test. On Hume's account, there is no *necessary* causation that can be known. Our idea of causation is fashioned out of experience; specifically, out of the experiences of constant conjunction and succession. What Kant was quick to discern, however, is that the very concept of *succession* requires a percipient whose experiences are ordered *in time*. Indeed, succession is no more *out there* than is causation itself. It is a property endemic to the mind by which the external world is organized. Thus, for *B* to be said to "follow" *A*—that is, for there to be succession—the percipient's temporal packaging of experience must be granted a priori. Put briefly, for Hume's account of the origin of the idea of causation to be correct, the a priori judgment of temporal sequence—a synthetic judgment—must be taken as *true*.[2]

Kant, as is well known, delineated a number of "pure categories of the understanding" which determined the manner in which experience itself was organized; the very means by which experience itself became possible. The limits of knowledge were set by these categories such that reason could operate only within them. The sense in which Kant may be said to have completed the empiricistic tradition is in his insistence that the directly knowable world was the world of *phenomena;* a world once-removed from the real world, the world of *noumena*. Because of our purely sensory modes of relating to the world, we can only know *about* things. We cannot know *things-in-themselves*. The a priori categories of the pure understanding equip us with concepts of a higher order than those available through (mere) experience, but they do not yield *factual* knowledge beyond that given by experience.

A simplistic but suggestive way of summarizing Kant's contribution is to say that it put the mind and the self back into experience in an active and a creative way. Traditional empiricism, with its insistence on the *tabula rasa* and its image of the "sentient statue" had characterized the percipient as a passive target for a barrage of stimuli tied together by the mechanical principle of association and the equally mechanical Humean principal of "causal relation." Kant's *Critique* restored the mind as a principle of organization by which experience itself becomes possible and intelligible. Even for the laws of association to operate, it is necessary to assume an "I," for the past and the present can combine associatively only in the same agent. This "I" is not merely a generalization from experience but the sine qua non of experience. To speak of the empirical facts of perception—facts which occur in space and proceed in time—is to take for granted a temporally and spatially predisposed percipient. The "pure categories" *logically* precede experience and, in this sense, *transcend* experience. Kant's difficult term, the "transcendental aesthetic," refers to these nonsensory, logically required principles of experience which cannot be reduced to experience. Kant's own word for these principles, anticipating Piaget and others, is "schema." One such schema is the *conservation of matter* which reveals itself in the fact that, in our perception of a *thing*, we take for granted the permanence of its material composition through time and space.

No brief comment on Kant's moral philosophy can do it justice, and it may do it considerable injustice. I would only point to a striking symmetry between Kant's epistemological theory of experience and his moral theory of duty. Just as the experience of objects in space and time logically implicates the categories of space and time in the understanding, so a knowledge of right and wrong logically implicates categories of moral judgment. We somehow recognize the moral dimensions of situations through the operation of still another kind of schema (though Kant did not use the term in this connection) which conveys the *maxim* of our actions. The moral worth of an action can, on Kant's construction, never be ascertained through a study of the action itself, but only through an analysis of the *intentions* of the actor as these intentions disclose the moral maxim he is following. Hume's theory of causation failed to explicate the fact that we not only have ordered experiences but we believe them to be true; we believe that it is *we* who are the subjects of these experiences; and we are certain in our belief. So also in the moral realm. It may be (trivially) true that pleasure and pain are the mechanisms by which behavior is controlled, but none of this speaks to the fact that we believe some actions to be *wrong* as such, and others *right* as such. Neither a purely sensual animal nor a purely rational one arrives at both the judgment and the belief. The sensual animal may feel guilt, but will not be able to tie that feeling to a principle. The purely rational creature will be perfectly moral, but will not *feel* compelled to do the right thing. Again, Kant reinserts active, rational, and affective man into the moral world and thereby goes beyond the mechanical principles of hedonism.

How the idealistic elements of Kant's epistemology and moral theory were translated into the Absolute Idealism of Hegel is an interesting chapter in the history of thought but not an appropriate topic here. Both Fichte[3] and Hegel[4] subscribed to the view that man is a phenomenon of *becoming,* and that the individual, as well as the race, must pass through stages of ignorance and barbarism before reaching the first levels of understanding and moral sensibility. Both Fichte and Hegel emphasize struggle. Fichte presents the goal of all life as *freedom in accord with reason*, a goal established by nothing other than the *World Plan*.[5] Hegel, in his *Encyclopedia*, also discusses "the will to freedom"[6] and labors to establish a fundamental identity between the concept of mind and the concept of freedom. The Fichtean and Hegelian struggles are imbedded not merely in affairs of society, but in the evolution of mind itself, where they appear in the endless war between assertion and denial, thesis and antithesis, affirmation and negation. But this, too, *assumes* the will and assumes an active, directed, purposive creature. At the center and the source of the conflict is the self, *das Ich*, bringing order to the universe through perception, reason, passion, and will. For Hegel, the stages of development through which mind must pass are subjective and then objective, before arriving at Absolute Mind. The "subjective" mind makes its first appearance when there is an animal able to adjust its behavior according to the lessons of experience; when the hand becomes a *tool* expressing the purposes of the builder (*Encyclopedia*, sec. 411); when the animal is able it display sense, thought, and feeling in public ways. The "objective" mind manifests itself in the formal institutions and practices by which daily and civilized life becomes actual. "Social morality" is the objective manifestation of individual mind; thus, the manifestation of objective mind. Only Absolute Mind, however, will yield religion, art, philosophy: philosophy being religion stripped of stories and pictures; art being the material expression of Absolute Mind. But only the philosophical mind, by attaining self-knowledge, is able to reach that condition of freedom which is the proper setting and the endless goal of Absolute Mind—of *man as mind*.

It was in Hegel's earliest significant writing, and especially in his *Phenomenology of Spirit* (1807), that he sought to refute the Kantian principle that forever divides the phenomenal and the noumenal worlds. Hegel's argument boils down to the assertion that mind, itself, evolves to the point at which it knows itself as it really is; that is, from a primitive stage in which mind appears to itself as mere phenomenon,* it moves to the developed stage in which it knows itself as noumenon. Hegel's used "phenomenology" in this context to identify the science of *mind as noumenon*. Here, then, phenomenology stands for the subject of a science. With Edmund Husserl (1859–1938), it becomes a veritable *method* of philosophical analysis which attempts to liberate philosophy from the "iffy" status of mere empirical facts. In his *Philosophie als Strenge Wissenschaft* (1910) he rejects both the naturalistic definition of philosophy (which ties it to the findings of natural science) and the historicistic conception of philosophy according to which "truth" is situationally determined. He defended philosophy as an autonomous discipline, dependent on neither mere facts nor mere historical or cultural conditions. His was to be a deductive, a priori science of truth and it is this he dubbed *phenomenology*.[7] Note, therefore, the very different senses of the term, and others have been added since Husserl's time. Note, too, that none of the major figures in contemporary "phenomenological" psychology can be said to be either Hegelian or Husserlian in method or objective, although both Hegelian and Husserlian elements may be found in current treatments. There is a weak Hegelian sense in which the contemporary phenomenological psychologist seeks to know the mind "as in itself it really is"; that is, noumenally; and there is something of Husserl's perspective in the contemporary attempt to transcend the physical sciences. But Husserl

* Kant's Empirical Self.

was unswervingly opposed to "psychologism"—the ism
which would assign validity to philosophical propositions on
the basis of their putative conformity with the principles of
psychology. How far, for example, Maslow's "existential
phenomenology" strays from Husserl will become clear
shortly.   In contemporary usage, "phenomenology" seems to be a
hodge-podge of meanings, attitudes, goals, and methods. The
most frequently cited modern "father" of the movement is
Maurice Merleau-Ponty, whose *Phénoménologie de la perception* (1945) is a quasi-Gestalt, quasi-Husserlian critique of
elementarism, but is in no sense a developed system of psychology. Merleau-Ponty opposes traditional idealism on the
grounds that the mind and the world are distinct entities;
that perception refers to a world distinct from consciousness; that in so referring, perception may be seen as independent of consciousness per se. A central thesis in *Phénoménologie de la perception*—inspired by Husserl's concept of
the *Lebenswelt*—is that experience is the ultimate setting in
which all knowledge, including scientific knowledge, occurs.
The echo of Kant can be heard in the claim that science
proceeds from experience, and that the latter cannot be
negated, reduced, or qualified by the former. In the Hegelian
tradition, Merleau-Ponty takes the *self* as the point of reference for all experience and argues, in *La Structure du com-
portment* (1942) and in *Phénoménologie de la perception* that
all experience is therefore *perspectival*. The implication here
is that the percipient's point of reference is one of the crucial
determinants of the experience itself. The implicative chain
now permits us to conclude that the realm of knowledge is,
in effect, bounded by the *perspective* of the knower.
    As the term "phenomenology" has served a variety of pur-
poses, the term "existential" has animated and continues to

animate a number of psychological quasi-systems, not all of which display agreement even on fundamental grounds. Here, too, the wellsprings are Kant, Fichte, Hegel and their immediate successors. The common ancestry, however, has not yielded much by way of family resemblances. Hegel, in a very basic respect, is an existentialist, and Søren Kierkegaard is also, but the latter, as one of the founders of modern existentialism, specifically rejects and condemns Hegelianism. The dividing line here is that of rationalism, of the very idea of *system*. Kierkegaard speaks for a disillusioned modern world; better, he anticipated the disillusion and, to some extent, heightened it. His attitude toward the ages of philosophical devotion to *system* was a combination of irony and contempt, with both elements illustrated in a passage from *Either/Or* (1843): [8]

What the philosophers say about Reality is often as disappointing as a sign you see in a shop window which reads: Pressing Done Here. If you brought your clothes to be pressed, you would be fooled; for only the sign is for sale.

Now in referring to Kant, Fichte, and Hegel as existentialists of a sort, I do not mean to overturn the received acceptations of the term, but to underscore the role of the logical requirement of *self*—a role prominently employed by these older philosophers—in all later existentialist thought. Kierkegaard dismissed Hegelianism, but his own philosophy is difficult to imagine in the absence of Hegel's analysis of freedom, experience, perception, reason, and mind. That Hegel attempted to embrace all this with a system—and that he failed—cannot be used to exclude his works from the foundations of existentialist philosophy. In an important respect, existentialism has been nothing more than a recognition of the limitations of Hegelianism. In this respect, as a thesis emerging from the negation of the Hegelian synthesis, the very existence of existentialism is, itself, a term in the Hegelian dialectic.

Modern existentialism, as propounded by Heidegger and by Sartre especially, draws inspiration from the phenomenology of Husserl, and the somewhat different but related phenomenology of Franz Brentano. Central to this development is the phenomenological concept of "intentionality," meaning not purpose or design, but that feature of thought and judgment which is independent of objective facts or external events. We are all prepared to believe that which, in fact, is false; to think things are so which, in fact, are not so; to feel anger, joy, or love and to have these feelings toward that which is, in fact, only an item in our own thoughts. The "object" of a false belief, a mistaken thought, a mental target of emotion is, in the Brentano-Husserl argot, an *intentional* object. Brentano expressed it this way:

This intentional inexistence is exclusively characteristic of mental phenomena. No physical phenomenon manifests anything similar. Consequently, we can define mental phenomena by saying that they are such phenomena as include an object intentionally within themselves.[9]

By "intentional inexistence" Brentano is referring to the fact that, for example, my thoughts of unicorns are thoughts of *something* but are not thoughts of externally existent somethings. One's love of country is not a love of anything in the country, but a feeling expressed by the mind to itself about what, in the mind, is a nonphysical, immaterial, *intentional* object.

Intentionality enters existentialism in Sartre as a justification for the claimed absurdity of life. Since the "I" of existentialism is both the author and the reader of the mind's intentional objects, since all knowledge is, then, a kind of

self-knowledge largely set off from the world, is it not preposterous to pretend to understand that world, and even
more absurd to attempt to make it conform to (illusory) first
principles? For Sartre, the essential fact of life, the cornerstone of human identity, is *choice* in those key situations
which can neither be predicted nor explained. The failure of
philosophical systems combines with the uniqueness of
every personal frame of reference to make the human condition no more than an ephemeral parade of mental events
calling forth another parade of reasonable choices for action.[10] Heidegger, too, characterizes the human condition in
existentialist-phenomenological terms. Man's three abiding
aspects are *facticity, existentiality,* and *forfeiture.*[11] By *facticity,* Heidegger means that we are "in the world," given to
certain wants and needs and habits, and that we use and are
used by this world which is, for each individual, uniquely
his. Here, then, is the phenomenological thread: the world
for me is *my* world and its salient objects are, in the last
analysis, intentional objects. This is related to my *existentiality* which refers to the fact that I have direct, immediate,
and noumenal knowledge of myself; I have expectations
which, after all, are only plausible for *me* to have, since only
I know what I plan to do and how I plan to do it. But, finally, there is also *forfeiture,* since the being who uses the
world is soon consumed by it, and soon comes to lose (for-
feit) the very self given by existentiality.

Heidegger's solution to the problem of forfeiture is something of a fixture in existentialist literature. We regain ourselves, we become authentic beings once more, when we at
last come to grips with the universal fact of life, which is
death. We find our authentic selves in the very dread of
death, the *Angst,* which summons our conscience to reestab-
lish the primacy of self in the affairs of each life. We are, as
selves, freed by conscience. Then we have a man who, in

Sartre's words, "is ". . . an irreducible . . . not presented as the postulate of the psychologist. . . ."[12]

An attempt to combine the phenomenological and existential elements drawn from so many sources and philosophical traditions cannot aspire to orderliness, only to coherence. A further difficulty is created by the fact that the primary authors of these traditions were not psychologists in the modern sense. They were not addressing the questions that occupy the contemporary theoretical psychologists, even if he happens to be an "existentialist." Moreover, both phenomenology and existentialism have had more than philosophical significance in the present century, since the leaders of both movements have often come from or have been wed to political ideologies only weakly identifiable with the formal systems of phenomenology and existentialism. Even this is implicit in Hegelianism, for the ethics of Hegel is the ethics of *action*, and the mission of philosophy is, when properly understood, nothing less than the historic progress of the world itself. Because of the double life lived by men such as Sartre and Heidegger, because a fair share of the "program" has been spelled out more in the fictional works of a Camus or a Sartre than in philosophical treatises, and because of the twisted pedigree of the movement, existentialism is as elusive as the mystery religions of late Rome. The present book is decidedly *not* prepared to address political ideologies of the left or the right, in large measure because the philosophical principles and explanatory systems by which psychology or any other discipline is to be understood is utterly indifferent to such considerations. Angular momentum is conserved whether Jefferson, Marx, Hitler, or Caesar wants it to be or not, believes it or not, or knows about it or not. Ideologues, whose works often strive to raise ambiguity and contradiction to the level of metaphysics, will continue to find support in all sorts of respectable traditions, and will

continue to traduce the most carefully weighed arguments
to a set of inspirational homilies and thrilling slogans.
Thoughtful people generally ignore such fluff, which may be
why the demagogue has had a remarkably successful history. In any case, our current concern is with third force psychology, not with the Marxist Vision of Man and similarly
deeply felt but essentially unanalyzable intuitions about the
human condition. The human condition is a complicated
matter, made more complicated by those whose phrases seldom include both *sense* and *reference*. Discussions of the
human condition are supposed to say something about the
circumstances in which modern man finds himself; something about the needs, perceptions, longings, and manipula-
tions of the world's average citizen. But existentially there is
no such thing as "the average citizen," just as there is no existential subject in the phrase, "Man is a machine." In point
of fact, there is also no existential predicate, since the universe contains no "a machine," it contains only machines.
Similarly, the universe houses no "Man," only a number of
men and women and children. Thus, slogans of the sort
"Man is a machine" must be refined if there are to be eval-
uated. They must be converted into referentially sound
statements of the sort, "This person is a machine of this
type." Analogously, "the human condition" must be translated—if the propositions employing the phrase are to be assessed—into statements about the actual settings in which
identifiable persons are now found.

   This brings me to the intellectual parentage of third force
psychology, beginning with Kant and proceeding through
Hegelianism to phenomenology and existentialism. I choose
here not to examine the purely philosophical merits of this
tradition, but to examine its relevance to any possible systematic psychology and, more specifically, to what is now
called third force psychology. Kant's most cogent and perti-

nent claims vis-à-vis psychology have to do with the "pure categories" and, more generally, with the Transcendental Aesthetic. Setting aside the relevance of this part of his theory to epistemology in general, we see in it the foundations of a *cognitive* psychology whose overarching explanatory scheme is nativistic. I do not mean by this that Kant was wed to "innate ideas" or that he even concerned himself with hereditary processes. For Kant, the pure categories are *necessary*, not contingent, and for this reason they cannot possibly be explained in biological or physical terms. For something to be the way it is because of material considerations, it can only be the way it is *contingently*. Connected experience does not "just happen" to include the concept of self, it logically requires self. Thus, the *self* is logically prior to connected experience and is so *necessarily*. A scientific psychology, however, is not obliged to test the propositional status of this claim in order to study if, in fact, the concept of self is an invariable property of judgments of a certain sort; or to study whether those conditions which seem to preclude connected experience are invariably correlated with a diminished sense of personal identity. The same is true with respect to the categories of space and time, of quantity, quality, modality, and relation. The cognitive psychologist's use of the concept of schemata, notwithstanding its deficiencies, is illustrative of the application of Kantian notions and what would seem to be the tacit acceptance of the existentialist element in Kant's system. What cognitive psychology takes for granted in employing such concepts is the percipient *as such* whose mind is expressed principally and most significantly by the manner in which it deals with *intentional* objects.

What is often missing from discussions of the history of phenomenology is that *intentionality*—its cornerstone—is implicit in Kant's epistemology. If we take the world as known only phenomenally, but as actually existing noumenally, than it follows that *all* our representations satisfy the criterion of "intentional inexistence." Quite literally, they cannot even be said to *refer* to something, since the something is utterly unknowable. Kant, of course, would simply have been Hume's parrot had he left matters at this stage. Rather, he grants "pure categories of the understanding" which are the a priori schemata by which the real world is assimilated to our capacity for phenomenal knowledge. Space, time, universality, negation, and certainty are not "in the world," but are principles of thought. They are "objects" of thought. They are, then, *intentional* objects. To various degrees, Köhler, Piaget, Lewin, Kohlberg,—all theorists in psychology who take for granted either built-in maps, fields, principles of organization, rules for moral reasoning, and the like—are in that part of the Kantian tradition which flowered as phenomenology.

To the extent that this is so, we are called upon to ask what it is in the third force that would give it unique status among the contemporary schools of cognitive psychology, and the lingering schools of Gestalt and Lewinian psychology. One answer, referring back to the passage from Sartre, is that these traditional schools are still tied to the notion of *reducing* experience to these principles, whereas the existential phenomenologist insists that such reductions promise to conceal the very matter at hand—the mind.

Those who have read the previous chapters of this text will surely not accuse the author of defending reductionism. But in all intellectual pursuits one's position on an issue is less important that the grounds on which the position is defended. The mere act of recording a reported experience is not, ipso facto, reductionistic, nor is the attempt to unearth other events (variables) which may be reliably correlated with the reported experience. We must not surrender to the easy temptation which establishes synonymy between "experimental" and "reductionistic." Experimentation refers to a method of inquiry; reductionism to a theory of ontology. The reductionist subscribes to the view that the actual constituents of the universe, including the universe of thought and experience, are atomistic, and that complex events and processes can be no more than assemblies of these elementary components. He goes on to assert that in such assemblies there are not "emergent" properties; that is, the whole is not more or less than the sum of its parts, it *is* the sum of its parts. This is an ontological claim in that it attempts to legislate what there is in the universe. The claim is at least as old as Democritus, and has seldom been based upon experimental evidence. In any case, as a metaphysical proposition, it cannot be settled by data. To underscore the point, let me say that arguments against reductionism are neutral with respect to methodology.

Proceeding from the glimmer of phenomenology to a clear statement of one form of it, we arrive at Hegel, and at the point at which stress is laid to man as an evolving being whose knowledge of his own mind shatters the Kantian partition between the noumenal and phenomenal worlds. With Husserl and Merleau-Ponty, we discover the more explicit insistence that a true science of experience is not to be reached by mimicking the experimentalists. And with the abandonment of Husserl, we arrive at the position of radical *experientialism* which installs the subjective states of the percipient as the last word on psychological matters.

This last step most fully identifies the contomporary third force movement. It is the one step for which neither logic, nor science, nor intellectual history has an explanation. Note Abraham Maslow's discussion of the meaning of existential psychology: "Existentialism rests on phenomenology, i.e., it uses personal, subjective experience as the foundation upon which abstract knowledge is built."[13]

But this is surely not the phenomenology of Hegel; less that of Husserl. And, to the extent that the experience is, in fact, "personal" and "subjective," how can it possibly serve as the foundation of *abstract* knowledge which, after all, is universalistic? It can serve this function only to the extent that we grant the same "personal, subjective experience" to the species as a whole, but in this case it is not clear that the "personal" and the "subjective" features are even relevant. It will be profitable to remain with Maslow, for he has been one of the most eminent and influential spokesmen for existential psychology and the third force movement.

We learn from Maslow that his *Toward a Psychology of Being* "is unmistakably a normative social psychology. That is, it accepts the search for values as one of the essential and feasible tasks of a science of society."[14] But behaviorism and psychoanalytic psychology are, too, "normative social psychology" in the sense in which Maslow employs the expression, and so we are encouraged to ask how Maslow's existential perspective differs from these more traditional ones. The answer is not hard to find. In contrast to behaviorism, existential psychology does not confine its motivational constructs to drive-reduction or related notions of drive as deficiency. Some tensions are, in fact, pleasurable.[15] Moreover, the healthiest personality, the "self-actualized" personality, is one allowing the person to be himself, and his behavior to be "unlearned, created and released rather than acquired, expressive rather than coping."[16]

Against psychoanalysis, Maslow emphasizes the part played by *future* time—by the plans and hopes of the person—and the role of personal evolution (*becoming*) in shaping the personality. Here, then, is a shift away from the psychoanalytic emphasis upon innate, persistent, and somewhat mechanical determinants. As Maslow sees it, "Freud supplied to us the sick half of psychology and we must now fill it out with the healthy half."[17]

The "healthy half" turns out to be the "self-actualized" personality identified by nearly a hundred characteristics, some of which turn out to be in contradictory relation to others. Since Maslow lists but does not analyze these descriptions, no injustice is done to his text by presenting a short list for illustrative purposes. Thus, the self-actualized individual is one with (a) a superior perception of reality, (b) increased acceptance of self, of others, and of nature, (c) greater spontaneity, (d) a greater desire for privacy, (e) more frequent "peak experiences," (f) a more "democratic " character structure.[18] His cognitions tend to be of a "non-comparing . . . non-evaluating" sort,[19] and his *self* is an *authentic* one—an echo here of Heidegger. As Maslow searches for synonyms of the authentic self, he discovers such attributes as free, impetuous, frank, unreasoning, unreserved, unsophisticated, and trusting.[20] Maslow notes certain dangers in all this[21] but does not tell us how we are to confine "authenticity" given the dangers implicit in it.

In his quest for a "normative social psychology," Maslow discovers that man is basically good, a refreshing alternative to the Freudian legacy, but is also troubled by the fact of individual differences since, "To the extent that capacities differ, so will values also differ."[22] This is a very odd claim, but it does make some sense when examined in light of Maslow's metaphysical position on ethics. It appears to be his conviction that a system of ethics, if it is to have validity and practical force, must be derived from human nature itself, and must conform to what is, in this sense, "natural" to man. Thus, "Some values are common to all (healthy) mankind. . . ."[23] Yet, even in begging the question by inserting the parenthetical "healthy," Maslow still has trouble with it because, as he recognizes, persons differ in nonpathological ways. His evidence for the *constitutional* foundations of relevant differences is hardly convincing, but this is due less to any serious grounds for disputing such differences than to the sort of evidence cited; for example, the "universal experience of clinicians" and the "cultural diversity" reported by ethnologists.[24] Maslow does not examine, nor does he show any sign of familiarity with, the past several centuries of discourse on normative ethics and the formidable arguments for the claim that morals—though reflected by human conscience—do not derive their sanctions from the habits, inclinations, or cultures of man. What Maslow's "naturalism" suggests is that fundamental moral issues—for example, slavery—can only be settled on the grounds of what is basic to "human nature"; that is, that the ultimate test of the moral worth of an action or practice is the *feelings* it excites in all (healthy) persons. This, of course, was the feature of Kant's "categorical imperative" which convinced some— including J. S. Mill—that Kant's was a moral theory that could serve to justify even reprehensible and repugnant actions.

The question of just what is "natural" to man is, of course, the most vexed in the history of thought, and it cannot be settled even by something as lofty as "the universal experience of clinicians." Furthermore, cultural diversity per se is utterly beside the point since no culture operates in a setting devoid of constraint. Indeed, the very concept of culture entails some measure of homogenization of action, perspective, and values such that the given individual in *any* culture may be living a life entirely unnatural to him. In any case, there is simply no ground in logic or in history for assigning moral worth on the basis of the size of the majority engaging in the behavior in question, or sharing the value in question. Like geometry, moral reasoning proceeds from first principles, and like geometry, once these are accepted, certain deductions follow. The history of moral discourse is a history of disputation regarding the first principles. For a time, most notably in the seventeenth and early eighteenth centuries, it was thought that these principles flowed from the very "nature" of man. The British "sentimentalists"—Butler, Shaftesbury, Hutcheson, Adam Smith, Hume—did much to promote the view that morality has as its source and as its only compelling justification the sentiments of man; the feelings of pleasure or revulsion inspired by certain ideas, perceptions, and actions; the instinctive reaction civilized beings have to morally weighted situations. To some extent, this tradition survives in Kant's moral philosophy, but it is enriched by a strain of rational analysis generally missing in (and opposed by) the older "empathy" and "sympathy" theories. The plain fact is that a comprehension of right and wrong can never be contained in, produced by, justified by, or conditioned through mere feelings of pleasure or pain. Were it otherwise, any species capable of experiencing pain would be capable of moral judgment, and ever moral judgment would be reducible to a matrix of sensations. We could not, on such account, take a *moral* stand on any action or event which falls beyond the perimeter of our own experiences.

It is interesting in this connection to recall that the self-actualized person in Maslow's scheme reflects such tendencies as unreasoningness and impulsiveness. As in much existentialist literature, Maslow's text is something of a celebration of irrationalism, something of a polemic against what is thought to be Aristotelianism. This does not stop Maslow from introducing rather rigid categories of his own[25] two pages after he has identified those who live in the world of Aristotelian classification as "less developed."[26] What he senses to be significant about the self-actualized personality here is a *resistance to acculturation*[27] such that the person's values are governed by principles endemic to his own character. The debt to Nietzsche is too obvious to require discussion, except to say that, like Nietzsche's Superman, Maslow's has removed, ignored, or rejected the very moral foundations on which he might demand those liberties which make his resistance possible and even safe.

To sense in this "liberated" person a strain of good humour, a detachment, a rather ironically powered willingness not to make waves in the inferior cultural contexts in which he finds himself, contrasts sharply with Maslow's own "normative social psychology." Either the species is generally sound in its ethics or it is not. If the former, deviation bears the burden of justification. If the latter, Maslow's humanism bears the burden. The persons interviewed by Maslow are said to take what is good in American culture and reject the rest, and are in this respect not infected by a "national character."[28] But to offer such an assessment, it is necessary to know just what the "national character" is—to make the sort of generalization across persons and discriminations of identifiable groups with which "less developed" Aristotelians have already been charged. Those who engage in the rejection of norms are said by Maslow to do so on the basis of that very sort of judgment and criticality which, we learned earlier, is missing in the "authentic" personality. The staying power of rationality is ensured by the lucky fact that an intelligible negation of its value requires the critic to exercise it. The men and women described in positive terms by Maslow can probably be classified according to their formal education, reading habits, measured intelligence, and social standing. They come across as urbane, reflective, serious (without being somber), and "liberal"; that is, they seem to have incorporated *all* the cultural features of their class. They are then indistinguishable, given Maslow's depiction, from the college students and professional men and women who populate the more affluent suburbs, and who tend to congregate on the East and West coasts. That they are of a generous disposition and that they might be free of the more frequent mental debilitations may be deserving of congratulations, but will scarcely serve to justify their use as moral examplars.

We must also pay some attention—even at the risk of exposing ourselves as "less developed" Aristotelians—to the meanings of *humanism* as this word gains adherents. Little of the Renaissance meaning survives. Those who call themselves humanists today generally are not referring to a course of study, or to that devotion to classical knowledge which served as the center of a broad cultural ideal. What does survive of the Renaissance meaning is something of an interest in human *values*, something of an appreciation of the *individual* person as an entity of immeasurable worth. But not every humanist will defend individualism, and the majority of contemporary humanists—or so it would seem— might be expected to oppose individualism when it is in conflict with the needs of the masses, struggling or otherwise. Contemporary humanism has taken on a communalistic flavor which historical humanism lacked (or opposed), and thus has cut itself loose from that traditional liberalism which served as its only philosophical defense. Without philosophical liberalism as an underpinning, humanism has only consensualism for a justification, but this is antithetical to every careful exposition of "the liberal principle." Maslow is surely not the first to be caught on the horns of this contradiction. He wants to guarantee the precious individuality of each person, the conditions under which this individuality has an opportunity to flower. He *also* wants a sane and civilized world, if only because such a world constitutes these very conditions. But there's the rub, for to achieve sanity and civilization, to create societies in which the needs and aspirations of each citizen receive due attention and support, is to create societies in which *some* individuals must be artificially held back as others are artificially advanced.

These facts transcend such local perturbations as racism or sexism, and rise to the level of the human condition itself. Maslow notices the implicit contradictions between individualism and welfarism, but he does not even pretend to resolve them. He does not foist an ideology, but for this (commendable) reason, he does not answer the very questions raised by his program for the "healthy" life, the self-actualized life. As with other "humanists," he appreciates the need for values, but he is unwilling to impose them—while fearing the form they can take when left to their own devices. Since he cannot advance an irrefutable theory of beauty or truth or virtue, he is unwilling to saddle the developing child with the received wisdom of the ages. He prefers to think that, somehow, unfettered and free to explore, this child will articulate standards of beauty, truth, and virtue. Like monkeys who select a balanced diet when given access to all sorts of foods, the child will select a balanced collection of values and sentiments. That this hope finds little support anywhere in the history of the human race does not seem to dim it in the eyes of the "humanist." Nor does this optimist—for this is surely a more apt noun—fret over the competing tendencies of man toward self-actualization and toward social assimilation; toward society and toward isolation; toward love and toward war; toward pleasure and toward virtue; toward acquisitiveness and toward philanthropy. Human beings are sufficiently flexible and diverse to support any theory we are able to fashion about them. Thus, no system of human psychology will ever be *all wrong!* The existentialists, humanists, and phenomenologists are not all wrong; nor are the behaviorists, materialists, and cognitivists. Each ism addresses a different set of dispositions, characteristics, habits, aims, motives, emotions, and perceptions. It is probably more fruitful to attempt to discern in which contexts each is most useful than to try to determine which of them is *best*. What we demand of each is that it not contradict itself, that it not contradict established facts, and that it not recklessly promote inferences which either beg the question at issue or bear no relevant connection to the data-base on which the inferences are said to rest.

Social Phenomenology and Situationism

The phenomenological perspective has been more influential in social theory than in individual psychology. This is further evidence of the discrepancy between contemporary and traditional formulations of the perspective. The modern marriage of phenomenological *epistemology* and existential *sociology* has given rise to what I will call the New Situationism. Its birth in intellectual circles precedes its appearance in academic psychology, but I would not go so far as to suggest a causal sequence. Rather, both arenas have hosted a mounting suspicion of *system* and have, accordingly, hosted a growing eclecticism. In the willingness to choose the best from many schools of thought—from schools once radically opposed to each other—the eclectic will, without a trace of embarrassment, marry Humean phenomenalism to the deductive phenomenology of Husserl, and will accept as the offspring of this odd couple quasi-systematic *deductions* of situationism; defenses that are, ironically, *empirical*. The irony, of course, is that Hume was at pains to show the value-free status of all empirical evidence, Husserl was equally committed to demonstrating the invalidity of any *psychological* defense of logic or science.

If we begin with the Humean claim that the mind's contents are limited to ideas, and that these are the ideas of sensation and of reflection, then the only *matters of fact* available to us are gleaned from sensory experience. Add to this the Humean claim that morality is finally to be comprehended in terms of those feelings inspired by pleasure and pain. From this *phenomenalistic* epistemology and *hedonistic* ethics, we move to the radically different realm of Kantian philosophy. Yet, despite the deep differences between the two realms, there are superficial similarities; for example, a willingness to accept knowledge as *phenomenal* (rather than noumenal) and a willingness to accept an element of *feeling* in every truly moral transaction. But then Hegel teaches that the mind can know *itself* noumenally—but necessarily *privately*. If we ignore the arguments behind these conclusions and attend to the conclusions alone, we arrive at a peculiar mixture of Absolute Idealism (according to which the ultimate truth of the world is *idea*), Absolute Personalism (according to which the phenomenologically valid is that which is presented to *my* mind), and Moral Contextualism; that is, given that truth is but a face of ideas, and given that what is in *my* mind is the gift of experience, it follows that the moral dimensions of any act are drawn by *my* context.

This chain of reasoning was assembled in social philosophy long before it was dragged into the psychology laboratory, but it has taken on new strengths since experiments have seemed to support it. I say "seemed to," for there is actually only the thinnest connection between what has come from the research findings and what is claimed in the argumentative chain. The studies themselves require little by

way of discussion. Some of them have already been translated into motion pictures; that is, have become engines of
the *Zeitgeist*. What suffices is a brief list of typical "findings"
spawned by this perspective.

1. Many persons—perhaps two-thirds of any random
sample—will inflict what they believe to be excruciating
pain on other persons if they are called upon to do so by
"responsible authority."[29]
2. Persons will regulate their judgments—even along objective continua—to conform with the judgments of majori-
ties. The tendency to conform is increased by the belief that
the majority is composed of experts, and by the belief that
the majority is, in fact, a unanimous one.[30]
3. Persons tend to like those who agree with them, and
will judge intelligence and other characteristics in terms of
the degree of agreement on but a few basic issues.[31]
4. The likelihood of coming to the aid of those thought to
be in distress is greater when the bystander is alone than
when in the company of other and nonresponsive bystanders.[32]
5. Those exposed as passive witnesses of violent behavior
are given to behave violently themselves.[33]

As with all research in the social "sciences," the studies
yielding these generalizations have been challenged on this
jot or that tittle. It is not my purpose here to assess the reliability of the putative facts, only their relevance to the recent
intellectual tradition they are said to confirm; that is, their
relevance to *situationism*.

The first thing to notice about these five conclusions is
that no man or woman of broad experience or a knowledge
of history would doubt any of them. Whether one takes an
absolutistic or relativistic position on what used to be called
"moral science" is not determined by one's knowledge of
such facts, for the simple reason that *everyone* has this

knowledge. Every war offers macabre evidence of the willingness of some to conform to the dictates of immoral authority. In noting the obviousness of the findings, however, I do not suggest that what is amiss here is that research has failed to surprise us. Rather, the point is that moral philosophy is the philosophy of "ought," and that no statement of what "is" is relevant to the philosophy in question.

At this juncture, one may be tempted to ask: Is it not *relevant* that, for example, man cannot fly if we are assessing a moral system which punishes man for not flying? The answer to the question is straightforward: Every moral system is concerned with the boundaries of obligation and responsibility. It is self-contradictory to hold a person *responsible* for failing to do that which was not in his power to do. That is, the very concept of responsibility logically entails capacity. There may be instances in which a factual account of what Smith is able to do is relevant to a determination of his responsibility; for example, physically, Smith is unable to control his index finger and so we accept his claim that he pulled the trigger because he could not stop his finger from twitching. Yet, even if on factual grounds we exempt Smith from responsibility, we still do not conclude that it was, therefore, *right* that Jones was shot. Stated briefly, the argument according to which the findings from social psychology are irrelevant to moral philosophy takes this form: the causes of events cannot, in and of themselves, serve as moral justifications of the events, but only as grounds for forgiveness. To show, then, that something about a "situation" makes conduct of a particular kind more likely is to establish *nothing* in regard to the moral status of the consequences of the action.

It may be argued that, even if the moral status of outcomes is independent of the cause of the action itself, the moral status of the *actor* is relevantly connected to the cause of the action. But, again, it must be understood that moral assessments begin only after it is granted that Smith did what was in his power to do, or that Smith failed to do what was in his power to do. Purely physical constraints aside, what is in Smith's *power* to do is determined by a constellation of factors including, but not limited to, Smith's knowledge, his education, his motivation, his perception of the situation, and his recognition of alternative courses of action. All this, however, is not a defense of "situationism" but a description of some of the grounds on which Smith might plead for mercy. That is, these considerations are independent of the position one takes on what is right and what is wrong; they refer, instead, to questions of culpability. And, indeed, we are permitted to hold Smith responsible for doing wrong when Smith has put himself in the position of, for example, foreclosing options, failing to ascertain the proper course of action, etc. Recall that damages produced in Ancient Greece by one who was drunk carried a double penalty: one for the damage done, and one for putting oneself in a state making such damage more likely.

The laboratory has not been the only mischosen setting for the assessment or moral principles. Additionally, the social "sciences" have taken recourse to opinion polls in order to determine the average perspective on all sorts of morally weighted matters. Here again we have the assault by "social phenomenology" on the independent duchy of moral philosophy. There must be some purpose to be served by such polls. If it is to allow public officials to learn how the citizenry "feels" about the matters in question, then the social scientist must, if only implicitly, consider problems of value solvable by recourse to opinion. If instead or in addition, it is a desire to learn the moral character of a sample or population, then the questions incorporated into the polls are useless. Whether one supports or opposes busing, abortion, war, death penalties, foreign aid, and the like is merely a matter of *fact* from which nothing of moral consequence can be inferred or deduced. What counts morally is the *reason* behind the support or the opposition. Some may oppose homicide because it creates sanitation problems; others because it frightens the children; still others because it is usually noisy. Such reasons are evidence of moral bankruptcy, but all the poll shows is that people are opposed to homicide.

It is not uncommon for those engaged in such research and sampling to assume the posture of cool detachment, insisting that their efforts are value-neutral and are devoted to nothing more than unearthing the facts. Some go further and insist that the social scientist is *obliged* to use his skills to learn more about human behavior ". . . for the ultimate aim of human betterment," as Aronson has written.[34] Yet, the very studies and polls that are intended to reveal what is the case actually become justifications for the outcomes to continue to be the case. We have the equivalent of the self-fulfilling prophecy; that is, *the self-perpetuating finding.* Since the consumer of the finding should not be expected to know the great distance between such mere facts and the very different realm of human values, one is almost tempted to require something akin to the Surgeon General's warning: *These facts may be dangerous to your judgment.*

Repeatedly in this section I have placed the science part of social "science" within quotation-marks; a habit adopted not out of enmity but caution. The formal properties of explanation in social psychology are so different from those encountered in scientific explanations that it would be unwise to take social psychology's scientific status for granted. It is, to be sure, an *experimental* discipline, but this does not by itself confer scientific status. Alchemy, too, was experimental, as was phrenology. Social psychology has a strong element of *rational* explanation in it, as I have noted elsewhere,[35] and it is this which gives its findings a certain immediacy and reality. I do not mean by this that the social psychologist accepts the subject's reasons as explanations for that subject's actions, but that the social psychologist *assumes* a cognizing, needful, perceptive, and organizing entity as the only one able to engage in anything properly identified as *social*. This bodes well for the explanatory potential of the discipline, but less well for its much desired scientific status. Its recent courtship with philosophy, and especially moral philosophy, is likely to be more passionate than enduring. In this it will join the ranks of other rejected suitors: existential psychology, humanistic psychology, psychoanalytic theory.

Summary

The phenomenological perspective in contemporary psychology bears only faint resemblance to the early formulations grounded in Kantian and Hegelian philosophies and developed by Brentano and Husserl. Similarly, "existential" and "humanistic" psychologies lack both historical pedigrees and discernible philosophical ties. Yet, humanistic, phenomenological, and existential psychologies are a "third force," offering something of an alternative to behavioristic reductionism and psycho-analytic irrationalism. The emphasis is on the striving, directed, and evolving person; the person acutely and healthily aware of the gap between his current standing and his reasonable expectations. The emphasis is also on the experiences of this person—including *current* experiences—and on the relationship between these and his personal values. The third force gives uncommon epistemological authority to the individual's private "screen," and great moral weight to the individual's own moral sentiments and inclinations. It takes for granted that within every individual there is another—and another—waiting to come through, and it attempts to identify the sources of inhibition and expression so that "self-actualization" becomes more frequent, intense, and durable.

What the third force faces is the twin-obstacle of poetic imagery and ontological contradictions. The first arises each time the third force rejects the reductionistic-mechanistic language of modern science and strives to depict psychological man in different terms. The depictions—often summoning in their literary force and beauty—are generally destitute of precision, and are often destitute of accepted meanings. The second obstacle surfaces each time the third force celebrates human individuality while attempting to improve the psychological condition of *social* man. The individual, rife with nuances, needs, eccentricities, and privatistic considerations, must and longs to live in a world with others, each of whom is also *sui generis*. Collisions are inevitable, and the third force has not instructed us in how these are to be managed and settled. To a great extent, this third force has been one of opposition rather than one of progression. Its chief contribution is perhaps in laying bare the immense gulf separating "scientific" psychologies from the human *person* they presume to comprehend. The third force points to but does not fill the void.

By a more winding path, contemporary social psychology arrives as an expression of phenomenological thought. Its explanatory conventions are too far removed from traditional scientific explanations for it to qualify even as a *social* science. Its most reliable and famous findings have to do with what, traditionally, would be construed as moral behavior and civics, yet the findings, properly understood, are largely irrelevant to historic moral concerns. There is a cogent and engaging *rational* aspect to social psychological explanation, but this very feature may threaten the ultimate status of the discipline within the scientific community.

CHAPTER SEVEN
CONCEPTUAL INTEGRATIONS: AN EPILOGUE

What is perhaps more striking than the absence of a coherent and general system of psychology is the fact that this absence endures even though the various schools of psychology have come to share many of the same subjects and even some of the same methods. It has not been the case for many years that the "humanistic" psychologist or the clinical psychologist took an official stand against, for example, behavioristic or physiological psychology. We are now in a period of transition. We have passed the period of territoriality, and we can all say, "Good riddance!" There are, to be sure, lingering defenders of psychology's fruitless cold war; those who will not accept the existence of a state of arousal or consciousness or feeling or motivation unless the dial of meter is moved by it; those who consider the electrode tip as the Philosopher's stone; those who consider any measurement of any feature of human life to be treasonous to the very idea of Man. At the root of these positions is ideology, and psychology—either in its scientific aspirations or in its clinical duties—need not acknowledge it.

The balance that must be struck is one between *systematic psychology as ideology* and *nonideological psychology as antisystematic*. This requires the psychologist to discern the difference—often a subtle one—between a psychological system defended in terms of public evidence (though not necessarily *experimental* evidence), and a merely political argument which happens to include some data. It also requires distinctions to be made between mere laboratory busywork which bears some loose connection to what scientists do, and research efforts designed to assess specific theoretical propositions. The acid test in the first case is given by the question: What specific predictions are implicit in this "system," and under what specifiable conditions should confirmation be possible? The acid test in the second instance is given by the question: To what general proposition are these data relevant and, if the proposition is confirmed by the data, what additional propositions become plausible? In both cases, a *general theory* is the means by which fruitful enterprises are set off from fog and ritual.

As we examine the perspectives, methods, and findings presented in previous chapters, a number of working hypotheses and, in Hempel's felicitous term, *explanation sketches* emerge. The great difficulty, of course, is finding the connecting links with which to join perception, learning, cognition, motivation, consciousness, etc. Explanation sketches *within* each of these areas are already abundant, but they do not amount to systematic formulations because they remain confined to a specific function (that is, a *noun*). Moreover, the same examination of preceding chapters leads to the conclusion, if only a tentative one, that several of the more enduring assumptions of modern psychology may have to be abandoned or significantly modified. The first step in a conceptual integration is surgical; one must cut away distracting, unnecessary, or invalid assumptions before attempting to unite the few that are essential, plausible, and significant. A few comments on each of these are in order.

Distracting Assumptions

Psychology in the twentieth century, and particularly in the past thirty or so years, has belabored several assumptions which, although true—or at least not provably false—have led to digressions and evasions. Certainly the most overarching of these is the assumption of *mechanism*. For theoretical purposes, it can be done away with entirely, either by being ignored or by being taken for granted. I do not legislate here a "solution" to the Mind/Body problem, nor do I legislate against a bona fide physiological *psychology*. Instead, I simply note that the methods and findings of neurophysiology become psychologically significant only *after* psychology itself has reached a systematic level of theory and explanation. To reach this level, psychology may, on purely metaphysical grounds, operate on the premise that, for each significant psychological event or process, there is some underlying mechanism. Yet, as Lewin and Skinner both argued decades ago, the mechanism—if discovered—would add nothing to the description of the process or event, and would "explain" it in terms not directly, easily, or even possibly translatable into psychologically useful terms.

Note, however, that the call to abandon mechanism is not a general injunction against the concepts and principles of the biological sciences. Biology, itself, is more than a study of mechanisms. It is a study of *functions* and the *laws* by which functions are controlled. A developed physiological psychology is one in which the equivalence of laws is established, but this equivalence may not apply to the mechanisms themselves. Both a latch and a magnet can serve as locks. Here we have functional equivalence. The law by which both lock a door is, itself, a *mechanical* law quite different from the principles of magnetism. Thus, there is no assurance, even when a mechanism is understood, that functional laws will be forthcoming.

For physiological psychology to search for equivalence among psychological processes and biological laws, it must include psychological processes among the terms of equivalence. The firing of single units is a datum describing a mechanism, not a process describing a function. The call here is, of course, for ecological validity measures; a call that includes a significant slice of adaptive behavior to be included in every sampling of neural function.

In mentioning adaptive behavior, I introduce the second distracting assumption which is that of *Darwinism*. Perhaps the best way to defend a classification of evolutionary theory as a distraction is to pair it off with Ohm's law. It is trivially true that, to the extent that species possess electrical networks, Ohm's law is preserved in evolution. Yet, it would be entirely beside the point to take the fact of Ohm's law as essential to an understanding of evolution, or to the unearthing of the principles of evolution. When we pair off psychology and the theory of evolution, there is not only a similar inaptness but an actual danger which is not contained in the Ohm's law–Evolution dyad. A psychology wed to evolutionary theory is one that fails to recognize itself as one of the major *tests* of this very theory. Let us recognize that the fact that behavior is, somehow, *adaptive* does not mean that it is adaptive for Darwinian reasons. To assume otherwise is to treat all non-Darwinian behavior as maladaptive, and all the individual differences as mere epiphenomena to be ignored or, somehow, reconciled with the behavioral trends of the species as a whole.

Modern genetics is a more instructive guide for psychology than is traditional Darwinism. It is through modern genetics that we learn of the norm of reaction or "reaction range" of the individual genotype, and come to recognize that only broad statistical descriptions stand behind the "uniformity" hypothesis. There is no biological reason for expecting narrow uniformities in the behavior of members of the same species even when the environment has been homogenized. Indeed, where such uniformities are regularly observed, the measurements in question are likely to be measurements of what is least significant about the organism and, therefore, about the behavior of the organism. We must recognize—as Darwin did—that survival of the species hinges on diversity, and that the very origin of a species is based upon variations in the parent stock. It is only when the distracting hypothesis of mechanism is insensibly combined with that of Darwinism that we become surprised and rather irritated by individual differences. The principal argument against the inclusion of genotype as an independent variable in psychological research—and particularly in physiological psychology—is that the species of greatest interest cannot be genotypically specified or controlled with accuracy. The question-begging term in this argument is, of course, "of greatest interest." The extent to which monkeys are "more like man" than, say, pigeons are will depend entirely on the basis of comparison. That there is a closer evolutionary tie between man and ape is a fact whose psychological implications are at issue, not a fact by which these implications are established. Find something that *only* species X can do, and you have an open-ended phenotype which can be located on the phylogenetic continuum only by taking Darwinian theory for granted. The word "like" is a theoretical term, not just a descriptive one. Often, in fact, it is not even descriptive; as, for example, in such statements as bird song is "like" speech; nesting behavior is "like" human mothering.

The distraction produced by Darwinism is further illustrated, even perversely illustrated, by the virtual disappearance of comparative psychology. The only journal of psychology containing the term has become more the "Journal of the Hypothalamus" than a periodical addressing the problems and facts of comparative psychology. Thus, the discipline has all but forfeited these problems and facts to the ethologists, while still holding on to what is least useful to psychology—the Darwinian sense of adaptation. For this reason, the psychology of aesthetics, of religious experience, of the paranormal, remains the property of fringe groups generally not taken seriously by "real" psychologists. Note that what divorces these subjects from the mainstream is not that the phenomena are elusive, but that they are not "adaptive." My point here is that such ascriptions as "adaptive," "naturally selected," and "species-specific" be applied *after the fact*, and not be used as the criteria by which only these and not those facts will be admitted for study.

Unnecessary Assumptions

Among the unnecessary assumptions plaguing contemporary psychology is what I will call *incrementalism*. Apparently the history of science has not been sufficient to convince today's psychologist that the greatest advances in science have come from perspectival shifts, and not from the (Baconian) accumulation of data. The heaviest burden imposed by incrementalism is a false sense of progress; a tendency to perceive it in any setting in which the data become more numerous. It is a rudimentary principle of theory construction that some facts must be *stipulated*, since one cannot measure everything. Psychology's recent aloofness toward theory has thus resulted in a profession whose experimenters seem hellbent on measuring everything. Were there time, this enterprise could even be encouraged. The problem, of course, is that to measure *all things* will probably require *all time*.

For illustrative purposes, let us choose a sensible question that would, under current conditions, lead to at least one Ph.D. dissertation:

Reaction time is unaffected by those "metacontrast" conditions which render the stimulus "unperceived." That is, the subject responds just as quickly to the first of two flashes when the second "masks" the first as he does to the first when it is presented alone. Is this also true of *cutaneous* backward masking?

In raising this question, I would not discourage someone from actually doing the study; for all I know, it has already been reported. Rather, I raise the question in order to raise another one. What implications follow if, in fact, the cutaneous masking yields data similar to those obtained in visual studies? What implications follow if the two sets of data are in conflict? If one is not able to express the implications a priori, the research is no more than string-gathering. But suppose (as we would hope) that the question really pertains to central vs. peripheral processing, and that the research is designed to determine if cutaneous processing follows the same principles as visual processing. The only feature of this question which is troublesome is the established fact that visual and cutaneous sensitivity are known to be similar in some respects and different in others. Without a *theory* of inter- and intramodality perception, the data simply have no place to go but into that large handbook of facts which is somehow thick but thin.

Related to *incrementalism* (as a glove to a hand) is *mensurationalism*, according to which the validity of an observation is directly proportional to the accuracy of the measurement. It is not merely historically interesting that the three revolutions mentioned by Freud—the Copernican, the Darwinian, and Freud's own—included almost no *numbers* in their ranks. It is more than historically interesting that the more impressive revolution led by Einstein did not succeed primarily on the grounds of measurement, but on the very different grounds of conceptualization. My claim is not that measurement is unimportant, but that it is not all-important; it will not compensate for woolly reasoning; it will not spell "truth" no matter how accurate it is; it will not *yield* a theory, even though sooner or later it will figure in assessments of the theory. The importance of measurement in science is greatest where competing theories are at issue. Measurement, then, is an instrument of discrimination, not the tool of invention. It is seldom, however, that measurement appears in psychology except in statistical tests of "significance" or correlational tests of "agreement." Psychologists spend much time talking about "hypothesis testing" in connection with statistics; less time framing bona fide hypotheses worthy of the method.

Measurement has more than a single role in science. Psychology has chosen what is by far the minor one. To take measurements for the purpose of making subsequent statistical decisions is different from taking measurements for the purpose of articulating a law. In the first case, we learn something about the generality of our observations; in the second, we learn something about nature. There is a difference too between establishing that X and Y can be measured on the same scale, and establishing that what is being measured is the same thing. This leads me to a brief section on invalid assumptions.

Invalid Assumptions

When we combine *incrementalism* and *mensurationalism* we produce what passes for an epistemological defense of one or another form of descriptive psychology with one or another form of behaviorism as the exemplar. From here it is a short step to the assumption that equivalent stimulus-response correlations can be yielded only by equivalent processes or laws. The fallacy here is that of treating the logical $=$ as synonymous with or identical to the arithmetic $=$. To show, for example, that $(S\text{-}R)_M = (S\text{-}R)_C$, where the subscripts refer repectively to *monkey* and *child*, is to show the arithmetic equality of two numbers, not the logical identity of two entities. Dogs, pigeons, and commuters all find the way back home, but surely not in the same way. For the pigeon, polarization cues seem to be essential. The dog uses a keen olfactory sense and a reasonably good Tolmanian "map." The commuter uses an automobile. If one were to show (experimentally, of course) that "minutes to get home" diminished by the same amount for pigeon, dog, and commuter as a function of "trials," we would be permitted to write the following expression:

$$M_P = f(T)$$
$$M_D = f(T)$$
$$M_C = f(T)$$
$$\text{and,} \quad M_P = M_D = M_C,$$

where M stands for "minutes to get home," where the subscripts stand for pigeon, dog, and commuter, and where (T) stands for "trials." Note, however, that these expressions are theoretically neutral, *as are all equivalent expressions*. Experimental findings, supported by accurate measurements, cannot *produce* a theory no matter how numerous the findings or accurate the measurements. Just as it is silly to conclude that, for example, there are no motives unless we have measured them, it is fallacious to assume that the motives we have measured are the same if they happen to yield the same measures. To be brief, I will stop by saying that this is true of all states and processes which have not been or cannot be *directly* measured.

Another invalid assumption—and one that is embarrassing to mention to an audience of psychologists—is the implicit assumption by which *reliability* and *validity* come to be judged as conceptually related. Every teacher of General Psychology conscientiously distinguishes between the question of whether an event occurred and how reliably a recurring event recurs. But beyond the custodial ambiance of the classroom, the same psychologist often cannot resist the temptation to conclude that rare events are invalid, and that their invalidity is the consequence of their infrequency. It is useless and somewhat patronizing to invoke the illustrations of the lecture hall here: "How do we know that Smith will die again, since he has only died *once?*" The problem is not that the competent psychologist is ignorant of the distinction, but that a blurring of the distinction is part of the contemporary *Zeitgeist;* that is, it is a self-imposed delusion, formed out of a mixture of Darwinism, the "uniformity" hypothesis, incrementalism, mensurationalism. It is at the root of "experimenter-bias effects," the tossing out of stubborn subjects, the unwillingness to be guided by literary or artistic insights, the general disregard of the lessons of history as a guide to the understanding of human psychology—and much more.

When these distractions, errors, and nonessentials are peeled away, we are left with a core of assumptions likely to be required by any systematic psychology. This core contains elements that are the opposites of those just discussed, as well as new elements not conceptually tied to them. I should say in advance that I set these forth not legislatively but as challenges. I do not offer them as a veiled general theory, but only as *terms* in a general theory. Furthermore, there seems to be no way of *not* begging certain philosophical questions. Yet there is no justification for requiring psychology to defer its proper business until the philosophers have concluded theirs.

Perception and the Assumption of Realism

A theory of perception, and of the relationship between perception and the balance of human psychological functions, is not required to settle or even address Kantian tensions between "phenomenal" and "noumenal" existence. On a purely naturalistic foundation, psychology is compelled to accept as a working hypothesis that successful transactions between organisms and environments require a spatio-temporal correspondence between events "out there" and the registration of those events "in here." The idealistic (Berkeleian) alternative, on this account, is *purely* philosophical and is, thus, beyond the power of psychology to test and beyond the obligations of psychology to adopt. Moreover, even on the idealistic account—if not especially on this account—the facts of perception stand, and the real problem is for the physicalists.

Perception and Heritability

That certain specific patterns of stimulation are more effectively processed than others, and that this bias is an integral feature of perceptual systems *de novo* are facts sufficiently well documented to support a *heritability* thesis. Perceptual functions in this respect anticipate the environmental demands imposed upon the species; a claim no more "teleological" than the theory of evolution itself. Taking the heritability thesis for granted then permits us to expect individual differences which can be enhanced by selective breeding. Among strains of known genetic structure, the heritability can be directly assessed. Even now, however, research on visual deprivation has shown that perceptual functions require patterned stimulation for normal development. To the extent that this is a "need," it follows that stimulus-seeking behavior is as natural and predictable as food-seeking behavior. Since there is nothing that would seem to exempt human beings from conditions requiring such tendencies, it is plausible to include *Homo sapiens* with the balance of the animal kingdom in these regards. What this guarantees is that activity and action are *there*, as it were, and no further explanation is necessary. This is to say that any further explanation will be exclusively physiological, but that the question of mechanism is irrelevant to a general theory of psychology.

Heritability in General

As a proposition of the system, it is proposed that any process displaying high heritability is a fundamentally biochemical one; that those processes of a psychological nature which display high heritability either (a) diminish in importance among progressively advanced species or (b) deviate significantly below the average of the species only in cases of pathology. The claim here is a general one which permits deductions of the following sort:

1. That "instinctive" behavior drops out as the phylogenetic series advances;
2. That such characteristics as "schizophrenia" or "manic-depressive psychosis"—to the extent that they display high heritability—are explicable principally in biochemical terms;
3. That other human characteristics of a *psychological* nature that display high heritability are candidates for biochemical rather than psychological explanation.

Item (3) is a strong claim in that it would turn over such psychological variables as I.Q. to the biochemists, but I will stand behind it. This is no more than admitting or proposing that a general theory of psychology may not be in a position to offer an account of intellectual differences in psychological terms. Yet, the same general theory may incorporate accounts of these differences developed by the biological sciences. From psychology's point of view, individual differences must be taken as a given. Extreme variations, however, are not likely to be embraced by a *psychological* theory; that is, a theory designed to organize and explain events based upon experience, perception, emotion, motivation, memory, and cognition.

Self-Awareness
It is proposed that the only public measure of this state is an indirect one. The proposition may be stated briefly thus:

The degree of self-awareness that can be imputed to an organism varies inversely with the degree to which that organism's behavior is instinctive.

As a crude measure of instinctivity, one may use habituation procedures, tests of invariance over time, determinations of the age of onset of the behavior in question, and estimates of the incidence of the behavior in the species at large. To the extent that self-awareness can be posited, the organism in question must be assumed capable of self-control, self-direction, and self-motivation. To this same extent, the organism can be judged as capable of *social* behavior. A corollary of this is that instinctive behavior cannot (by definition) be social.

Self-Awareness and Cognition
That a problem has been solved by following logically specifiable steps is no proof that the solver of the problem is *aware* of the steps. The question of cognition vis-à-vis orga-

nisms otherwise self-aware is an empirical question, to be answered anthropomorphically; that is, the organism must solve problems of a *logical* nature as these are defined by logicians. Evidence that the problem has in fact been solved logically can be gleaned only in settings in which no feature of the stimulus can serve as a guide. With human beings, however, cognition is taken for granted, and is absent only in instances of pathology.

Learning and Memory

Associative processes are known to be (a) extremely vulnerable to biochemical influences, (b) extremely sensitive to neuropathological states, (c) widespread throughout the animal kingdom, and (d) relatively invariant within species and among members of the species at the same level of maturation. Accordingly, these processes probably fall beyond the reach of a general theory of psychology and might best be reserved to the biological sciences. They may, of course, be incorporated as needed in a general theory of psychology, but they hardly constitute the central concern of such a theory. For all useful theoretical purposes, the principles of association (improvement with practice, improvement with motivation, facilitation in the presence of perceptually similar associates, interference by interpolated activity, etc.) may simply be taken for granted.

Motivation

In the advanced species and certainly in the human species, significant motivations are *acquired*. Psychology can get out of one rut by simply rejecting the notion of "instinctive" human motives, and by putting in that category what are ordinarily treated as physiological reflexes. Moreover, from the diversity of motives incubated under sufficiently similar cultural conditions, it is doubtful that the motivational complexion of the individual is acquired incrementally. It is more likely that the source of motives will be found in significant experiences—"peak" or otherwise—and that the *life history* method will remain the most useful means of identifying these. On this construction, a number of traditional approaches to motivation would have to be abandoned. Find a motive that can be engaged by a stimulating electrode inserted into a limbic nucleus, and you have found something quite different from the motives proposed here. We do not ordinarily think of someone who has been knocked off his chair as being "motivated" to unseat himself. The same reasoning applies to animals "knocked" into copulation, eating, drinking, and the like. Motivation entails awareness and choice. Otherwise, it is a mere reflex or a "need" over which the organism has no control, in which case the explanation will have to come from biology. In any case, the connection between biological needs and human motives is vitiated by the facts of history, by the daily life of most reflecting human beings, and by the failure of sixty years of drive-reduction theorizing and research to offer a plausible account of any of the commoner motives found among human beings living a safe distance from psychology laboratories. The claim here is not that there are not bona fide needs, but that such needs are *psychologically* irrelevant if they are immune to the effects of perception, cognition, past learning, and future prospects. Significant motives are *insatiable*—consider, among others, motives to be virtuous, successful, happy, healthy, and wise.

Reasoning

Psychologically significant behavior generally issues from deliberation, whether that behavior is genuinely creative, destructive, social, or moral. In this connection, J. Rychlak's *The Psychology of Rigorous Humanism* (1977) is illustrative of the possibilities available to those who wish to examine logic and behavior experimentally. I mention this work because it puts to rest the honored complaint that "rational man" is not a fit candidate for experimental assessment. The larger point is that the reasonings of human beings cannot be excluded from accounts of *human* behavior unless the behavior is trivial, reflexive, or unintended. The introspective method, liabilities and all, is well suited to the task of unearthing the rational substrate of human conduct.

This is a short list of "musts" for some future systematic psychology. Much interesting work has been done in defiance of this list, and much more will be done by those with lists of their own. Yet, it is difficult for me to conceive of a general theory of psychology as long as the tired assumptions prevail and some of the foregoing ones remain neglected. What is less clear, however, is the status of several traditional branches of psychology should the newer assumptions and their implications prevail. Especially vulnerable would seem to be those forms of psychological inquiry and evidence which focus on animal behavior and that large division of psychology in which "therapy" is the primary service.

To put animal research in the conceptual context I have advocated, let me begin by clarifying the role of heritability as noted above. If the goal is, indeed, a general theory of psychology, it follows that the targeted processes, events, and variables are those ordinarily associated with human thinking, action, and motivation. There have, we must recall, been very few justifications of studies of lower organisms in which the promise of relevance to human psychology has not been present at least as innuendo. Moreover, the very suggestion of an infrahuman *psychology* is predicated on some understanding of *"*psychology," and this understanding—regardless of reductionistic energies—begins with the facts of human psychology. Were these facts lacking, there could be no basis upon which to assume that nonhuman species are "psychological" in any sense at all. This is the inescapable anthropomorphic feature of all psychology, even if the object of study is the flatworm. In this regard, it really makes little difference where we draw the line separating *homo sapiens* from other animals vis-à-vis consciousness, motivation, perception, learning, and so on. If there were *nothing* in the infrahuman world comparable to *any* human psychological function, there would be no justification for calling studies of infrahuman organisms "psychological" studies. The question, then, boils down to what will qualify as a *psychological* function, and the answer, I submit, is that the function in question must depend minimally upon (a) some degree of awareness on the organism's part, (b) the potential influences of prior experience, (c) the possibility of alternative outcomes, and (d) what I will here refer to only as *room for error*. Stated in negative terms, I am suggesting that the adjective "psychological" not be applied to events, outcomes, processes, and functions able to run their courses at the level of tissue, organs, decerebrate preparations, neuromuscular junctions, and the like. Stated in still other terms, a psychological function, unlike a purely physical one, is not transferable from one organism to another. I put the notion in these terms intentionally to cause the reader to think of "memory-transfer" studies, for these speak directly to the point I raised in the matter of associative principles of learning and memory. There is perfect conceptual symmetry between the *fact* (or putative fact) that specific associations can be transferred from one biological system to another, and the proposition that associative principles are fundamentally *not* psychological. It is in the same sense that classical conditioning falls beyond the range of psychology, notwithstanding its (purely) historical role in the emergence of modern psychology.

It is at this point that the quantitative value of heritability enters the analysis. The greater this value, the greater is the fraction of total variance that can be accounted for by additive genetic influences. This, as I noted in an earlier chapter, does not amount to saying that environmental influences are negligible, since the *average* value of the phenotype can be drastically altered no matter how high heritability is. What the high value of heritability establishes, however, is that the cumulative *differences* among organisms are due principally to *genetic* differences, and proportionately less so to nongenetic differences. Height and weight are phenotypes displaying high heritability, but the average value of both can be significantly affected by diet, exercise, and early experience—not to mention childhood diseases, wasting diseases, and traumatic injury. What is relatively nonresponsive to such factors, however, is the *variance* of height and weight in the population. To come full circle, then, in the propositions advanced here, I am arguing that where the room for variation is severely constricted by factors indifferent to behavior, motivation, and affect, the dominant variables are not *psychological* in any defining sense.

It is obvious that associative learning and memory are not "inherited" and are surely not "instincts." Nonetheless, the performances of members of the same species on tests of associative learning and memory are so similar and so manipulable by adjusting the genotypes of the subject population that we may safely predict very high heritability values to emerge when the genetic contribution to the *variance* of test performance is assessed. Studies of human verbal learning should not confuse us here, for the argument is utterly indifferent to the sorts of stimulus materials employed. Nor is the argument weakened by demonstrations of motivational effects on associative learning, for the argument does not claim that bona fide psychological processes do not interact with nonpsychological processes. In such studies, it is more profitable to think of the learning and memory measures as instruments by which the *motivational* functions can be quantified. It is these functions that make such studies psychological.

When these views are brought to bear upon animal psychology, there are some immediate casualties: research confined to genetically and experientially homogeneous samples; research in which the behavioral options are so narrowed as to preclude the appearance of relevant differences among the participants; research in which "needs" are the only impulses to perform. The combination of unrepresentative genetic variation with ecologically trivial settings has yielded a mountain of data, but a mountain from whose peak one can only look down, not out. It seems doubtful that additional information of this sort will add to the understandings possible now as a result of previously collected information of the same sort. Each year, the operant chains get longer, the animal's tricks more clever, the contingencies somewhat more imaginative, but the distance between all of this and the *Lebenswelt* must be measured in intergalactic units. The addition of physiological techniques to studies of this sort has only increased the distance, for with this addition have come greater constraints on the organism and a greater separation between the psychological features of the organism and the sampled behaviors. The problems of behavioristic reductionism are not solved but augmented by physiological reductionism. The choice between descriptive behaviorism and functional neuroanatomy is not the sort of choice an aspiring *psychology* can afford to make.

I have introduced heritability also in the context of pathology and have extended it to embrace all psychologically exceptional cases. This, too, requires clarification lest I be accused of dismantling psychology in the hopes of improving it. Part of the temptation to turn phenomena over to the biological sciences is based upon the recognition that a general theory of psychology cannot be expected to account for *everything*. Knowing this in advance, good strategy calls for eliminating the most difficult and conceptually distant issues first. Again, phenotypes displaying exceptionally high heritability—those responsive only to radical alterations in the environment, including the internal environment—bear the burden of qualifying as *psychological* phenotypes. An individual displaying no sign of reason, no evidence of directed attention, no semblance of motivation, no trace of memory, cannot be incorporated into a general theory whose propositions are addressed to rational, perceptual, motivational, cognitive, and mnemonic functions. It would be akin to demanding that the principles of digestion be used to "explain" metabolism in an organism surgically stripped of stomach, intestines, gall bladder, liver, and parotid glands. It is at least suggestive that the only theories of psychosis which have enjoyed any empirical support are those based upon the physiology and biochemistry of the nervous system. It is also suggestive that patients in this category come face to face with clinical psychologists, psychiatrists, psychoanalysts, and counsellors only *after* electroconvulsive, surgical, or pharmacological assaults on the nervous system. Again on strategic grounds, facts of this sort should conduce to a certain modesty on the part of theorists; a willingness—if only for a time—to remove such cases from the realm of phenomena to which a general theory of psychology is addressed.

There is, of course, that large middle ground occupied by

those who deviate from the phenotypic norms of psychology but not by so great a degree as to be eliminated from theoretical interest. A greater willingness to face the *fact* of psychological diversity and a more realistic appreciation of unhappiness, stress, and confusion as integral features of human life when it is *lived* may reduce the numbers now occupying this middle ground. "Deviation" serves as both a statistical and a diagnostic term, but sense attaches to the latter only if there is a *disease* to be diagnosed. Some wounds are better left undressed; some problems go away with time; some are coextensive with life in the real world; some are created by a social commitment to sameness; some are the very foundations of personal growth. In light of the propositions advanced in this chapter, the "problems" in question are psychological—and therefore fit subjects for a general theory of psychology—only to the extent that they are attributable to the functions of self-awareness, motivation, reasoning, and psychologically relevant past experiences. In the absence of a general theory, practitioners have the right and the responsibility to "keep talking," even though in this case talk is not cheap. But because of this very absence of a general theory, it is not obvious that psychology, qua psychology, can prepare practitioners even for talking. The patient's willingness to enter these sessions is amenable to more than one construction. It may be a sign that some good is coming from the sessions; it may also be a sign of the patient's pathologic dependency and self-forfeiture.

My modest defense of introspection, the citation of work on "logical problem-solving," and the brief section on reasoning are included to redress the substantial depreciation of the actual *person* inflicted by the past half-century of academic psychology. That persons often deceive themselves is no truer than the fact that they often don't. That they are sometimes unaware of the forces impelling them to behave in certain ways is offset by the fact that they are generally quite aware of why they have chosen a given course of action. There is great appeal in mystery—great dramatic power—and there is surely more than mere wheel-spinning in psychoanalytic theory. Yet, *daily man* is a consciously striving chap, given to fits of anger and frustration, relieved by the charms of music and the balm of humor, driven to plan for the future and relive the past, eager to find a friend and keep a loved one. A psychological industry, no matter how vast, that refuses on principle or out of ignorance to speak to the needs of this fellow has a dismal future. And he, after all, is the patron—the stockholder; not simply in the mundane sense of wielding some power in the financial affairs of the profession, but as part of a culture; part of a moral and intellectual community that must decide which enterprises are worth saving and which must be left to die on the vine.

It is an insult to the person and the culture—and a characteristic insult, at that—to think that appeals for patronage must be so trendy as to be mindless; so gaudy as to be objectionable. The standing of a discipline is not measured by the number of its members or the size of its public. If that were the case, Classics would have gone the route of phrenology. The standing of a discipline is determined by the number of serious persons encouraged to take it seriously, and by that larger number of ordinary men and women who find it interesting and informative. In both cases, the numbers are very small, but they increase with the seasons as more and more people become prepared to hear what Matthew Arnold often described as "the best things said and thought in the world."

NOTES

1. THE NATURE OF SYSTEMS

1. The distinction between knowledge by *acquaintance* and knowledge by *description* appears in a number of Russell's works, but is set forth most clearly in his (unsigned) article, "On Denoting." (1905).

2. Pierre Duhem's exposition first appeared in French in his *La theorie physique: Son objet, sa structure* (1905). The English translation of the 1914 edition is published as *The Aim and Structure of Physical Theory* (1954). Quine's development of the thesis is given in his *From a Logical Point of View* (1953). It is in chapter 2 of the work that Quine states the thesis most economically: "Any statement can be held true come what may, if we make drastic enough adjustments elsewhere in the system. . . . [N]o statement is immune to revision." Duhem's position was less extreme than this, in that Duhem made provision for the role of "sagacity" and prudence in the choice of theoretical options. But even on the more radical account, the Duhem–Quine thesis requires *logical* coherence, no matter how odd the "adjustments" are which we find it necessary to make in the "system."

3. Ceres was discovered in the same year that Hegel legislated the fixed number of possible heavenly bodies in our solar system. Hegel's deduction was based upon prevailing scientific theories, and not on numerology.

4. W. James, *Psychology* (1890 ed.), pp. 467–68.

5. *Nichomachean Ethics*, book 1, ch. 7.

6. Aristotle's version of the reasons-causes distinction appears in several of his works. The passages in book 2, ch. 8 of his *Physics* are particularly instructive. His fourfold classification of causes is set forth in chs. 3–7 of book 1 of the *Metaphysics*, and in book 2, ch. 3 of the *Physics*.

7. Controversy surrounding the concept of causation is both old and current. An excellent anthology of modern works addressed to the issue is Tom L. Beauchamp's *Philosophical Problems of Causation* (1974). In contemporary science, the *necessitarian* position is one which, following Aristotle, treats of hypothetical or theoretical necessity. Thus, *if* the gravitational laws are true, then *necessarily* the time taken by object X to fall Y feet is n seconds. Note that the "necessity" is "necessity on a hypothesis." This is something of a "necessity by definition" in that—if the scientific theory, with its universal laws, is taken to be true—all predictions about such things as time-to-descend are contained in the very wording of the laws.

8. The most accessible and complete source for Carl G. Hempel's philosophy of science is his *Aspects of Scientific Explanation* (1963). The Hempelian "covering law" model has many precedents, some ancient. It is, perhaps, directly indebted to Karl Popper's *Logik der Forschung* (1935) which had developed the concept of explanation-as-deduction.

9. C. Hempel, *Aspects of Scientific Explanation* (1963), pp. 423–24.

10. Guthrie's learning theory is still *molar* rather than *molecular*, but is expressed in such a manner as to be assimilable by a molecular theory. This cannot be said of, for example, the learning theories of Hull, Spence, or Miller. This will be discussed further in chapter 3.

11. W. V. O. Quine, "On What There Is," in *From a Logical Point of View* (1953).

2. THE PHYSICALISTIC POINT OF VIEW

1. R. Descartes, *Meditations*, in *The Method, Meditations, and Philosophy of Descartes* (1901); *Traité des passions de l'âme*, in *The Philosophical Works of Descartes* (1955).

2. R. Descartes, *Discourse on Method*, in *Method, Meditations, and Philosophy* (1901).

3. The pamphlet accusing Descartes of holding this theory and his reply to the charge are both given in volume 1 of *Philosophical Works*.

4. The most accessible introduction to the thought of Gassendi is *The Selected Works of Pierre Gassendi* (1970), edited and translated by Craig Brush. His role in the materialist movement of the seventeenth century is discussed in chapter 9 of my *An Intellectual History of Psychology* (1976).

5. Again, I would refer the reader to the discussion offered in chapter 9 of *An Intellectual History of Psychology*.

6. The pages of Whytt's *Works* relevant to the history of physiological psychology have been republished in series E, volume 1 of Robinson, ed., *Significant Contributions to the History of Psychology* (1977–1978).

7. Opposition to Galvani's theory took several forms, some mutually contradictory. Some rejected the theory on the grounds that biological tissue is nonconductive. Others argued that, were the mechanism electrical, the effects would be instantaneous.

8. The seminal contributions of Du Bois may be sampled in series E, volume 1 of Robinson, ed., *Significant Contributions to the History of Psychology*, which contains his "On Secondary Electromotive Phenomena in Muscles, Nerves, and Electrical Organs," first published in 1887.

9. Flourens's *Phrenology Examined* is republished in its entirety in series E, volume 2 of Robinson, ed., *Significant Contributions to the History of Psychology*. The same volume contains Spurzheim's influential *Outlines of Phrenology* (1832).

10. The best edition of Ferrier's *The Functions of the Brain*, where this claim is made, is the edition of 1886 which is given in its entirety in series E, volume 3 of Robinson, ed., *Significant Contributions to the History of Psychology*.

11. I would refer the interested reader to the collection of articles presented in Robinson, ed., *Heredity and Achievement* (1970).

12. Reid has been unpardonably neglected by modern historians of psychology and philosophy, although there has been a recent spate of interest. *An Inquiry into the Human Mind* is available in a 1970 edition edited by Timothy Duggan. Norman Daniels has offered an interesting analysis of this work in *Thomas Reid's "Inquiry"* (1974). An entire issue of *Philosophical Monographs* (1977) has been devoted to Reid's philosophy: see Barker and Beauchamp, eds., *Thomas Reid: Critical Interpretations*. I have contributed a chapter to this, entitled "Thomas Reid's Gestalt Psychology," which addresses Reid's *realist* theory of perception. Finally, the April 1978 number of *The Monist* is devoted to Reid's philosophy.

13. J. J. Gibson has been one of the two or three most important figures in the field of perception in this century. He has summarized his position on perception in "Perception as a Function of Stimulation," a chapter appearing in volume 1 of S. Koch, ed., *Psychology: A Study of a Science* (1959), pp. 456–501. The full development of the theory appears in his *The senses Considered as Perceptual Systems* (1966). The range and depth of his influence can be gleaned from the articles appearing in MacLeod and Pick, eds., *Perception: Essays in Honor of James J. Gibson* (1974). His so-called naive realism is developed in his "New Reasons for Realism" (1967). As I note in the chapter, fitting Gibson's work into *physiological* psychology is warranted only on conceptual grounds, since very little of Gibson's immensely productive career has had direct contact with physiological measurement or procedure. But on conceptual grounds, his theory is a theory about the manner in which the brain's perceptual mechanisms assimilate the sensory data and

determine the perceptual outcome. Assessments of such a theory need not—any more than need the theory itself—consider actual physiological mechanisms. These, for theoretical purposes, may merely be posited. His theory is, however, uncompromisingly *physicalistic*.

14. In Koch, *Psychology: Study of a Science*, p. 465.

15. I. Köhler, *Über Aufbau und Wandlungen Wahrnehmungswelt* (1951).

16. In Koch, *Psychology: Study of a Science*, p. 492.

17. Physiological theories of vision have, since Galen, been peculiarly burdened by the apparent simplicity with which external objects might somehow project images on the brain. Of course, no such thing occurs, but it is a ready way of thinking about such matters. The quickest way to dispel such "copy" theories from one's thoughts is to consider the neural representation of odors or tastes.

18. See the chapter in Koch, *Psychology: Study of a Science*, pp. 469–73.

19. *Ibid.*, p. 471.

20. For a summary of Hartline's work and the quantitative models arising from it, consult F. Ratliff's *Mach Bands* (1965). Perhaps the most seminal of the many articles by D. Hubel and T. Wiesel is "Receptive Fields, Binocular Interaction and the Functional Architecture of the Cat's Visual Cortex." (1962).

21. D. N. Robinson, "Visual Disinhibition with Binocular and Interocular Presentations," (1968).

22. For two illustrations of proposed "feature-analyzers," consult (a) D. N. Spinelli's " occam: A Content Addressable Memory Model for the Brain," in Pribram and Broadbent, ed., *The Biology of Memory* (1970); and (b) G. Werner's "The Topology of the Body Representation in the Somatic Afferent Pathway," in volume 2 of Quarton, Melnechuk, and Schmitt, *The Neurosciences* (1970). An excellent discussion of this approach and its limitations is provided by Karl Pribram in his *Languages of the Brain* (1971), pp. 126–39.

23. The seminal article here is that by C. Blakemore and F. Campbell, "On the Existence of Neurones in the Human Visual System Selectively Sensitive to the Organization and Size of Retinal Images" (1969).

24. *Ibid.*

25. The evidence for this can be gathered in any movie theater.

26. Here, Gibson and the Gestalt psychologists are not very far apart. An enlightening article germane to this is Mary Henle's "On Naive Realism," in *Perception: Essays in Honor of James J. Gibson* (1974).

27. This approach is explained and defended by Wolfgang Köhler in *The Task of Gestalt Psychology* (1969).

28. *Ibid.*

29. *Ibid.*

30. K. S. Lashley, K. L. Chow and J. Semmes. "An Examination of the Electrical Field Theory of Cerebral Integration (1951).

31. J. S. Stamm and A. Warren. "Learning and Retention by Monkeys with Epileptogenic Implants in Posterior Parietal Cortex (1961).

32. R. Sperry, N. Miner and R. Meyers. "Visual Pattern Perception following Subpial Slicing and tantalum Wire Implantations in the Visual Cortex (1955)

33. Pribram, *Languages of the Brain*, ch. 8.

34. See Karl Lashley's "The Problem of Cerebral Organization in Vision" (1942), pp. 301–22.

35. *Ibid.*, pp. 312–14, where Lashley also speaks of those "reverberatory circuits" which we now identify with Hebb's theory.

36. Helson has summarized his research and theory in "Adaptation Level Theory," in S. Koch, *Psychology: Study of a Science*, pp. 565–621.

37. *Ibid.*, p. 569.

38. Hartley's originality and thoroughness are not depreciated by noting that his was a veritable *age* of materialistic psychologies, led principally by the *philosophes* in France.

39. Bain's highly influential *The Senses and the Intellect* (1855) and *The Emotions and the Will* (1859) are now available unadbridged in series A, volumes 3 and 4, of *Significant Contributions to the History of Psychology*.

40. Herbart's *Textbook of Psychology* (English translation, 1891) is reproduced unabridged in series A, volume 6, of *Significant Contributions to the History of Psychology*.

41. The standard reference to Pavlov is G. V. Anrep's translation of *Conditioned Reflexes* (1927).

42. Brief comments on his recent discoveries in the area of conditioned reflexes were made in his Nobel address of 1904. Indeed, in the previous year he spoke on "Experimental Psychology and Psychopathology in Animals" at the International Medical Congress meeting in Spain. But the wide attention given to the Nobel lectures makes 1904 the year in which a broad scientific community had an opportunity to learn of this important new work.

43. Lashley's most important papers are presented in *The Neuropsychology of Karl Lashley* (1960), edited by F. A. Beach, D. O. Hebb, C. T. Morgan, and H. W. Nissen.

298   2. THE PHYSICALISTIC POINT OF VIEW

44. D. O. Hebb, "A Neuropsychological Theory," in Koch, *Psychology: Study of a Science*, p. 627.

45. *Ibid.*, p. 632.

46. *Ibid.*, p. 628.

47. Hebb's notion of alterations of synaptic resistance has had a mixed history but the essential soundness of the basic idea can be seen in the excellent research of E. R. Kandel on the organism *Aplysia*. See especially Kandel and Tauc, "Heterosynaptic Facilitation in Neurones of the Abdominal Ganglion of *Aplysia depilans*" (1965).

48. D. O. Hebb, in Koch, *Psychology*, p. 629.

49. *Ibid.*, p. 631.

50. The earliest article is C. P. Duncan's "The Retroactive Effects of Shock on Learning" (1949). See also the review of methods and findings by W. J. Hudspeth and L. K. Gerbrandt: "Electroconvulsive Shock: Conflict, Consolidation, and Neuroanatomical Functions" (1965).

51. The difficulties here are discussed by J. Bures and O. Buresova in "The Use of Leao's Spreading Depression in the Study of Interhemispheric Transfer of Memory Traces" (1961), and by S. E. Glickman in "Perseverative Neural Processes and Consolidation of the Memory Trace" (1961).

52. A brief review of this entire literature is E. M. Gurowitz's *The Molecular Basis of Memory* (1969).

53. D. O. Hebb, in Koch, *Psychology*, p. 639.

54. E. R. John, R. N. Herrington, and S. Sutton, "Effects of Visual Form on the Evoked Response" (1967).

55. E. R. John and P. P. Morgades, "The Pattern and Anatomical Distribution of Evoked Potentials and Multiple Unit Activity Elicited by Conditioned Stimuli in Trained Cats" (1969).

56. E. R. John, *Mechanisms of Memory* (1967), p. 414.

57. A review of the earier efforts in this area is provided by Gurowitz, *Molecular Basis of Memory* (1969).

58. Representative of the better studies—all of which have serious problems—is that by A. L. Jacobson, C. Fried, and S. D. Horowitz: "Planarians and Memory" (1966). Here, the RNA hypothesis is tested directly by feeding "educated" flatworms to "naive" ones and testing for the facilitation of the specific response—the contraction of the body conditioned by pairing flashes of light with shocks. On failures in such "transfer" studies, see L. D. Hutt and L. Elliot, "Chemical Transfer of Learned Fear: Failure to Replicate Ungar" (1970). Actually, it was Ungar's experiment, and not Ungar that

Hutt and Elliot failed to replicate. For Ungar's controversial research, consult G. Ungar, L. Gelson, and R. H. Clark, "Chemical Transfer of Learned Fear" (1968). Important articles addressing RNA synthesis and RNA destruction vis-à-vis memory appear in Gaito, ed., *Macromolecules and Behavior* (1966). A more recent and comprehensive treatment is provided by Essman and Nakajima, eds., *Current Biochemical Approaches to Learning and Memory* (1973).

59. On appetitive behavior and the hypothalamus, see P. Teitelbaum and A. Epstein, "The Lateral Hypothalamic Syndrome" (1962). On brain mechanisms associated with emotion, an excellent critical review is M. L. Goldstein's "Physiological Theories of Emotion: A Critical Historical Review from the Standpoint of Behavior Theory" (1968). See also P. D. MacLean, "Psychosomatic Disease and the Visceral Brain: Recent Developments Bearing on the Papez Theory of Emotion" (1964), in Isaacson, ed., *Neuropsychology*. Still useful is James Olds's "Emotional Centers in the Brain" (1967). "Reward" and "punishment" centers within the brain are studied for the first time by James Olds and Peter Milner whose work is summarized in "Positive Reinforcement Produced by Electrical Stimulation of Septal Area and Other Regions of Rat Brain" (1954). On the chemical substrates of reinforcement, see L. Stein's "Chemistry of Reward and Punishment" (1970).

60. See, for example, E. S. Valenstein, V. C. Cox, and J. W. Kakolewski, "Re-examination of the Role of the Hypothalamus in Motivation" (1970).

61. H. Ursin, "The Effect of Amygdaloid Lesions on Flight and Defense Behavior in Cats" (1965).

62. P. Broca's famous discovery was announced in 1861 in the *Bulletins de la Société Anatomique de Paris* (Tome IV), and was based on a single observation.

63. See, for example, David Premack's "The Education of Sarah: A Chimp Learns the Language" (1970).

64. On deficits in human beings, consult Brenda Milner's "Psychological Defects Produced by Temporal Lobe Excision" (1958). See also K H. Pribram and W. E. Tubbs, "Short-term Memory, Parsing, and the Primate Frontal Cortex" (1967).

65. An excellent discussion of this is provided by K. H. Pribram in "On the Neurology of Thinking" (1959), and by the same author in "The Biology of Mind: Neurobehavioral Foundations" (1970).

66. J. Z. Young, *The Memory System of the Brain* (1966), p. 1.

67. E. Lenneberg, *The Biological Foundations of Language* (1967).

68. R. Sperry, "Cerebral Organization and Behavior (1961).

69. R. Sperry, M. Gazzaniga, and J. Bogen, "Interhemispheric Relationships: the Neocortical Commissures: Syndromes of Hemispheric Deconnection, 11 in volume 4 of Vinken and Bruyn, eds., *Handbook of Clinical Neurology* (1969), pp. 273–90.

70. R. Ornstein, *The Psychology of Consciousness* (1972).

71. See R. Puccetti's "Brain Bisection and Personal Identity" (1973).

72. D. N. Robinson, "What Sort of Persons are Hemispheres? Another Look at the 'split-brain' man" (1976).

73. An excellent discussion of this entire area is still that presented by W. Penfield and L. Roberts in *Speech and Brain Mechanisms* (1959).

3. THE BEHAVIORISTIC POINT OF VIEW

1. E. L. Thorndike, *Animal Intelligence* (1898).

2. David Hume, *A Treatise of Human Nature*, book 1, part 1, sec. 1. All references are to the Dover (1965) reprint of the edition edited by L. A. Selby-Bigge.

3. *Ibid.*, sec. 4.

4. Kant's critique of the Humean theory of causation is discussed with great penetration by L. W. Beck in "Once More Unto the Breach: Kant's Answer to Hume Again" (1967).

5. Many such experiments are discussed by A. Michotte in his *The Perception of Causality* (1963).

6. For relevant studies, see E. C. Tolman's "Cognitive Maps in Rats and Man" (1948).

7. G. Ryle, *The Concept of Mind* (1949), p. 63.

8. See especially A. G. Greenwald's "Sensory Feedback Mechanisms in Performance Control: With Special Reference to the Ideo-motor Mechanism" (1970). Also informing in this connection is Alvin Goldman's discussion, "The Volitional Theory Revisited," in *Action Theory* (1975).

9. E. R. Guthrie, *The Psychology of Learning* (1952), pp. 23ff.

10. *Ibid.*

11. E. R. Guthrie, "Conditioning: A Theory of Learning in Terms of Stimulus, Response, and Association," in N. B. Henry, ed., *The Forty-first Yearbook of the National Society for the Study of Education* (1942), p. 30.

12. *Ibid.*, p. 26.

13. *Ibid.*, p. 28.

14. E. R. Guthrie, *Psychology of Learning*, pp. 133ff.

15. This literature has a long history. For one of the earliest articles, see J. A. McGeoch's "The Influence of Degree of Interpolated Learning upon Retro-active Inhibition" (1932). One of the "classic" papers is Benton Underwood's "The Effect of Successive Interpolations on Retroactive and Proactive Inhibition" (1945).

16. F. D. Sheffield and T. B. Roby, "Reward Value of a Non-nutritive Sweet Taste" (1950).

17. E. R. Guthrie, "Conditioning: A Theory of Learning," pp. 38ff.

18. H. S. Terrace, "Errorless Discrimination Learning in the Pigeon: Effects of Chlorpromazine and Imipramine" (1963).

19. W. K. Estes, B. L. Hopkins, and E. J. Crothers, "All-or-None and the Conservation of Effects in the Learning and Retention of Paired Associates" (1960).

20. See especially W. K. Estes, "Toward a Statistical Theory of Learning" (1950).

21. *Ibid.*

22. There is a large and growing literature devoted to this. A number of significant articles have been assembled and discussed in my *Heredity and Achievement* (1970).

23. Thorndike, *Animal Intelligence*, p. 244.

24. *Ibid.*

25. J. B. Watson, *Behaviorism* (1924), p. 206.

26. Clark Hull's most influential book was his first, *Principles of Behavior*, which appeared in 1943. His second text, *A Behavior System* (1952), offered some extensions and refinements, but is neither as tight nor as purely "Hullian" as was the first. Kenneth Spence's most important book is *Behavior Theory and Conditioning* (1956).

27. The most influential extensions of the Hullian perspective are *Social Learning and Imitation* (1941) and *Personality and Psychotherapy* (1950) by Neal Miller and John Dollard. It is in the second that the Hullian system is reconciled to psychoanalytic concepts, and that the attempt is made to "Freudianize" learning theory—or, perhaps, Hullianize Freudian theory. Nearly everyone would agree that the *rapprochement* is less than convincing, but the books by Miller and Dollard were important in bringing the behavioristic perspective to bear on issues of broad psychological consequence.

28. A wholesome exception to this rule is *Dynamics of Response* (1965) by J. M. Notterman and D. E. Mintz. Here, a genuinely biophysical analysis of operant behavior is begun, principally through an examination of the dis-

tribution of operant forces. The text is sensitive to the need for inquiries into the topography of behavioral events and represents the possibility of a step beyond the counting-stage of behavioristic psychology.

29. For relevant experiments, consult R. A. Butler's "Incentive Conditions which Influence Visual Exploration" (1954). On "curiosity" in general, see Daniel Berlyne's Conflict, Arousal, and Curiosity (1960).

30. N. E. Miller, "Learning of Visceral and Glandular Responses" (1969). This is also the article which had much to do with the new wave of interest in "biofeedback."

31. S. Blue and F. Hegge, "Transposition of a Stimulus Generalization Gradient along an Auditory Intensity Continuum" (1965).

32. Skinner's position over the years has been somewhat oscillatory on this point.

33. B. F. Skinner, "Are Theories of Learning Necessary?" (1950), p. 193.

34. B. F. Skinner, Verbal Behavior (1957).

35. B. F. Skinner, Beyond Freedom and Dignity (1971).

36. D. Premack, "Reversibility of the Reinforcement Relation" (1962), p. 255.

37. For a summary of Tolman's research see his Purposiive Behavior in Animals and Men (1967).

38. The experiments were conducted by H. C. Blodgett and by Tolman and C. H. Honzig. They are discussed in Tolman's engaging "Cognitive Maps in Rats and Men" (1948).

39. Harry F. Harlow, "The Formation of Learning Sets" (1949), p. 56.

40. Ibid., p. 65.

41. See Harlow's "Learning Set and Error Factor Theory," in volume 2 of Koch's Psychology: Study of a Science (1959). Criticisms of Harlow's interpretation are offered by M. H. Sheldon in chapter 7 of Weiskrantz, ed., Analysis of Behavioral Change (1968).

42. W. Köhler, "Simple Structural Functions in the Chimpanzee and in the Chicken," in W. D. Ellis, ed., A Sourcebook of Gestalt Psychology (1938), pp. 217ff.

43. Consult Chomsky's famous review of Verbal Behavior, which appeared in Language in 1959.

44. For example, Kenneth MacCorquodale's "B. F. Skinner's Verbal Behavior: A Retrospective Appreciation" (1969).

45. See, for example, Skinner's About Behaviorism (1974).

46. B. Schwartz, Psychology of Learning and Behavior (1978), p. 3.

4. PERCEPTION, MEMORY, AND COGNITION

1. U. Neisser, *Cognition and Reality* (1976), p. 9.

2. *Ibid.*, p. 5.

3. P. H. Lindsay and D. A. Norman, *Human Information Processing* (1977), p. 594.

4. See, for example, Jean Piaget's *The Construction of Reality in the Child* (1954). That "conservation" is not indifferent to learning and experience can be seen in the work of D. R. Price-Williams, W. Gordon, and W. Ramirez, "Skill and Conservation: A Study of Pottery-making Children" (1969).

5. Those impressed by the possibility of joining cognitive notions of feature analysis to extant facts and theories in neuropsychology will be much informed by William Uttal's discussion in *The Psychobiology of Mind* (1978), pp. 498–505.

6. An excellent discussion of Lewin's position on this and related matters is provided in J. W. Atkinson's *An Introduction to Motivation* (1964). See especially chapter 4.

7. W. Uttal, *The Psychobiology of Sensory Coding* (1973).

8. To an almost alarming degree, "information processing" has become something of a synonym for cognitive psychology, itself. Much of the literature composed under this rubric is actually addressed to perception, and a fair share of the rest is devoted to memory. My quick estimate, based upon books and articles published over the past five years, is that less than 5 percent of the literature is concerned with *cognition* as it has been discussed in this chapter.

9. G. Miller, Decision Units in the Perception of Speech (1962).

10. For an early and seminal article, see Colin Cherry's "Some Experiments on the Recognition of Speech, with One and with Two Ears" (1953).

11. D. N. Robinson and S. Sabat, "Elimination of Auditory Evoked Responses during Auditory Shadowing" (1975); also, D. N. Robinson and S. Sabat, "Neuroelectric Aspects of Information-Processing by the Brain" (1977).

12. L. R. Peterson and M. Peterson, "Short-term Retention of Individual Items" (1959).

13. G. Sperling, "The Information Available in Brief Visual Presentations" (1960).

14. For perceptual approaches to information processing, an excellent anthology has been collected by R. N. Haber under the title *Contemporary Research and Theory in Visual Perception* (1968). Essays describing the cogni-

tive approach to information processing appear in Solso, ed., *Information Processing and Cognition: The Loyola Symposium* (1975).

15. See David Rabb's "Backward Masking" (1963).

16. D. N. Robinson, "Visual Reaction Time and the Human Alpha Rhythm: The Effects of Stimulus Luminance, Area, and Duration" (1966).

17. C. G. Gross, C. E. Rocha-Miranda, and D. B. Bender, "Visual Properties of Neurons in Inferotemporal Cortex of the Macaque" (1972).

18. Perhaps the best brief statement of the Gestalt position is Wolfgang Köhler's *The Task of Gestalt Psychology* (1969).

19. R. N. Shepard and J. Metzler, "Mental Rotation of Three-dimensional Objects" (1971).

20. Still interesting is the old article by J. A. McGeoch, "Forgetting and the Law of Disuse" (1932). A good illustration of more recent work is N. J. Slamecka's "Proactive Inhibition of Connected Discourse" (1961).

21. A review of the interference theory of forgetting is provided in chapter 9 of Robert Klatzky's *Human Memory: Structures and Processes* (1975).

22. On acoustic interference in short-term memory, see R. Conrad's "Acoustic Confusions in Immediate Memory" (1964). The notion that only acoustic factors are involved in short-term interference, and that only semantic factors are involved in long-term interference has been revised in light of further research. See particularly chapter 7 in Klatzky, *Human Memory*.

23. Lindsay and Norman, *Human Information Processing*, p. 415.

24. There is a growing literature addressed to perception in the newborn. Pattern-recognition studies have been conducted by R. L. Fantz—see his "Pattern Vision in Young Children" (1968). Very influential is T. G. R. Bower's "The Object in the World of the Infant" (1971). See also J. Kagan's "The Growth of the 'Face Schema': Theoretical Significance and Methodological Issues," in J. Hellmuth ed., *Exceptional Infant* (New York: Brunner/Mazel, 1967).

25. J. S. Bruner, "The Course of Cognitive Growth" (1964).

26. Neisser, *Cognition and Reality*, p. 4.

27. *Ibid.*, ch. 4.

28. G. A. Miller, E. Galanter, and K. H. Pribram, *Plans and the Structure of Behavior* (1960).

29. Neisser, *Cognition and Reality*, p. 56.

30. *Ibid.*, p. 161.

31. Kagan, "Growth of 'Face Schema.' "

32. See, for example, J. Piaget and B. Inhelder, *The Psychology of the Child* (1969), especially pp. 12ff.

33. Neisser, *Cognition and Reality*, pp. 164ff.

34. L. Kohlberg, "The Development of Children's Orientations toward a Moral Order: I. Sequence in the Development of Moral Thought," *Vita Humana* (1963), 6:11–33.

35. R. S. Woodworth and S. B. Sells, "An Atmospheric Effect in Formal Syllogistic Reasoning" (1935).

36. M. Henle, "On the Relation between Logic and Thinking" (1962).

37. See especially James R. Erickson's "A Set Analysis Theory of Behavior in Formal Syllogistic Reasoning Tasks" (1974).

38. Founding works by Binet, Galton, and Stern are reproduced with critical prefaces in D. N. Robinson, ed., *Significant Contributions to the History of Psychology*, series b, vol. 4.

39. Sharp's paper is reproduced in series A, volume 11 of the above cited collection.

40. I have discussed some of the abuses of the "heritability" concept in *Psychology: Traditions and Perspectives* (1976), pp. 429–33.

5. PERSONALITY, MOTIVATION, AND THE PSYCHOANALYTIC PERSPECTIVE

1. The argument for this maxim is set forth in chapters 2 through 5 of B. F. Skinner's *Beyond Freedom and Dignity* (1971).

2. For an interesting brief account, see Walter Bromberg's *From Shaman to Psychotherapist* (1975).

3. It is sometimes overlooked that Locke never mentions Descartes in his *An Essay Concerning Human Understanding,* and that Descartes specificaly disowned the theory of innate ideas customarily ascribed to him. Locke may well have had the "Cambridge Platonists" as much in mind in his critique of nativistic epistemologies.

4. J. Locke, *An Essay Concerning Human Undersanding* (1956), book 4, ch. 9, sec. 3; book 2, ch. 1, sec. 9; book 2, ch. 27, sec. 6.

5. D. Hume, *Treatise of Human Nature* (1965), book 1, pt. 4, sec. 6.

6. *Ibid.*

7. For an analysis of Reid's critique of Hume's theory of personal identity, see D. N. Robinson and T. L. Beauchamp, "Personal Identity: Reid's Answer to Hume" (1978).

8. The issue has recently resurfaced in connection with commissurotomized human patients. I would refer the reader to my "What Sort of Persons Are Hemispheres? Another Look at 'Split-Brain' Man" (1976).

9. The most relevant discusson is given in essay 4, ch. 2 of Thomas Reid's *Essays on the Active Powers of the Human Mind* (1969).

10. Reid, in the essay cited above, states it this way: "We are conscious of making an exertion, sometimes with difficulty, in order to produce certain effects . . . [which] implies a conviction that the effect is in our power. No man can deliberately attempt what he does not believe to be in his power."

11. The words are Asper's, the Presenter of the first scene in Jonson's *Every Man Out of His Humour*.

12. Readers may consult the articles by I. Gottesman and D. Rosenthal collected in D. N. Robinson, ed., *Heredity and Achievement* (1970).

13. C. G. Jung, *Psychological Types* (1923).

14. W. T. Norman, *2800 Personality Trait Descriptors: Normative Operating Characteristics for a University Population* (1967). University of Michigan Department of Psychology, Ann Arbor, 1967.

15. W. H. Sheldon, *The Varieties of Human Physique: An Introduction to Constitutional Psychology* (1949).

16. N. Tinbergen, "On War and Peace in Animals and Man" (1968).

17. Most of this is given in his *The Expression of the Emotions in Man and Animals* (1896).

18. See especially the last chapter of Wallace's *Darwinism* (1897).

19. R. A. Hinde, *Biological Bases of Human Social Behaviour* (1974), p. 4.

20. H. J. Eysenck, "Principles and Methods of Personality Description, Classification and Diagnosis" (1964).

21. A. Bandura, "Social Learning Theory of Aggression," in J. F. Knutson, ed., *Control of Aggresson: Implications from Basic Research* (1971).

22. W. Köhler, *The Task of Gestalt Psychology* (1969), p. 120.

23. An excellent and searching review of Lewin's theory and its roots in Lewin's philosophy of science may be found in chapter 4 of J. W. Atkinson's *An Introduction to Motivation* (1964). My own discussion of Lewin's work is indebted to Atkinson's treatment.

24. K. Lewin, *A Dynamic Theory of Personality* (1935), p. 28.

25. K. Lewin, *The Conceptual Representation and the Measurement of Psychological Forces* (1938), p. 163.

26. E. C. Tolman, *Collected Papers in Psychology* (1951), p. 117.

27. R. A. Butler, "Discrimination Learning by Rhesus Monkeys to Visual-Exploration Motivation" (1953).

28. R. S. Woodworth, *Dynamic Psychology* (1918).

29. S. Milgram, "Behavioral Study of Obedience" (1963).

30. B. Latané and J. Rodin, "A Lady in Distress: Inhibiting Effects of Friends and Strangers on Bystander Intervention" (1969).

31. P. Zimbardo, "The Psychological Power and Pathology of Imprisonment" (1971).

32. This distinction has been defended by K. Spence, for example, in his *Behavior Theory and Conditioning* (1956).

33. G. Allport, "The Ego in Contemporary Psychology" (1943).

34. Atkinson, ed., *Introduction to Motivation.*

35. *Ibid.*

36. D. McClelland, *The Achieving Society* (1961).

37. See Series D, volume 4 (*Darwinism*) of *Significant Contributions to the History of Psychology.* This volume contains reviews which appeared in London's *Quarterly Review*, Scotland's *Edinburgh Review*, and Ireland's *Dublin Review.*

38. See particularly his *Evolution and Ethics* (1893).

39. The statement appears in Flourens's *Phrenology Examined*, which is reprinted in Series E, volume 2 of *Significant Contributions to the History of Psychology.*

40. H. Ellenberger, *The Discovery of the Unconscious* (New York: Basic Books, 1977).

41. The Preface to Cabanis' *Memoires* has been translated by Francine Robinson, and the *Xth Memoire* has been translated by Margarita Heliotis. Both translations appear in Series E, volume 1 of *Significant Contributions to the History of Psychology.*

42. A. Adler, *The Neurotic Constitution* (1917).

43. C. G. Jung, *Memories, Dreams, Reflections* (1961).

44. C. G. Jung, "Psychological Types" (1928), p. 303.

45. See particularly Adler's *The Science of Living* (1929).

6. THE "THIRD FORCE": PHENOMENOLOGICAL AND HUMANISTIC PSYCHOLOGIES

1. Membership in the "third force" fraternity appears to be by self-affirmation. In the present chapter, I have made no effort to summarize all or even many of the third force treatises ordinarily cited. There are influential works by E. Fromm, Rollo May, Carl Rogers, and J. Bugental emphasizing "self," "authenticity," "human freedom," the "will," etc. These are not simple repetitions of one another, and the reader interested in the variety of third force psychologies must examine each work in its own right. My purpose in the present chapter has been to sketch the historical lineage of what is central to third force psychology, and to provide an outline of criticism relevant to these central ingredients. Given this aim, the nuances are really beside the point.

2. For an excellent development of the argument, see L. W. Beck's "Once More unto the Breach: Kant's Answer to Hume Again" (1967).

3. Fichte's most important works in this connection have been republished in Series A, volume 2 of *Significant Contributions to the History of Psychology*. Included in the volume are his *Characteristics of the Present Age* and *The Way toward the Blessed Life, or the Doctrine of Religion*.

4. The German edition of Hegel's works runs to 26 volumes. Works translated into English and central to the discussion in this chapter are his *Phenomenology of Mind* (1931), *The Philosophy of Right* (1942), and *Encyclopedia* (1959).

5. Fichte, *Characteristics of the Present Age*, in *Significant Contributions*.

6. Hegel, *Encyclopedia*, sec. 482.

7. The *Philosophie als Strenge Wissenschaft* has been translated by Q. Lauer as *Philosophy as Rigorous Science* in Edmund Husserl, *Phenomenology and the Crisis of Modern Philosophy* (1965).

8. S. Kierkegaard, *Either/Or* (1941, 1944).

2

9. F. Brentano, *Psychologie vom Empirischen Standpunkt* (1874), volume 1, book 2, ch. 1; third edition, 1925. The passage in the text is given in translation in Roderick Chisolm (ed.), *Realism and the Background of Phenomenology* (1960).

10. See, for example, J.-P. Sartre, *Existentialism and Humanism* (1948).

11. M. Heidegger, *Being and Time* (1962).

12. J.-P. Sartre *Being and Nothingness* (1956), p. 560.

13. All quotations from Abraham Maslow are taken from the 2nd edition of his *Toward a Psychology of Being* (1968), this one from page 9.

14. *Ibid.*, p. 220.

15. *Ibid.*, p. 29.

16. *Ibid.*, p. 39.

17. *Ibid.*, p. 5.

18. *Ibid.*, p. 157.

19. *Ibid.*, p. 107.

20. The list given on p. 107 in the footnote offers such pairs as "self-disclosing" and "undeliberate," and "forthright" and "unsophisticated." It is not clear how Maslow understands these descriptions.

21. Maslow, *Psychology of Being*, pp. 116–24.

22. *Ibid.*, p. 152.

23. *Ibid.*, p. 151.

24. *Ibid.*, p. 152.

25. *Ibid.*, p. 42.

26. *Ibid.*, p. 40.

27. *Ibid.*, p. 181.

28. *Ibid.*, p. 181.

29. S. Milgram, "Behavioral Study of Obedience" (1963).

30. S. Asch, "Studies of Independence and Conformity: A Minority of One against a Unanimous Majority" (1956).

31. D. Byrne, "Attitudes and Attraction," in *Advances in Experimental Social Psychology* (1969).

32. B. Latané and J. Darley, "Group Inhibition of Bystander Intervention in Emergencies" (1968).

33. A. Bandura, D. Ross, and S. Ross, "Transmission of Aggression through Imitation of Aggressive Models" (1961).

34. E. Aronson, *The Social Animal* (1972), p. 44.

35. D. N. Robinson, "Psychological Explanation: Reasons or Causes?" (1978).

BIBLIOGRAPHY

Adler, A. *The Neurotic Constitution.* New York: Moffat-Yard, 1917.
—— *The Science of Living.* Philadelphia: Chilton, 1929.
Allport, G. "The Ego in Contemporary Psychology." *Psychological Review* (1943), 50:451–78.
Anrep, G. V., trans. *Conditioned Reflexes.* London: Oxford University Press, 1927.
Aristotle. *Nichomachean Ethics,* in *The Basic Works of Aristotle.* R. McKeon, ed. New York: Random House, 1941.
Aronson, E. *The Social Animal.* San Francisco: W. H. Freeman, 1972.
Asch, S. "Studies of Independence and Conformity: A Minority of One Against a Unanimous Majority." *Psychological Monographs* (1956), vol. 70, no. 9, Whole Part no. 416.
Atkinson, J. W. *An Introduction to Motivation.* New York: Van Nostrand, 1964.
Bain, A. *The Senses and the Intellect.* In D. N. Robinson, ed., *Significant Contributions to the History of Psychology,* Series A, vol. 3. Washington, D.C.: University Publications of America, 1977–78.
Bandura, A. "Social Learning Theory of Aggression." In J. S. Knutson, ed., *Control of Aggression: Implications from Basic Research.* Chicago: Aldine, 1971.
Bandura, A., D. Ross, and S. Ross. "Transmission of Aggression through Imitation of Aggressive Models." *Journal of Abnormal and Social Psychology* (1961), 63:575–82.

311

Barker, S. and T. L. Beauchamp, eds. *Thomas Reid: Critical Interpretations.* Philadelphia: University Science Center, 1976.

Beach, F. A., D. O. Hebb, C. T. Morgan, and H. W. Nissen, eds. *The Neuropsychology of Karl Lashley.* New York: McGraw Hill, 1960.

Beauchamp, T. L., ed. *Philosophical Problems of Causation.* Encino, Calif.: Dickenson, 1974.

Beck, L. W. "Once More unto the Breach: Kant's Answer to Hume Again." *Ratio* (June 1967), 9(1):33–37.

Berlyne, D. *Conflict, Arousal, and Curiosity.* New York: McGraw-Hill, 1960.

Blakemore, C. and F. Campbell. "On the Existence of Neurones in the Human Visual System Selectively Sensitive to the Organization and Size of Retinal Images." *Journal of Physiology* (1969), 203:237–60.

Blue, S. and F. Hegge. "Transposition of a Stimulus Generalization Gradient Along an Auditory Intensity Continuum." *Psychonomic Science* (1965), 3:201–2.

Bower, T. G. R. "The Object in the World of the Infant." *Scientific American* (1971), 225(4):30–38.

Brentano, F. *Psychologie vom Empirischen Standpunkt.* 3d ed. Leipzig: F. Meiner, 1925.

Bromberg, W. *From Shaman to Psychotherapist.* Chicago: Regnery, 1975.

Bruner, J. S. "The Course of Cognitive Growth." *American Psychologist* (1964), 19:1–15.

Brush, C. R., ed. and trans. *The Selected Works of Pierre Gassendi.* New York: Johnson Reprint Co., 1970.

Bures, J. and O. Buresova. "The Use of Leao's Spreading Depression in the Study of Interhemispheric Transfer of Memory Traces." *Journal of Comparative and Physiological Psychology* (1961), 53:558–63.

Butler, R. A. "Discrimination Learning by Rhesus Monkeys to Visual-Exploration Motivation." *Journal of Comparative and Physiological Psychology* (1953), *J. Comp. Physiol. Psychol.*, 46:95–98.

Butler, R. A. "Incentive Conditions Which Influence Visual Exploration." *Journal of Experimental Psychology* (1954), 48:19–23.

Byrne, D. "Attitudes and Attraction." In L. Berkowitz, ed., *Advances in Experimental Social Psychology,* vol. 4. New York: Academic Press, 1969.

Cabanis, P. Preface to *Memoires.* Francine Robinson, trans. In D. N. Robinson, ed., *Significant Contributions to the History of Psychology,* series E, vol. 1. Washington, D.C.: University Publications of America, 1977–1978.

—— *Xth Memoire.* Margaret Heliotis, trans. In D. N. Robinson, ed., *Significant Contributions to the History of Psychology,* series E, vol. 1. Washington, D.C.: University Publications of America, 1977–1978.

Cherry, C. "Some Experiments on the Recognition of Speech, with One and with Two Ears." *Journal of the Acoustical Society of America* (1953), 25:975–79.

Chisholm, R., ed. *Realism and the Background of Phenomenology.* Glencoe, Ill.: Freeman Press, 1960.

Chomsky, N. Review of *Verbal Behavior,* by B. F. Skinner. *Language* (1959), 35:26–58.

Conrad, R. "Acoustic Confusions in Immediate Memory." *British Journal of Psychology* (1964), 55:75–84.

Daniels, N. *Thomas Reid's "Inquiry."* New York: B. Franklin, 1974.

Darwin, C. *The Expression of the Emotions in Man and Animals.* New York: Appleton, 1896.

Descartes, R. *Discourse on Method.* In *The Method, Meditations, and Philosophy of Descartes.* J. Veitch, trans. New York: Tudor, 1901.

—— *Meditations.* J. Veitch, trans. New York: Tudor, 1901.

—— *Les Passions de l'âme.* In *The Philosophical Works of Descartes.* E. Haldane and G. R. T. Moss, trans. New York: Dover, 1955.

Du Bois, R. "On Secondary Electromotive Phenomena in Muscles, Nerves, and Electrical Organs. "In D. N. Robinson, ed., *Significant Contributions to the History of Psychology,* series E, vol 1. Washington, D.C.: University Publications of America, 1977–1978.

Duggan, T., ed. *An Inquiry into the Human Mind,* by T. Reid. Chicago: University of Chicago Press, 1970.

Duhem, P. *La théorie physique, Son objet et sa structure* (1905). English translation, *The Aim and Structure of Physical Theory.* Princeton, N.J.: Princeton University Press, 1954.

Duncan, C. P. "The Retroactive Effects of Shock on Learning." *Journal of Comparative and Physiological Psychology* (1949), 42:32–34.

Erickson, J. R. "A Set Analysis Theory of Behavior in Formal Syllogistic Reasoning Tasks." In R. L. Solso, ed., *Theories of Cognitive Psychology: The Loyola Symposium.* New York: Wiley, 1974.

Essman, W. and S. Nakajima, eds. *Current Biochemical Approaches to Learning and Memory.* New York: Spectrum Publications, 1973.

Estes, W. K. "Toward a Statistical Theory of Learning." *Psychological Review* (1950), 57:94–107.

Estes, W. K., B. L., Hopkins, and E. J. Crothers. "All-or-None and the Conservation of Effects in the Learning and Retention of Paired Associates." *Journal of Experimental Psychology* (1960), 60:329–39.

Eysenck, H. J. "Principles and Methods of Personality Description, Classification and Diagnosis." *British Journal of Psychology* (1964), 55:284–94.

Fantz, L. "Pattern Vision in Young Children." *Psychological Record* (1968), 8:43–48.

Fichte, J. G. *Characteristics of the Present Age.* In D. N. Robinson, ed., *Significant Contributions to the History of Psychology,* series A, vol. 2. Washington, D.C.: University Publications of America, 1977–1978.

—— *The Way Toward the Blessed Life, or the Doctrine of Religion.* In D. N. Robinson, ed., *Significant Contributions to the History of Psychology,* series A, vol. 2. Washington, D.C.: University Publications of America, 1977–1978.

Flourens, P. *Phrenology Examined,* In D. N. Robinson, ed., *Significant Contributions to the History of Psychology,* series E, vol. 2. Washington, D.C.: University Publications of America, 1977–1978.

Gaito, J., ed. *Macromolecules and Behavior.* New York: Appleton-Century-Crofts, 1966.

Gibson, J. J. "New Reasons for Realism." *Synthese* (1967), 17:162–72.

—— "Perception as a Function of Stimulation. In S. Koch, ed., *Psychology: A Study of a Science,* vol. 1. New York: McGraw-Hill, 1959.

—— *The Senses Considered as Perceptual Systems.* Boston: Houghton Mifflin, 1966.

Glickman, S. E. "Perseverative Neural Processes and Consolidation of the Memory Trace." *Psychological Bulletin* (1961), 58:218–33.

Goldman, A. "The Volitional Theory Revisited." In M. Brand and D. Walton, eds., *Action Theory*. Holland: Reidel, 1975.

Goldstein, M. L. "Physiological Theories of Emotion: A Critical Historical Review from the Standpoint of Behavior Theory." *Psychological Bulletin* (1968), 69:23–40.

Greenwald, A. G. "Sensory Feedback Mechanisms in Performance Control: With Special Reference to the Ideo-Motor Mechanism." *Psychological Review* (1970), 77:73–101.

Gross, C. G., C. E. Rocha-Miranda, and D. B. Bender. "Visual Properties of Neurons in Inferotemporal Cortex of the Macaque." *Journal of Neurophysiology* (1972) 35:96–111.

Gurowitz, E. M. *The Molecular Basis of Memory.* Englewood Cliffs, N.J.: Prentice-Hall, 1969.

Guthrie, E. R. "Conditioning: A Theory of Learning in Terms of Stimulus, Response, and Association." In N. B. Henry, ed., *The Forty-first Yearbook of the National Society for the Study of Education.* Chicago: University of Chicago Press, 1942.

—— *The Psychology of Learning.* Magnolia, Mass.: Peter Smith, 1952.

Haber, R. N. *Contemporary Research and Theory in Visual Perception.* New York: Holt, Rinehart and Winston, 1968.

Harlow, H. F. "The Formation of Learning Sets." *Psychological Review* (1949), 56:51–65.

——"Learning Set and Error Factor Theory." In S. Koch, ed., *Psychology: A Study of a Science.* New York: McGraw-Hill, 1959.

Hebb, D. O. "A Neuropsychological Theory." In S. Koch, ed., *Psychology: A Study of a Science.* New York: McGraw-Hill, 1959.

Hegel, G. W. F. *Encyclopedia of Philosophy.* G. E. Mueller, trans. New York: Philosophical Library, 1959.

—— *Phenomenology of Mind.* 2d ed. J. B. Baillie, trans. London: Allen & Unwin, 1931.

—— *The Philosophy of Right.* T. M. Knox, trans. and ed. Oxford: The Clarendon Press, 1942.

Heidegger, M. *Being and Time* (1927). J. Macquarrie and E. S. Robinson, trans. New York: Harper & Row, 1962.

Helson, H. *Adaptation Level Theory.* In S. Koch, ed., *Psychology: A Study of a Science.* New York: McGraw-Hill, 1959.

Hempel, C. G. *Aspects of Scientific Explanation.* New York: Free Press, 1963.

Henle, M. "On Naive Realism." In R. B. Macleod and H. L. Pick, Jr., eds., *Perception: Essays in Honor of James J. Gibson*. Ithaca: Cornell University Press, 1974.

—— "On the Relation between Logic and Thinking. *Psychological Review* (1962), 69:366–78.

Herbart, J. *Textbook of Psychology* (English translation, 1891). In D. N. Robinson, ed., *Significant Contributions to the History of Psychology*, series A, vol. 6. Washington, D.C.: University Publications of America, 1977–1978.

Hinde, R. A. *Biological Bases of Human Social Behaviour*. New York: McGraw-Hill, 1974.

Hubel, D. and T. Wiesel. "Receptive Fields, Binocular Interaction and the Functional Architecture of the Cat's Visual Cortex." *Journal of Physiology* (1962), 160:106–54.

Hudspeth, W. J. and L. K. Gerbrandt. "Electroconvulsive Shock: Conflict, Consolidation, and Neuroanatomical Functions. *Psychological Bulletin* (1965), 63:377–83.

Hull, C. *A Behavior System*. New Haven: Yale University Press, 1952.

—— *Principles of Behavior*. New York: Appleton-Century, 1943.

Hume, D. *A Treatise of Human Nature*. L. A. Selby-Bigge, ed. New York: Dover, 1965.

Husserl, E. *Philosophy as Rigorous Science*. Q. Lauer, trans. In E. Husserl, ed., *Phenomenology and the Crisis of Modern Philosophy*. New York: Harper & Row, 1965.

Hutt, L. D. and L. Elliot. "Chemical Transfer of Learned Fear: Failure to Repulicate Ungar." *Psychonomic Science* (1970), 18:57–59.

Jacobson, A. L., C. Fried, and S. D. Horowitz. "Planarians and Memory." *Nature* (1966), 209:599–601.

James, W. *The Principles of Psychology*. New York: Holt, 1892.

John, E. R. *Mechanisms of Memory*. New York: Academic Press, 1967.

John, E. R., R. N. Herrington, and S. Sutton. "Effects of Visual Form on the Evoked Response." *Science* (1967), 155:1439–42.

John, E. R. and P. P. Morgades. "The Pattern and Anatomical Distribution of Evoked Potentials and Multiple Unit Activity Elicited by Conditioned Stimuli in Trained Cats." *Communications in Behavioral Biology*, Part A, vol. 3, 4:181–207. New York: Academic Press, 1969.

Jung, C. G. *Memories, Dreams, Reflections.* New York: Pantheon, 1961.
—"Psychological Types." In *Contributions to Analytical Psychology,* London: Kegan Paul, 1928.
—— *Psychological Types.* New York: Harcourt Brace Jovanovich, 1923.
Kagan, J. "The Growth of the 'Face Schema': Theoretical Significance and Methodological Issues." In J. Hellmuth, ed., *Exceptional Infant.* New York: Brunner/Hazel, 1967.
Kandel E. R. "Heterosynaptic Facilitation in Neurones of the Abdominal Ganglion of *Aplysia depilans." Journal of Physiology* (London) (1965), 181:1–27.
Kierkegaard, S. *Either/Or.* 2 vols. Translated by D. F. Swenson and L. M. Swenson, and A. Lowrie. Princeton, N.J.: Princeton University Press, 1941, 1944.
Klatzky, R. *Human Memory: Structures and Processes.* San Francisco, Freeman, 1975.
Koch, S., ed. *Psychology: A Study of a Science.* New York: McGraw-Hill, 1959.
Kohlberg, L. "The Development of Children's Orientations toward a Moral Order: I. Sequence in the Development of Moral Thought. *Vita Humana* (1963), 6:11–33.
Köhler, I. *Über Aufbau und Wandlungen der Wahrnehmungswelt.* Vienna: R. M. Rohrer, 1951.
Köhler, W. "Simple Structural Functions in the Chimpanzee and in the Chicken." In W. D. Ellis, ed., *A Sourcebook of Gestalt Psychology.* London: Routledge & Kegan Paul, 1938.
—— *The Task of Gestalt Psychology.* Princeton, N.J.: Princeton University Press, 1969.
Lashley, K. "The Problem of Cerebral Organization in Vision." In *Biological Symposia,* vol. 7: *Visual Mechanisms,* pp. 301–22. Lancaster, Pa.: Jacques Cattell Press, 1942.
Lashley, K. S., K. L. Chow, and J. Semmes. "An Examination of the Electrical Field Theory of Cerebral Integration." *Psychological Review* (1951), 58:123–36.
Latané, B. and J. Darley. Group Inhibition of Bystander Intervention in Emergencies. *Journal of Personality and Social Psychology* (1968), 10:215–21.
Latané, B. and J. Rodin. "A Lady in Distress: Inhibiting Effects of

Friends and Strangers on Bystander Intervention." *Journal of Experimental Social Psychology* (1969), 5:189–202.

Lenneberg, E. *The Biological Foundations of Language.* New York: Wiley, 1967.

Lewin, K. *The Conceptual Representation and the Measurement of Psychological Forces.* Durham, N.C.: Duke University Press, 1938.

—— *A Dynamic Theory of Personality.* New York: McGraw Hill, 1935.

Lindsay, P. H. and D. A. Norman. *Human Information Processing.* 2d ed. New York: Academic Press, 1977.

Locke, J. *An Essay Concerning Human Understanding.* Chicago: Regnery, 1956.

McClelland, D. *The Achieving Society.* New York, Van Nostrand, 1961.

MacCorquodale, K. "B. F. Skinner's *Verbal Behavior:* A Retrospective Appreciation." *Journal of the Experimental Analysis of Behavior* (1969), 12:831–41.

McGeoch, J. A. "Forgetting and the Law of Disuse." *Psychological Review* (1932), 39:352–70.

—— "The Influence of Degree of Interpolated Learning upon Retroactive Inhibition." *American Journal of Psychology* (1932), 44:695–708.

MacLean, P. D. "Psychosomatic Disease and the Visceral Brain: Recent Developments Bearing on the Papez Theory of Emotion. In R. L. Isaacson, ed., *Neuropsychology.* New York: Harper & Row, 1964.

Macleod, R. and H. L. Pick, eds. *Perception: Essays in Honor of James J. Gibson.* Ithaca, N.Y.: Cornell University Press, 1974.

Maslow, A. *Toward a Psychology of Being.* 2d ed. New York: Van Nostrand, 1968.

Michotte, A. *The Perception of Causality.* London: Methuen, 1963.

Milgram, S. "Behavioral Study of Obedience." *Journal of Abnormal and Social Psychology* (1963), 67:371–78.

Miller, G. "Decision Units in the Perception of Speech." *IRE Transactions on Information Theory* (1962), 8:81–83.

Miller, G. A., E. Galanter, and K. H. Pribram. *Plans and the Structure of Behavior.* New York: Holt, Rinehart and Winston, 1960.

Miller, N. E. "Learning of Visceral and Glandular Responses." *Science* (1969), 163:434–45.

Miller, N. and J. Dollard. *Personality and Psychotherapy*. New York: McGraw-Hill, 1950.

—— *Social Learning and Imitation*. New Haven: Yale University Press, 1941.

Milner, B. "Psychological Defects Produced by Temporal Lobe Excision." In *The Brain and Human Behavior*, vol. 36. Baltimore: Williams and Wilkins, 1958.

Neisser, U. *Cognition and Reality*. San Francisco: Freeman, 1976.

Norman, W. T. "2,800 Personality Trait Descriptors: Normative Operating Characteristics for a University Population." Ann Arbor: University of Michigan, Department of Psychology, 1967.

Notterman, J. M. and D. E. Mintz. *Dynamics of Response*. New York: Wiley, 1965.

Olds, J. "Emotional Centers in the Brain." *Science* (1967), 156:87–92.

Olds, J. and P. Milner. "Positive Reinforcement Produced by Electrical Stimulation of Septal Area and other Regions of Rat Brain." *Journal of Comparative and Physiological Psychology* (1954), 47:419–27.

Ornstein, R. *The Psychology of Consciousness*. San Francisco: Freeman, 1972.

Penfield, W. and L. Roberts. *Speech and Brain Mechanisms*. Princeton, N.J.: Princeton University Press, 1959.

Peterson, L. R. and M. Peterson. "Short-term Retention of Individual Items." *Journal of Experimental Psychology* (1959), 58:193–98.

Piaget, J. *The Construction of Reality in the Child*. New York: Basic Books, 1954.

Piaget, J. and B. Inhelder. *The Psychology of the Child*. New York: Basic Books, 1969.

Premack, D. "The Education of Sarah: A Chimp Learns the Language. *Psychology Today* (1970), 4:55–58.

Premack, D. "Reversibility of the Reinforcement Relation." *Science* (1962), 136:255–57.

Pribram, K. "The Biology of Mind: Neurobehavioral Foundations." In A. Gilgen, ed., *Scientific Psychology: Some Perspectives*. New York: Academic Press, 1970.

Pribram, K. "On the Neurology of Thinking." *Behavioral Science* (1959), 4:265–87.

Pribram, K. and W. E. Tubbs. "Short-term Memory, Parsing, and the Primate Frontal Cortex." *Science* (1967), 156:1765–67.

Price-Williams, D. R., W. Gordon and W. Ramirez. "Skill and Conservation: A Study of Pottery-Making Children." *Developmental Psychology* (1969), 1:769.

Pucetti, R. "Brain Bisection and Personal Identity. *British Journal for the Philosophy of Science* (1973), 24:339–55.

Quine, W. V. O. *From a Logical Point of View*. Cambridge, Mass.: Harvard University Press, 1953.

Rabb, D. "Backward Masking." *Psychological Bulletin* (1963), 60:118ff.

Ratliff, F. *Mach Bands*. San Francisco: Holden Day, 1965.

Reid, T. *Essays on the Active Powers of the Human Mind* (1778). Cambridge, Mass.: M.I.T. Press, 1969.

—— *An Inquiry into the Human Mind*. T. Duggan, ed. Chicago: University of Chicago Press, 1970.

Robinson, D. N. *An Intellectual History of Psychology*. New York: Macmillan, 1976.

—— "Psychological Explanation: Reasons or Causes?" *Proceedings of Annual Convention of the American Psychological Association*, 28–31 August, 1978, Toronto

—— *Psychology: Traditions and Perspectives*. New York: Van Nostrand, 1976.

—— "Visual Disinhibition with Binocular and Interocular Presentations." *Journal of the Optical Society of America* (1968), 58:254–57.

—— "Visual Reaction Time and the Human Alpha Rhythm: The Effects of Stimulus Luminance, Area, and Duration. *Journal of Experimental Psychology* (1966), 71:16–25.

—— "What Sort of Persons are Hemispheres? Another Look at the 'Split-Brain' Man." *British Journal for the Philosophy of Science* (1976), 27:73–78.

Robinson, D. N. and T. L. Beauchamp. "Personal Identity: Reid's Answer to Hume." *The Monist*, April 1978.

Robinson, D. N. and S. Sabat. "Elimination of Auditory Evoked Responses during Auditory Shadowing." *Physiological Psychology* (1975), 3:26–28.

—— "Neuroelectric Aspects of Information-Processing by the Brain." *Neuropsychologia* (1977), 15:625–41.

Robinson, D. N., ed. *Heredity and Achievement*. New York: Oxford University Press, 1970.

——, ed. *Significant Contributions to the History of Psychology.* 28 vols. Washington, D.C.: University Publications of America, 1977–1978.

Russell, B. "On Denoting." *Mind* (1905), 479–93.

Rychlak, J. *The Psychology of Rigorous Humanism.* New York: Wiley, Interscience, 1977.

Ryle, G. *The Concept of Mind.* London: Hutchinson, 1949.

Sarte, J. P. *Being and Nothingness.07 (1946). Hazel Barnes, trans.* New York: Philosophical Library, 1956.

——*Existentialism and Humanism.* P. Mariet, trans. London: Methuen, 1948.

Schwartz, B. *Psychology of Learning and Behavior.* New York: Norton, 1978.

Scheffield, F. D. and T. B. Roby. "Reward Value of a Non-nutritive Sweet Taste. *Journal of Comparative and Physiological Psychology* (1950), 43:471–81.

Sheldon, M. H. In L. Weiskrantz, ed., *Analysis of Behavioral Change.* New York: Harper & Row, 1968.

Sheldon, W. H., S. S. Stevens, and W. B. Tucker *The Varieties of Human Physique: An Introduction to Constitutional Psychology.* New York: Harper & Row, 1940.

Shepard, R. N. and J. Metzler. "Mental Rotation of Three-dimensional Objects. *Science* (1971), 171:701–3.

Skinner, B. F. *About Behaviorism.* New York: Knopf, 1974.

—— "Are Theories of Learning Necessary?" *Psychological Review* (1950), 57:193–216.

—— *Beyond Freedom and Dignity.* New York: Knopf, 1971.

—— *Verbal Behavior.* New York: Appleton-Century-Crofts, 1957.

Slamecka, N. J. "Proactive Inhibition of Connected Discourse." *Journal of Experimental Psychology* (1961), 62:295–301.

Solso, R. L., ed. *Theories of Information Processing and Cognition: The Loyola Symposium.* New Jersey: Erlbaum, 1975.

Spence, K. *Behavior Theory and Conditioning.* New Haven: Yale University Press, 1956.

Sperling, G. "The Information Available in Brief Visual Presentations." *Psychological Monographs* (1960), vol. 74, whole no. 11.

Sperry, R. "Cerebral Organization and Behavior." Science (1961), 133:1749–57.

Sperry, R., M. Gazzaniga, and J. Bogen. "Interhemispheric Relationships: The Neocortical Commisures: Syndromes of Hemispheric Deconnection." In P. J. Vinken and G. W. Bruyn, eds.,

Handbook of Clinical Neurology, vol. 4. Amsterdam: North Holland, 1969.

Sperry, R., N. Miner, and R. Meyers. "Visual Pattern Perception Following Subpial Slicing and Tantalum Wire Implantations in the Visual Cortex. *Journal Comparative and Physiological Psychology* (1955), 48:50-58.

Spinelli, D. N. "OCCAM: A Content Addressable Memory Model for the Brain." In K. Pribram and D. Broadbent, eds., *The Biology of Memory*. New York: Academic Press, 1970.

Stamm, J. S. and A. Warren. "Learning and Retention by Monkeys with Epileptogenic Implants in Posterior Parietal Cortex." *Epilepsia* (1961), 2:229-42.

Stein, L. "Chemistry of Reward and Punishment." *Psychopharmacologia* (1970), 8:105-23.

Teitelbaum, P. and A. Epstein. "The Lateral Hypothalamic Syndrome." *Psychological Review* (1962), 69:74-90.

Terrace, H. S. "Errorless Discrimination Learning in the Pigeon: Effects of Chloropromazine and Imipramine." *Science* (1963), 140:318-19.

Thorndike, E. L. *Animal Intelligence*. (Fascimile of 1898 ed.; New York: Hafner, 1970.

Tinbergen, N. "On War and Peace in Animals and Man." *Science* (June 28, 1968), 24-49.

Tolman, E. C. "Cognitive Maps in Rats and Man." *Psychological Review* (1948), 55:189-208.

—— *Collected Papers in Psychology*. Berkeley: University of California Press, 1951.

—— *Purposive Behavior in Animals and Men*. New York: Appleton-Century-Crofts, 1967.

Underwood, B. "The Effect of Successive Interpolations on Retroactive and Proactive Inhibition. *Psychological Monographs* (1945), vol. 59, no. 3.

Ungar, G., L. Gelson, and R. H. Clark. "Chemical Transfer of Learned Fear." *Nature* (1968), 217:1259-61.

Ursin, H. "The Effect of Amygdaloid Lesions on Flight and Defense Behavior in Cats. *Experimental Neurology* (1965), 11:64-79.

Uttal, W. *The Psychobiology of Mind*. New York: Earlbaum, 1978.

—— *The Psychobiology of Sensory Coding*. New York: Harper & Row, 1973.

Valenstein, E. S., V. C. Cox, and J. W. Kakolewski. "Reexamination of the Role of the Hypothalamus in Motivation." *Psychological Review* (1970), 77:16–31.

Wallace, A. R. *Darwinism*. London: Macmillan, 1896.

Watson, J. B. *Behaviorism*. Chicago: University of Chicago Press, 1924.

Werner, G. "The Topology of the Body Representation in the Somatic Afferent Pathway." In G. C. Quarton, T. Melnechuk, and F. O. Schmitt, eds., *The Neurosciences*, vol. 2. New York: Rockefeller University Press, 1970.

Whytt, R. *Works*. In D. N. Robinson, ed., *Significant Contributions to the History of Psychology*, series E, vol. 1. Washington D.C.: University Publications of America, 1977–1978.

Woodworth, R. S. *Dynamic Psychology*. New York: Columbia University Press, 1918.

Woodworth, R. S., and S. B. Sells. "An Atmospheric Effect in Formal Syllogistic Reasoning." *Journal of Experimental Psychology* (1935), 18:451–60.

Young, J. Z. *The Memory System of the Brain*. Los Angeles, Calif.: University of California Press, 1966.

Zimbardo, P. "The Psychological Power and Pathology of Imprisonment." A statement prepared for the U.S. House of Representatives, Committee on the Judiciary, Subcommittee #3. October 1971.

NAME INDEX

Adler, A., 226, 232, 233, 234, 236, 307, 311
Allport, G., 217, 218, 307, 311
Anrep, G., 297, 311
Aquinas, T., 193
Aristotle, 7, 8, 115, 150, 169, 193, 210, 293, 311
Aronson, E., 267, 309, 311
Asch, S., 309, 311
Atkinson, J., 218, 303, 306, 307, 311
Augustine, 156, 193

Bacon, F., 23
Baillie, J., 315
Bain, A., 63, 98, 297, 311
Bandura, A., 209, 306, 309, 311
Barker, S., 295, 312
Barnes, H., 321
Beach, F., 297, 312
Beauchamp, T., 294, 295, 305, 312, 320
Beck, L., 300, 308, 312
Bell, C., 28
Bender, D., 304, 315
Berkeley, G., 20, 24, 39
Berlyne, D., 302, 312
Binet, A., 186, 187, 305
Blakemore, C., 296, 312
Blodgett, H., 302
Blue, S., 302, 312

Bogen, J., 300, 321
Bower, T., 304, 312
Boyle, R., 25
Brand, M., 315
Brentano, F., 238, 248, 268, 308, 312
Breuer, J., 225
Broadbent, D., 296, 322
Broca, P., 28, 85, 299
Bromberg, W., 305, 312
Browne, T., 221
Bruner, J., 175, 304, 312
Brush, C., 294, 312
Bruyn, G., 321
Bugenthal, J., 308
Bures, J., 298, 312
Buresova, O., 298, 312
Butler, J., 258
Butler, R., 302, 307, 312
Byrne, D., 309, 312

Cabanis, P., 227, 228, 313
Campbell, F., 296, 312
Cattell, R., 206, 207
Cherry, C., 303, 313
Chisolm, R., 308, 313
Chomsky, N., 137, 302, 313
Chow, K. L., 297, 317
Clark, R., 299, 322
Condillac, E., 23, 25
Condorcet, A., 25

325

SUBJECT INDEX

331